DICTIONARY

OF

EPONYMS

Martin H. Manser

BCA
LONDON · NEW YORK · SYDNEY · TORONTO

This edition published 1989 by
BCA
by arrangement with Sphere Books Ltd

Fifth Reprint 1992

Copyright © by Martin H. Manser 1988
Copyright © illustrations by Tony Cantale, 1988

CN 6281

Printed in England by Clays Ltd, St Ives plc

PREFACE

This book explores the rich heritage of the English language – the deriving of words from the names of people. The idea for the book originally arose several years ago, after an evening meal with my mother. We quite simply tried to list as many objects named after people as we could. We quickly exhausted the very familiar **mackintosh**, **wellington**, **sandwich**; the scientific **ampere**, **watt**, **volt**, and so on. The idea of listing such words lay fairly dormant with the passage of time, until Sphere publishers began to discuss with me the writing of a book dealing with such words. Naturally, I began to tackle the task enthusiastically, since the subject was close to my heart.

Eponyms are the people who give their names to words. Most eponymous words derive from a person's surname: **boycott**, from the Irish landlord Captain Charles Cunningham Boycott, **dahlia**, from the Swedish botanist Anders Dahl, the **sousaphone**, from the American bandmaster John Philip Sousa, and **volt**, from the Italian physicist Count Alessandro Volta. Some eponymous words come from literary, biblical, or mythological sources: **malapropism**, from Mrs Malaprop in Sheridan's *The Rivals*, **Dickensian** – for example, *a real old-fashioned Dickensian Christmas* – from the English writer Charles Dickens, **as old as Methuselah**, from the age of the Old Testament patriarch, and **aphrodisiac**, from the Greek goddess of love and beauty Aphrodite. In this book, I have concentrated on the more well-known eponymous words in general use and have sought to give background detail on interesting aspects of an individual's life.

The entries are listed according to the name of the thing referred to, not the name the thing derives from. So there is an entry **spoonerism**, which shows the derivation Rev William Archibald Spooner. Note that when the name of the thing is itself a person's name, this is listed in alphabetical order: e.g. an **Aunt Sally** is listed at **Aunt**, **Mrs Grundy** at **Grundy**, and a **smart alec** at **smart**.

I would like to thank my family and friends, particularly Friedemann Lux, for their helpful advice on numerous points of detail, Christopher Potter of Sphere Books for his encouragement, and my secretary Mrs Rosalind Desmond for her painstaking research and typing work.

Martin H. Manser

Illustrated by Tony Cantale

A

Aaron's beard; Aaron's rod

Aaron, the brother of Moses, has given his name to at least two eponymous words. Aaron's beard is another name for rose of Sharon (also called St John's Wort) a creeping shrub, *Hypericum calycinum*, having large yellow flowers. The term derives from the Bible. 'It is like the precious ointment upon the head, that ran down the beard, even Aaron's beard: that went down to the skirts of his garments' (Psalm 133:2).

Aaron's rod is a plant, especially a mullein, *Verbascum trapsus*, that has tall spikes of yellow flowers and broad hairy leaves. The name Aaron's rod comes from one of the rods that were placed in the tabernacle. Aaron's rod had the next day budded, blossomed, and produced almonds (Numbers 17:1–13).

abigail

Abigail is an archaic word for a lady's maid. The name comes originally from Nabal's wife, *Abigail*, in the Bible (1 Samuel 25). Abigail apologized for her husband's meanness in refusing to give food to David's followers. She herself provided food for them, waylaying David even as he planned to attack Nabal and his people. In the space of 17 verses of the Bible text, Abigail refers to herself as 'thine handmaid' six times. Later, after Nabal's death, Abigail became David's wife.

The name and occupation came into more general use from the

'waiting gentlewoman' in the play *The Scornful Lady* by Sir Francis Beaumont and John Fletcher, first performed in 1610.

Swift, Fielding, and other novelists of the period used the name further and it became popularized by the notoriety of *Abigail Hill*, lady-in-waiting to Queen Anne, 1704–14, who used her friendship with the queen to try to secure personal favours.

Abraham's bosom

Abraham's bosom refers to the sleeping-place of the blessed in death. It is well known from Shakespeare's *Richard III*: '*The sons of Edward sleep in Abraham's bosom*' (Act 4, Scene 3), but originally it was a figure of speech used by Jesus in the parable of Lazarus and the rich man (Luke 16:19–31). '*The beggar* [Lazarus] *died, and was carried by the angels into Abraham's bosom*' (verse 22). In the language of the Talmud to sit in Abraham's bosom meant to enter paradise.

academy

Nowadays an academy is a school that gives a particular training: a military academy, and in Scotland, a secondary school. An academy is also an association of learned people organized to promote literature, art, or science: the Royal Academy, the French Academy, etc.

The word academy comes from Greek *Acadēmeia*, a pleasure garden in the suburbs of Athens where the philosopher Plato taught in the late fourth century B C. The garden itself is named after the Greek mythological hero *Acadēmos*.

Achilles' heel; Achilles tendon

To mention an Achilles' heel is to refer to a weakness, fault, or vulnerable spot in a person or thing that is otherwise strong: *The*

party knows that its group of political extremists might well be its Achilles'
heel.

The expression derives from Greek mythology, when Thetis, the mother of *Achilles*, dipped him into the River Styx to make him invulnerable. His one weak spot was the heel by which Thetis had held him during the dipping and which had not been touched by the water. It was during the siege of Troy that Achilles was mortally wounded by a poisoned arrow that was shot into his heel.

The fibrous cord connecting the heel-bone to the muscles of the calf is known as the Achilles tendon.

Adam's apple; Adam's ale; the old Adam; not to know someone from Adam

The visible projection at the front of the neck formed by the thyroid cartilage is called the Adam's apple. It is traditionally thought that this name derives from the belief that a piece of apple from the forbidden tree became stuck in *Adam*'s throat. It is however interesting to note that the Bible nowhere mentions that the fruit was in fact an apple.

Adam's ale is water: the first human would have had nothing else to drink.

The old Adam refers to the sinful nature of all human beings.

If you don't know someone from Adam, you don't recognize him or her – you have no idea who he or she is: *I think you'd better explain to Mr Chadwick who I am – he won't know me from Adam.* The expression derives from the fact that Adam, as the first man, is someone whom one could not know.

adonis

Adonis, 'a handsome young man', was a youth in Greek mythology who was renowned for his great beauty. Loved by Aphrodite, he was killed by a boar while hunting but resurrected by Persephone. He was celebrated in many festivals as a vegetation god, his death and restoration to life symbolizing the seasonal decay and rebirth of nature.

Aladdin's cave

With everything from children's games to computer software, the shop's a real Aladdin's cave for bargain hunters! The expression, referring to a source or place of great riches, comes originally from the oriental story *Aladdin and the Wonderful Lamp. Aladdin*, the poor son of a Chinese tailor is used by a Moorish magician to fetch from an underground cave a lamp with magical powers.

albert

An albert is a kind of watch chain usually attached to a waistcoat. The name comes from *Prince Albert* (1819–61), Prince Consort of Queen Victoria. When he visited Birmingham in 1849, the jewellers of that city presented him with such a chain. Very satisfied with their gift, he wore it from that time onwards, and such fashion became popular.

alexandrine

An alexandrine is a verse metre made up of a line of 12 syllables, usually with major stresses on the sixth and final syllables. The name comes from twelfth-century French poems about *Alexander the Great*, (356–323 BC), king of Macedonia. The alexandrine has been the dominant metre of French poetry since the sixteenth century, and was much used by Racine and Corneille.

algorithm

An algorithm is a step-by-step method of solving mathematical problems. The word algorithm is an alteration of Middle English *algorisme* and comes from Old French and Medieval Latin. Ultimately it comes from the name of the ninth-century Arab mathematician *Mohammed ibn Mūsa al-Khuwārizmi*. He introduced the Indian decimal system and the use of zero into Arabic mathematics.

Alice in Wonderland

Alice in Wonderland is sometimes used to refer to a strange, fantastic world in which the normal laws of logic and reason have been suspended. The phrase comes from *Alice's Adventures in Wonderland*, a story for children by Lewis Carroll, published in 1865. The story was in fact originally titled 'Alice's Adventures Under Ground'. The model for the character Alice was *Alice Liddell*, daughter of Dean Henry George Liddell, co-author of the standard Greek–English Dictionary *Liddell & Scott's Greek Lexicon*.

amazon

An amazon is a tall, strong, and athletic woman. In Greek mythology, *Amazons* were a nation of female warriors who lived on the shores of the Black Sea. The word amazon itself means 'without breast', because the Amazons were said to remove their right breasts to enable them to draw bows more easily. It is thought that the South American River Amazon was so called because the Spanish explorer Francisco de Orellana thought he saw female warriors there in 1541.

America

America is named after the name of the Italian navigator *Amerigo Vespucci* (1454–1512). He was a merchant who worked for a firm that fitted out ships for, among others, the explorer Christopher Columbus. Vespucci may well have gone on the voyages of some other explorers, but in 1499 he himself explored the north-east coast of South America. In 1507 an inaccurate record of his explorations was published, in which it was claimed that in 1497 he had discovered a new world, 'a continent more densely peopled and abounding in animals than our Europe or Asia or Africa'.

The two continents were therefore named in his honour, *Americus* being the Latin form of Amerigo.

ammonia

Ammonia is a colourless, poisonous, highly soluble gas that is used in making fertilizers, explosives, etc. The word comes from Latin *sal ammoniacus*; 'sal ammoniac'. Ammoniac is a salt or gum resin, and it was thought that the salt or gum resin was obtained from a district in Libya near the temple of the Egyptian god *Ammon*.

ampere

Ampere – often shortened to amp – is a common domestic word: we are familiar with 13-amp plugs, a 5-amp fuse, etc. The ampere is the basic metric unit of electric current. The word comes from the name of the French physicist *André Marie Ampère* (1775–1836), noted for his discoveries about the nature of electricity and magnetism. Three other familiar electrical terms named after scientists are: OHM, VOLT, WATT.

Although Ampère enjoyed a brilliant career, his private life was tragically unhappy. When he was only 18, he saw his father guillotined in the Reign of Terror; he was so shocked that he was unable to speak for over a year. He married at 24, but his wife died a year later. These personal tragedies led him to immerse himself in his work.

Anderson shelter; Morrison shelter

An Anderson shelter was a partly prefabricated air-raid shelter. It is named after *John Anderson, 1st Viscount Waverley* (1882–1958), a civil servant who entered parliament. As Home Secretary and Minister of Home Security (1939–40) he was faced with the urgent need to supply air-raid shelters to protect the civilian population. Designed by the engineer William, later Sir William, Paterson, the Anderson shelter could easily be erected by a non-specialist. About 3 million Anderson shelters were distributed. Anderson later became Chancellor of the Exchequer (1943–5).

A further eponymous air-raid shelter used in the Second World War: the Morrison shelter – an indoor shelter with a steel table-top and wired sides – is named after the British statesman *Herbert Stanley Morrison* (1888–1965), later Baron Morrison of Lambeth. Morrison was Home Secretary and Minister for Home Security in Churchill's War Cabinet (1942–5).

angstrom

An angstrom is a unit of length that was formerly in technical use to measure the wavelengths of electromagnetic radiations. It is named after the Swedish physicist and astronomer *Anders Jonas Ångstrom* (1814–74). He was a student and later professor at the University of Uppsala; he founded the science of spectroscopy, his studies of the spectra of the sun resulting in the discovery, in 1862, of hydrogen in the sun.

Annie Oakley

In theatrical (especially American) slang, an Annie Oakley is a free ticket. The name is the shortened name of the American markswoman *Phoebe Anne Oakley Mozee* (1860–1926). She was the star rifle shooter of Buffalo Bill's Wild West show.

The complimentary tickets have a hole punched in them to

ensure that they are not exchanged for cash at the box office. The tickets are probably so called because of Annie's most famous trick: tossing a playing-card – especially the five of hearts – into the air and shooting holes through all the card's pips.

aphrodisiac

An aphrodisiac is a substance, such as a drug, that stimulates sexual desire. The word comes from the name *Aphrodite*, the goddess of love and beauty in Greek mythology. According to one of the earliest of Greek poets, Hesiod, she was born from the foam (*aphros*) of the sea. According to Homer, she was the daughter of Dione and Zeus.

Appleton layer

The Appleton layer is the former name of the F-layer of the earth's atmosphere – the layer in the ionosphere about 150–1000 km above the earth. Of all the three different layers in the ionosphere, the F-layer contains the highest proportion of free electrons and is the most useful for long-range radio transmission.

The Appleton layer was so called because it was discovered by the British physicist *Sir Edward Appleton* (1892–1963).

See also HEAVISIDE LAYER.

arachnid

An arachnid is an invertebrate insect-like animal with eight legs that belongs to the order Arachnida, which includes spiders, scorpions, ticks, and mites. The word arachnid comes ultimately

Arachnid

from *Arachne*, in Greek mythology a girl from Lydia who presumptuously challenged the goddess Athena to a weaving contest. Jealous, Athena tore Arachne's attractive tapestry to pieces, whereupon Arachne tried to hang herself. Not content with this outcome, Athena changed Arachne into a spider (in Greek, *arachnē*).

Archimedes' principle; Archimedes' screw

The Greek mathematician and scientist *Archimedes* (*c*.287–*c*.212 BC) is noted for his work in geometry, mechanics, and hydrostatics. He is well known for his discovery of Archimedes' principle – that when a body is immersed in a liquid its apparent loss of weight equals the weight of the water that is displaced. It is alleged that he discovered this while taking a bath; on noticing that his body displaced the water in his bath, he is said to have exclaimed, '*Eureka!*' ('I have found it!'). His discovery enabled him to give a response to King Hiero II. The King had asked Archimedes to find out the amount of gold in a crown that had been made for him, since he suspected that it was not made of pure gold.

Archimedes' discovery led him to realize that since gold was heavier than silver, a floating vessel holding a pure-gold crown would displace more water than one holding a crown made of mixed metals. His tests proved that the King had in fact been supplied with a crown made of gold and base metal.

Archimedes is also remembered for the Archimedes' screw, a device for raising water. He reputedly invented it, but it was probably already known to the Egyptians.

assassin

The word assassin, 'a person who kills someone prominent, especially for political motives', was used to refer to a member of a secret fanatical sect of Muslims that operated in Persia and Syria in the eleventh and twelfth centuries. The sect was infamous for its campaign of terror in attempting to dominate the Muslim world. The name of the sect of *Assassins* further derives from Arabic *hashshāshīn*, meaning 'hashish eaters', as it is commonly believed that they ate or smoked hashish before being sent to carry out their evil deeds.

atlas

In Greek mythology *Atlas* was one of the Titans who, as a punishment for his part in the attempt to overthrow Zeus, was condemned to hold up the heavens on his shoulders for the rest of his life. Atlas came to be used to refer to a book of maps after a drawing of Atlas was included in the title-page of a collection of maps by the map-maker Mercator, published in the late sixteenth century.

See also MERCATOR PROJECTION.

attic

It is surprising to think that attic, 'a room in the space immediately below the roof of a house' is linked with a proper name, but this is so. Attic comes from the *Attic*, or *Athenian*, architectural style. A feature of this style was a wall that decorated the façade of the highest storey. In time, the space behind the decorative wall came to be referred to as an attic. Attic salt ('elegant and pointed wit') comes from *Attica*, the ancient Greek state whose capital was Athens. Salt was a common term for wit in both Latin and Greek, and Athenian men were famous for their wit and elegant expression.

aubrietia

The trailing perennial plant bearing small purple flowers that is widely grown in rock gardens is known as aubrietia or aubretia. It was named in 1763 by the French naturalist Michel Adamson after the French painter of flowers and animals *Claude Aubriet* (1665–1742).

Augean (clean the Augean stables)

It is difficult to think of a worse mess than stables for 3000 oxen that have not been cleaned out for 30 years. The stables of *King Augeas* in Greek mythology were, however, in this condition. The cleansing of these stables was one of the 12 labours of Hercules: he caused the River Alpheus to flow through the stables, cleansing them in a day. (Incidentally, when Hercules had successfully completed the task, Augeas meanly refused him a reward.) The phrase to cleans the Augean stables has come to refer to the task of removing the accumulation of different sorts of corruption.

August

The first Roman Emperor Octavian (63 BC–14 AD) was the great-nephew and adopted son of Julius Caesar. After Caesar's assassination in 44 BC, Octavian ruled Rome jointly with Mark Antony and Lepidus. Octavian defeated Mark Antony at Actium in 31 BC to become, two years later, the first Roman Emperor, the Senate later awarding him the title *Augustus* ('venerable') for his distinguished service to the state.

In 46 BC Caesar had established the so-called Julian calendar, adding the months January and February to the previous calendar. Caesar decided to rename one of the old months, formerly called Quintilis because it was the fifth (the first month being March), and chose to name it after himself: JULY. Not wishing to be beaten, Augustus wanted to have a month named after himself as well. His birth month was September, but he chose the sixth month Sextilis, as this had been the month in which he had achieved his greatest civil and military triumphs.

Furthermore, as Augustus did not want Julius Caesar's month to have more days than his own month, Augustus took a day from February to give both August and July 31 days.

Atlas

Aunt Sally

Originally, an aunt Sally was an effigy of an old woman at which one threw objects at a fair. This sense has broadened and the expression is now applied to any easy target for insults or criticism: *'In times of peace, a large part of the Dictator's role would be as a sort of national Aunt Sally, a symbol on which its citizens could vent their frustration'* (*Punch*).

The explanation of this expression is not certain: the elderly fairground figure resembles an aunt, but it has not been satisfactorily explained why the name Sally was chosen to stand for the unfortunate target.

B

bacchanalia

Bacchanalia is used to refer to a drunken orgy. It derives from *Bacchanalia*, the ancient mysteries or orgies in honour of *Bacchus* (the Roman name of the Greek god Dionysus), the god of wine. Coming from southern Italy, the cult reached Rome in the second century BC. The Roman festival of Bacchus, celebrated with dancing, song, and revelry, was marked by drunkenness, debauchery, and sexual immorality. A decree from the Senate in 186 BC prohibited Bacchanalia in Rome.

Baedeker

A Baedeker at one time referred to a travel guidebook published by the German *Karl Baedeker* (1801–59), but it is now sometimes used to refer to any authoritative travel guidebook. Baedeker's publishing firm was established in 1827. The fame of Baedeker's guides developed during the first three editions of J. A. Klein's *Rhineland Journey* (1833, second edition 1835, third edition 1839). By 1872, he had published guides to the whole of Europe; the guides being published in German, English, and French. His guides were well known for being authoritative and comprehensive – even Chekhov was to write from Venice, '*Here I am alone with my thoughts and my Baedeker*'.

During the Second World War German air raids on places of cultural or historical importance such as Canterbury and York in

England (1941–2) were known as Baedeker raids, because the German Luftwaffe used the Baedeker to determine the targets.

Baffin Bay; Baffin Island

Baffin Island is the largest island of the Canadian Arctic and is situated between Greenland and Hudson Bay. Baffin Bay is the name of the part of the Northwest Passage between Baffin Island and Greenland. The Bay and the Island are named after the English navigator *William Baffin* (*c.* 1584–1622). In 1615–16 he was the pilot on *Discovery* on expeditions with Captain Robert Bylot, attempting to find the sea route along the north coast of North America linking the Atlantic and Pacific Oceans (the Northwest Passage). Failing to find such a route, he explored the Hudson Strait and Baffin Island.

Bailey bridge

A Bailey bridge is a kind of temporary military bridge. Named after its inventor, the English engineer *Sir Donald Bailey* (1901–85), the Bailey bridge played a crucial role in the Allied victory in the Second World War. As Field Marshal Montgomery put it, *'Without the Bailey bridge we should not have won the war'*. Bailey bridges were quickly assembled from prefabricated lattice steel welded panels linked by pinned joints; they were capable of supporting heavy vehicles such as tanks and trains. Bailey bridges are still used in flood and disaster areas throughout the world.

Bakelite

Bakelite is the trademark for a kind of synthetic thermosetting resin and plastic used to make electrical insulating material and plastic fittings. Bakelite is named after the Belgian-born American chemist *Leo Hendrik Baekeland* (1863–1944). He discovered that the sticky resin formed by heating phenols and aldehydes under pressure had a number of useful properties: it was hard and strong, yet light; it could be moulded and coloured. In 1909 he announced the invention of Bakelite and, as President of the Bakelite Corporation (1910–39), he saw his product find many applications throughout the world.

banting

Banting is a method of slimming by eating high amounts of protein and avoiding sugar, starch, and fat. It is named after a London undertaker *William Banting* (1797–1878). Grossly overweight himself, Banting tried various slimming methods with no success, so he turned to a strict diet. He lost 46 pounds (21 kg) weight, reducing his waist measurement by 12 inches (32 cm). His efforts attracted some publicity, and he wrote a book about his experience, *Letter on Corpulence* (1863), outlining his methods of slimming. Banting's diet undoubtedly helped him: he was in his 60s when he started slimming and he lived to be 81.

baroque

The highly ornate style of architecture and art that flourished in Europe from the late sixteenth to the early eighteenth centuries is known as baroque. There are different theories of the word's origin: it may have come via French from the Portuguese *barroco* 'irregular pearl'. Alternatively, the word may perhaps derive via French from the name *Federigo Barocci* (*c.* 1535–1612), an Italian artist who painted in this style.

Bartlett pear

A Bartlett pear (also known as a Williams pear) is a kind of pear with a large juicy yellow sweet fruit. It is named after *Enoch Bartlett* (1779–1860) a merchant in Massachusetts, USA, but Bartlett was not the first to develop the fruit. It was a Captain Thomas Brewer who imported the trees from England; Bartlett, who bought up Brewer's farm, distributed the pears using his own name in the early 1800s.

Baskerville

The style of type Baskerville derives its name from its designer, the English printer *John Baskerville* (1706–75). At first a writing-master in Birmingham, Baskerville had by 1754 established a printing office and type-foundry in that city. His first work, a Latin Virgil, was printed in 1757. As printer to Cambridge University, he later produced editions of the Book of Common Prayer and the Bible. His books are notable for their high quality of presswork and type, and he was the first to use original high-gloss paper. The typeface that is named after him, Baskerville, is a traditional style, with exaggerated serifs and open curves.

Other designers of type who have given their names to typestyles include: Christophe *Plantin* (*c.* 1520–89), French printer; (Arthur) Eric (Rowton) *Gill* (1882–1940) British sculptor, engraver, and typographer; Claude *Garamond* (*c.* 1800–61), French type founder.

batiste

Batiste is a fine, soft, sheer fabric of plain weave, used especially in shirts, lingerie, dresses, and handkerchiefs. The word derives from French *toile de baptiste*, baptist cloth, and probably comes ultimately from the thirteenth-century French weaver, *Baptiste of Cambrai*, as he is reputed to have been its first manufacturer.

The town of Cambrai in north-east France was known from the

sixteenth century for its cambric linen cloth; it seems that the English merchants, wanting a different name for the new Cambrai fabric, called it after the French weaver, but misspelt his name in the process.

baud

A baud is a unit of measuring the speed of electronic data transmission, especially one equal to 1 unit of information per second. It is named after the French inventor and pioneer of telegraphic communication *Jean M. E. Baudot* (1845–1903).

A baud was originally equivalent to twice the number of MORSE CODE dots transmitted continuously per second. With the development of electronics, the term has been used to describe any of several different units.

BCG

This abbreviation is well known amongst schoolchildren who are having their BCG vaccine. The initials stand for bacille (or bacillus) Calmette-Guérin, after the French bacteriologists who developed the vaccines: *Albert Léon Charles Calmette* (1863–1933) and *Camille Guérin* (1872–1961). The vaccine stimulates the body's defence system against tuberculosis.

Beau Brummel

George Bryan Brummel (1778–1840) was known as *Beau Brummel* and this latter name has come to be used to refer to a dandy, fop, or leader of male fashion. For almost twenty years a prominent member of English fashionable society and a friend of the Prince of Wales (later King George IV) Beau Brummel is remembered for the extravagance of his dress. It is said that he spent an entire day preparing himself and his attire for a Royal ball. Eventually, however, he quarrelled with the Prince and the wealth that he had inherited was exhausted, so he was forced to flee to France in 1816 to escape his creditors. His final years were spent in poverty and suffering from attacks of paralysis.

Beaufort scale

The Beaufort scale is a measure of wind speed. The scale was devised in 1805 by the surveyor *Sir Francis Beaufort* (1774–1857) who later became Rear-Admiral and official hydrographer to the Royal Navy. The scale is based on easily observable features such as the movement of trees and smoke. It has the numbers 0–12, 0 being 'calm' and 12 'hurricane', or as Beaufort described it, 'that which no canvas could withstand'.

béchamel sauce

A béchamel sauce is a white sauce made from flour, butter, and milk flavoured with vegetables and seasonings. It comes from the French sauce *béchanelle* and is named after the French financier *Marquis Louis de Béchamel* (d. 1703), the steward of Louis XIV of France, who is reputed to have invented it. It seems that the original Béchamel sauce was a more elaborate mixture; it included in its ingredients old hens and old partridges.

becquerel

A becquerel is the basic metric unit of radiation activity, equal to one disintegration per second. It is named after the discoverer of radioactivity, the French physicist *Antoine-Henri Becquerel* (1852–1908).

The becquerel has now displaced the *curie* – itself an eponymous word, named after the French physicist and chemist *Marie Curie* (1867–1934) – as the basic measure of radioactivity. The curie is a much larger unit; it is equal to 3.7 × 10^{10} becquerel.

begonia

Begonia is a genus of succulent herbaceous plants originally found in the tropics. The genus contains about 1000 species, grown as pot or bedding plants and having showy, often brightly coloured, flowers with asymmetrical leaves.

Begonias are named after the French patron of science *Michel Bégon* (1638–1710). While working as Royal Commissioner in Santo Domingo, his enthusiastic amateur interest in botany led him to direct a study of the island's plant life. Among the plants found was the one that is now named after him. He later took species of the plant back to France, introducing them to his fellow European botanists. Species of the plant were brought to England in 1777, 67 years after Bégon's death, and it was here that the genus of plant was named begonia in his memory.

Belisha beacon

The Belisha beacon, a flashing light in an amber ball that is mounted on a post to mark a pedestrian crossing, is named after the British politician *1st Baron (Isaac) Leslie Hore-Belisha* (1893–1957). Hore-Belisha was National Liberal Minister of Transport from 1934 to 1937, and later Secretary of State for War 1937–40. His introduction of Belisha beacons as a road-safety measure to reduce the number of accidents was successful.

Benedictine

The name of a wine or spirit is often taken from the region where it was developed. Examples include champagne, from Champagne, the former province in north-east France, and cognac, from Cognac, the town in south-west France. The brandy-based liqueur known as Benedictine is, however, named after a person, *St Benedict* (*c.* 480–*c.* 547). St Benedict did not seem to have considered establishing a monastic order himself, although the rule of St Benedict (about AD 540) became the basis of the rule of Western Christian monastic orders.

It was in a Benedictine monastery at Fécamp, northern France, in about 1510 that a monk Don Bernando Vincelli first made the liqueur. His fellow monks declared it 'refreshing and recuperative'. During the French Revolution the monastery was destroyed. The secret formula for making the liqueur was kept safe, however, and some 50 years later Benedictine was manufactured by a Frenchman, Le Grand; his distillery standing on the site of the former abbey.

Bessemer process

The Bessemer process is a method for converting pig iron into steel, invented in 1856 by the British engineer *Sir Henry Bessemer* (1813–98). Molten pig iron is loaded into a refractory-lined furnace (Bessemer converter) at about 1250 °C. In the original version, air was blown into the furnace and the impurities removed. The result was that the quality of steel was improved and the costs of production were reduced. The modern version of the process has oxygen and steam blown into the furnace instead of air.

The Bessemer process was developed almost at the same time by the American inventor William Kelly (1811–88), and a long legal battle followed over which company, Kelly's or the one using the Bessemer process, should produce the steel in the USA. The dispute was finally resolved when the rival companies merged.

Belisha beacon

Betty Martin (all my eye and Betty Martin)

The idiomatic expression *all my eye and Betty Martin* is used as a response to state that something is untrue or utter nonsense. The expression is often shortened to *all my eye* or *my eye*. The expression is traditionally seen as a garbled version of the Latin prayer 'O mihi, beate Martini' (O grant me, blessed Martin), but since there is no fixed prayer resembling this, the explanation seems unlikely.

Eric Partridge (*A Dictionary of Catch Phrases*) suggests an alternative theory of the origin of the expression; in the late eighteenth century, 'an abandoned woman . . . named Grace . . . who induced a Mr Martin to marry her. She became notorious as Betty Martin: and favourite expressions of hers were *my eye!* and *all my eye.*'

Biedermeier

Biedermeier is used as a noun or an adjective to describe a style of German decoration and furniture in the mid-nineteenth century. The style, marked by simple, solid, and conventional features, is named after the unimaginative and bourgeois author *Gottlieb Biedermeier*, an imaginary writer of poems actually penned by Ludwig Eichrodt, the pseudonym of Rudolf Rodt (1827–92).

Big Bertha

Big Bertha was the name given to one of the three large German guns (with a range of some 75 miles) that were used to bombard Paris in the last months of the First World War. The name is a translation of German *dicke Bertha* 'fat Bertha', the Bertha in question being an uncomplimentary reference to *Bertha Krupp Von Bohlen und Halbach* (1886–1957), whose husband owned the Krupp armaments factory at Essen. The Germans originally used the name *die dicke Bertha* to refer to their 42-cm howitzer, it being wrongly believed that they were made at the Krupp factory. The name was later used to refer to the gun of a larger range.

bignonia

Bignonia – not to be confused with begonia – is a tropical American flowering shrub, grown for its trumpet-shaped yellow or red flowers. (It is sometimes also called cross vine.) The species is named after *Abbé Jean-Paul Bignon* (1662–1743), who was court librarian to Louis XIV, the name being given about 1700 by the French botanist Joseph Pitton de Tournefort (1656–1708) to honour the abbé.

billy goat see NANCY

billycock see BOWLER

Biro

Biro is a trademark used to describe a kind of ballpoint pen. It is named after its Hungarian-born inventor *László Jozsef Biró* (1900–85). Biró patented his ballpoint pen, containing quick-drying ink, in Hungary in 1938. The rise of Nazism meant that Biró left Hungary, and settled in Argentina.

Biró's pen soon proved popular: for instance, Royal Air Force navigators found that it wrote better at high altitudes than a conventional fountain pen.

Towards the end of the Second World War, Biró found an English company who backed his product, but the company was soon taken over by the French firm Bic. So it is that the ballpoint pen is known in France as a bic and in the UK as a biro.

Black Maria

A Black Maria is a police van for transporting prisoners and suspects. It is traditionally thought that the expression originally referred to *Maria Lee*, a strong, powerfully built American Negro woman who, in about 1800, kept a boarding-house for sailors in Boston. She was also known for the help she gave to the police: the expression *Send for the Black Maria*, it is supposed, became common when there was trouble and the drunk and disorderly needed to be removed. When the first police horse vans were introduced in Britain in 1938 they may well have been named in honour of this awesome lady.

blimp

A blimp (or Colonel Blimp) is a pompous, reactionary person with extremely conservative views. The origin of the word is the cartoon character *Colonel Blimp* invented by the New Zealand-born political cartoonist Sir David Low (1891–1963) in daily papers, particularly the *London Evening Standard*, of the 1930s and 1940s. Blimp was depicted as an elderly, unimaginative, unprogressive character. The adjective blimpish, derived from blimp, means 'reactionary or very conservative'.

The word blimp probably gained greater currency because it also referred to a small, non-rigid airship used in the First World War. This blimp probably owes its origin to the fact that it was also described as a *limp* airship: this was the successful type *B* version (hence B-limp), type A not having been a success.

Bloody Mary

A Bloody Mary is a cocktail drink that consists mainly of vodka and tomato juice. The expression was originally the nickname of *Queen Mary I of England* (1516–58). As queen (1553–8), Mary's aim was to restore Roman Catholicism to England: earlier Protestant legislation was repealed and heresy laws were re-introduced. Nearly 300 men and women were burnt at the stake, including the bishops Hugh Latimer and Nicholas Ridley, and the Archbishop of Canterbury, Thomas Cranmer. It was as Latimer was burnt at the stake with Ridley that he encouraged his fellow sufferer with the famous words, 'Be of good comfort, Master Ridley, and play the man. We shall this day light such a candle by God's grace in England as I trust shall never be put out.'

Mary's cruel actions earned her the nickname 'Bloody Mary' and so it is that she has been remembered by the red of the cocktail.

bloomers

The word bloomers nowadays refers to the women's under-garment that has full, loose legs gathered at the knee. The word owes its origin to the American feminist *Amelia Jenks Bloomer* (1818–94), but the garment Bloomer introduced into American society was not the garment known as bloomers today. The original garment was an entire costume consisting of a loose-fitting tunic, a short knee-length skirt, and billowing Turkish-style trousers gathered by elastic at the ankle. The costume, made originally from a design by Elizabeth Smith Miller, was worn by Mrs Bloomer and introduced at a ball in Lowell, Massachusetts, in July 1851. The outfit aroused considerable controversy at the time, largely because it was thought that trousers were a garment to be worn only by men.

Later, bloomers came to refer to just the trousers in the outfit, towards the end of the nineteenth century, to knee-length knicker-bockers worn by cyclists, and today, in somewhat informal and wry usage, to the variety of women's underwear.

See also KNICKERBOCKERS.

blue peter see JOLLY ROGER

bluebeard

Bluebeard, referring to a man who marries and then kills one wife after another, was originally a character in European folklore. The earliest literary form of the fairytale is that of Charles Perrault (1628–1703) published in 1697, in which six wives are the victims of the seductive yet evil desires of the husband and the seventh is rescued by the opportune arrival of her brothers, who then kill the murderer. The original Bluebeard is thought by some to have been Gilles de Retz, Marquis de Laval, who lived in Brittany and who was accused of murdering six of his seven wives; in 1440 he was burnt at the stake for his crimes. Others sources, however, assign the original Bluebeard to an earlier date.

blurb

A blurb is a short publicity notice on the jacket or cover of a book. The word was coined in 1907 by the American humorist and illustrator Gelett Burgess (1866–1951) to promote his book *Are You a Bromide?*

In the early years of the twentieth century, American novels commonly had a picture of an attractive young woman on the cover. In an effort to parody this practice, Burgess produced a picture of a sickly sweet girl, *Miss Belinda Blurb*, for the purpose, he hoped, of *'blurbing a blurb to end all blurbs'*. The outstanding success of this example meant that the word became associated with all such publicity notes.

bobby

The name for a policeman in British informal usage is a bobby: your friendly neighbourhood bobby. Bobby is the familiar form of Robert, coming from, as is well known, the British statesman Sir Robert Peel (1788–1850). In 1812 Peel was appointed Chief

Secretary for Ireland; in 1814 he founded the Irish Constabulary, members of which were nicknamed *peelers*. As Home Secretary, Peel passed the Metropolitan Police Act, which founded the Metropolitan Police (1829). The word bobby was then used to describe the new London police force, later passing into general use to refer to all British policemen.

Bob's your uncle

Bob's your uncle is a slang expression meaning 'everything is or will be fine; there'll be no difficulties'. The phrase became current in the 1880s, but its origin is uncertain. A possible explanation is the allusion to the appointments of Arthur Balfour (1848–1930), to various posts such as Secretary for Ireland, First Lord of the Treasury and Leader of the House of Commons. The appointments were made by Balfour's uncle, the Prime Minister *Robert* (hence *Bob*) *Gascoyne Cecil*, 3rd Marquess of Salisbury (1830–1903). The apparently nepotistic choice meant that with Prime Minister Bob as his uncle, Arthur Balfour had no problem obtaining whatever he wanted.

bogus

There are a number of different theories of the origin of the word bogus, meaning 'counterfeit; sham'. Some sources suggest that the word is an alteration of the name *Borghese*, an Italian man who in the 1830s supplied counterfeit banknotes to the American West. The Boston *Courier* reported that in about 1837 the people shortened Borghese's name to bogus, his banknotes being called bogus currency.

Other sources suggest that the word bogus referred originally to a device used for making counterfeit coins. The first citation of the word used in this way is 1827, some ten years earlier than the usage described above. Still others suggest that bogus is derived

from French *bagasse* 'rubbish'. The origin of *bogus* remains un-
proven; it may well be that all the sources mentioned have exer-
cised an influence on the word's acceptance.

Bolivia

The South American country Bolivia owes its name to the soldier
and statesman *Simón Bolívar* (1783–1830), known as the Liberator,
for his unremitting struggle to free Venezuela, Colombia, Ecuador,
and Peru from Spanish rule. He succeeded in liberating these
countries, but failed to join them in one united republican con-
federation. In 1825 Upper Peru became a separate state, taking
the name Bolivia, in honour of Bolívar who later became its president. He is one of the very few men in history who not only has
had a country named after him but also drew up that country's
constitution.

Boolean algebra

George Boole (1815–64) was a British mathematician who applied
the methods of algebra to logic, in the same way that conventional
algebra is used to express relationships in mathematics. In Boolean
algebra, variables express not numbers but logical statements and
the relationships between them. Boole's work was developed
further by such philosopher-mathematicians as Frege, Russell and
Whitehead and is important in the logic of computers.

bougainvillea; Bougainville

Bougainvillea is the name given to a genus of tropical South American woody climbing shrub bearing bright purple or red bracts
that cover the flowers. The genus is named after the French
navigator *Louis Antoine de Bougainville* (1729–1811). On an ex-

pedition round the world under his leadership (1766–9), the Solomon Islands were sighted. The largest island in the Solomon Islands archipelago is named after him, and is part of Papua New Guinea. Naturalists on Bougainville's expedition named the shrub in his honour.

bowdlerize

To bowdlerize a book means that all the words or passages considered indecent are removed. The word is traditionally thought to have come from the name of the British doctor *Thomas Bowdler* (1734–1825). Having retired from medicine, Bowdler published his *Family Shakespeare* in 1818; it excluded or modified words and expressions and even characters and plots that he found objectionable. The title page explains that, 'Nothing is added to the text; but those expressions are omitted which cannot with propriety be read aloud in a family'. Inspired by his success in this venture, Bowdler then published his expurgated version of Gibbon's *History of the Decline and Fall of the Roman Empire* in 1823.

Some recent research has, however, suggested that it was not Thomas Bowdler, but his sister, Henrietta Maria, known as Harriet, who edited the original *Family Shakespeare*, first published in 1807. This, it seems, was followed by the revised and second edition of 1818, with Thomas Bowdler as editor.

bowie knife

A bowie knife is a stout hunting knife, with a long, one-edged blade curving to a point. It is named after the American soldier and adventurer *James Bowie* (1799–1836). It was James Bowie who popularized the knife, but he did not invent it. It seems it was originally designed by his father or by his older brother Rezin Pleasant Bowie (1793–1841).

Bowie's exploits made him something of an American folk hero. He is said to have used the knife to kill six men and wound 15 others in a duel at Natchez, Mississippi, in about 1827. James later became a colonel in the Texan army in the revolution against Mexico. In 1836, less than 200 Texans, including James Bowie and the legendary Davy Crockett, held out against some 4000 Mexicans for 13 days at the Alamo, but the Texans were eventually all slaughtered, James Bowie being slain on his sickbed.

bowler

There are various theories of the origin of the word bowler, the stiff felt hat that has a rounded crown and a narrow brim. The word may well be derived from the name *Bowler*, a family of nineteenth-century London hatters. Some sources suggest that the name of the hat makers was *Beaulieu*; others suppose that the hat is so named because of its shape; it resembles a bowl or basin, and since it is round and stiff, it could be bowled along.

It is also interesting to note that a bowler hat was probably originally called a *billycock*. There are two theories of the origin of this word. On the one hand billycock could be derived from bully-cocked hat, a hat tilted at an aggressive angle. On the other hand, billycock could come from the name *William (Billy) Coke*, an English sportsman. In about 1850 the London hatters Lock's of St James's made a hat for Billy Coke. It is said that he wanted a hat that was more practical than a traditional 'topper', as the tall topper kept being knocked off by branches when Coke rode to the hounds.

Box and Cox

Box and Cox is an expression used in British English. Its origins lie in the farce *Box and Cox* by the English dramatist J. M. Morton (1811–91), published in 1847. In the farce, two men, one named *Box* and the other *Cox* lived in the same room, the one occupying the room by day and the other by night and neither knowing of the other's existence. In 1867 the play was adapted as a comic opera with music by Sir Arthur Sullivan and the text by Sir Francis Cowley Burnand. The expression Box and Cox means alternating or in turn.

boycott

Boycott is one of the most well-known eponyms in the English language. To boycott a person, organization, etc., means that you refuse to deal with them, as an expression of disapproval and often as a means of trying to force them to accept certain conditions. The word comes from the name of the Irish landlord *Captain Charles Cunningham Boycott* (1832–97).

After retiring from the British army, Boycott was hired to look after the Earl of Erne's estates in County Mayo, Ireland. In 1880 the Irish Land League, wanting land reform, proposed a reduction in rents, stating that landlords who refused to accept such rents should be ostracized. Boycott refused and was promptly ostracized. His workers were forced to leave him, tradesmen refused to supply him, and his wife was threatened – indeed he was persecuted to such a degree that he and his wife were forced to flee to England, in so doing making the first boycott a success. The word quickly passed into other European languages, e.g. German *boykottieren*.

Boyle's law

Boyle's law states that at a constant temperature, the pressure of a gas is inversely proportionate to its volume. This law is named after the Irish-born British physicist and chemist *Robert Boyle* (1627–91). In fact, Boyle's law is only roughly true for real gases; a gas that obeys Boyle's law completely (which would exist only in hypothetical instances) is called an ideal gas or a perfect gas.

In France and other countries on the continent of Europe, the law is known as *Mariotte's law*, after the French physicist *Edmé Mariotte* (1620–84). Mariotte discovered the law independently of Boyle in 1676, 13 years after the publication of Boyle's law.

boysenberry see LOGANBERRY

Bradshaw

Bradshaw was the informal name for the British railway passenger time-table *Bradshaw's Railway Guide*. First issued in 1839, it is named after its original publisher *George Bradshaw* (1801–53). It was discontinued in 1961.

braggadocio

The word braggadocio, meaning 'empty boasting' comes from the character *Braggadocchio* in the poem *The Faerie Queene* by the English poet Edmund Spenser (*c.* 1552–99). The character personified boasting and the poem records his adventures and ultimate exposure. Spenser probably coined the name from the English word braggart and the Italian suffix *-occhio* meaning 'great'. He may have had in mind the Duke d'Alençon, one of the many suitors of Queen Elizabeth I.

Braille

The name of the system of raised dots by which blind people can read comes from the Frenchman *Louis Braille* (1809–52). Blinded at the age of three by an accident with an awl in his father's workshop, Braille went, at the age of ten, to study at the National Institute for the Blind in Paris. The Institute then possessed only three books, each in 20 parts and weighing 400 pounds (180 kg). The cumbersome text was written in large embossed letters to be felt by hand, yet Braille learned to read using this means.

At that same time an artillery captain, Charles Barbier, invented a primitive method of 'night writing'. Combinations of raised dots

34

and dashes were used to communicate messages that could be understood by touch – that is, without the need for illumination. Barbier demonstrated his invention at the institute and Braille was inspired to refine it for use by the blind.

At the age of 20, Braille published his first book in his new system, soon applying his skill as a musician – he enjoyed organ-playing – to adapt his system for use in music. He remained a teacher at the institute until his death in 1852.

Bramley

The word referring to the variety of cooking apple known as a Bramley probably comes from the name *Matthew Bramley*, an English butcher who is said to have first grown it around 1850. Bramley lived in Southwell, Nottinghamshire, and it is thought that the first Bramley was the result of a bud mutation: a variation in which only part of the tree was affected.

brougham

The name of the light, closed, four-wheeled, horse-drawn carriage with an open seat in front for the driver, honours the Scottish lawyer and statesman *Henry Peter Brougham, Baron Brougham and Vaux* (1778–1868). Brougham (both the name and the carriage are pronounced broom or brooerm) designed the carriage in about 1850, originally describing it as a 'garden chair on wheels'. The brougham remained a popular form of public transport until it was surpassed by the HANSOM CAB.

Brougham's achievements include his advocacy, along with William Wilberforce, of the abolition of slavery; his defence in the House of Lords of Caroline of Brunswick against the charges of adultery brought by her husband, the Regent and later King George IV; and, as Lord Chancellor, his speech in the House of Lords that contributed to the passing of the Reform Bill of 1832.

Browning automatic rifle

The Browning automatic rifle (BAR), a portable gas-operated, air-cooled rifle, is named after its designer, the American *John Moses Browning* (1834–1926). Capable of firing 200–350 rounds a minute, the BAR was used greatly in the Second World War and was the standard automatic weapon in the US army until about 1950. A prolific firearm designer, Browning also designed machine guns, pistols, and shotguns.

Buckley's chance

Buckley's chance is an Australian expression which means 'a very remote chance'. Two chances, Buckley's and none, amounts in reality to next to no chance at all. The expression may derive from *William Buckley* (d. 1856), who against all odds lived with Aborigines for 30 years, or, more likely, a Melbourne store named *Buckley and Nunn* which became linked with the phrase.

Buddhism; Buddhist

The founder of Buddhism was the Hindu Prince Gautama Siddharta (*c.* 563–*c.* 483 B C). At the age of 16 he married his cousin, the Princess Yasodharma, who later bore him a son, Rahula. In his late twenties, he became dissatisfied with their life of luxury, so he left his family in order to try to find answers to the problems of human suffering and existence. Six years of asceticism followed, but these convinced him that self-mortification did not provide the solutions he was searching for. So, keeping himself from the extremes of self-mortification and indulgence, he turned to enlightenment alone, meditating within himself. He is traditionally said to have reached enlightenment while sitting under a fig tree in what is now called Buddh Gaya, a village in Bihar, in northeast India. He then took the title *Buddha*, meaning in Sanskrit 'the

Awakened One'. The next 45 years of his life were devoted to teaching the principles of enlightenment.

buddleia

Buddleia is a genus of trees and shrubs that have showy clusters of yellow or mauve flowers. Native to tropical or warmer regions in Asia and America, the first specimens were collected in the early eighteenth century by the Scottish-born botanist William Houstoun (*c.* 1695–1733). He wished to name the plant after the Essex rector and botanist *Adam Buddle* (*c.* 1660–1715). This desire was later honoured by Linnaeus in his plant classification.

One particular species of buddleia, *Buddleia davidii* was introduced into Britain from China in the late nineteenth century. This species is also known as the butterfly bush because its flowers are very attractive to butterflies. The word *davidii* is also eponymous – it comes from the French missionary and explorer of China *Père Armand David* (1826–1900). The rare Chinese deer, *Père David's deer*, is also named in his honour.

Bunsen burner

The Bunsen burner, the gas burner with an adjustable air valve used widely in chemistry laboratories, is named after the German chemist *Robert Wilhelm Bunsen* (1811–99). Bunsen is generally credited with the invention of the Bunsen burner, although some authorities point out that similar designs had been developed earlier by such scientists as Michael Faraday. Even if this is true, it was certainly Bunsen who popularized the use of the burner.

Bunsen is also famous for his discovery, with the German physicist Gustav Robert Kirchoff (1824–87), of the two chemical elements caesium and rubidium in 1860.

Buridan's ass

Buridan's ass is an illustration of a philosophical position. In the example, a hungry ass stands an equal distance between two identical bales of hay. He starves to death, however, because there is no reason why he should choose to eat one bale rather than the other. The dilemma is said to show the indecisiveness of the will when faced with two equal alternatives. The philosophical example is associated with the French philosopher *Jean Buridan* (*c.* 1295–1356), although it was first found in the philosophy of Aristotle.

burke

To burke means to murder someone in such a way that no marks are left on the body. The word comes from the name of the notorious murderer *William Burke* (1792–1829). Originally an Irish labourer, Burke moved to Scotland in about 1818, renting a room in Edinburgh from a fellow countryman William Hare. When one of Hare's lodgers died owing him money, Hare and Burke took the body to an Edinburgh anatomist Dr Robert Knox, who gave them seven pounds and ten shillings for it.

Quickly realizing the profitability of their business, Hare and his wife together with Burke and his mistress disposed of between 15 and 30 other unfortunates in a similar way. They were careful to suffocate their victims, leaving no marks of violence, so that it would appear that the bodies had been taken from graves. The murderers became careless, however, killing an attractive 18-year-old woman, Mary Peterson, whose corpse was recognized by the students at Knox's anatomy school. Other murders followed, and Burke and Hare were eventually caught with the body of a missing woman. Hare turned King's evidence, however, testifying against his accomplice. Hare was set free, but Burke was hanged in January 1829, before a crowd of about 30,000 people. On the way to the gallows the crowd shouted, '*Burke him! Burke him!*', wanting him to suffer the same fate as his victims.

With all the publicity, Burke's name came to stand for the murderous act, and figuratively to mean 'hush up' or 'stifle'.

Burnham scale

The name of the former salary scale for teachers in state schools in England and Wales, the Burnham scale, comes from *Harry Lawson, 1st Viscount Burnham* (1862–1933). A Member of Parliament, Burnham chaired the committee that in 1919–20 originally established the salary scale.

busby

A busby is the name for the tall bearskin fur hat worn by soldiers, especially hussars and members of certain British army regiments. In the eighteenth century a busby was a large, bushy wig.

The word is traditionally thought to come from the name of the disciplinarian headmaster *Dr Richard Busby* (1606–95). Headmaster of Westminster School, London, Busby had among his pupils Dryden, Locke, and Christopher Wren. It is not certain, however, that Busby himself wore a bushy wig. It may be that his hair naturally stood upright, thus suggesting the wig that became fashionable.

Byronic

The adjective Byronic is sometimes used to mean 'wildly romantic yet melancholy and despairing'. The word alludes to characteristics of the life and writings of *George Gordon, Lord Byron* (1788–1824). A significant romantic poet, whose writings included *Childe Harold's Pilgrimage* (1812–18) and *Don Juan* (1819–24), Byron is noted for his physical lameness, his attractive appearance and many romantic liaisons, and his journeyings on the European continent. Towards the end of his life, Byron became involved in the Greek struggle for independence. He died of malaria at Missolonghi in western Greece in 1824.

C

Cabal

A cabal is a small group of people who meet secretly or unofficially, especially for the purpose of political intrigue. The word derives ultimately from Hebrew *qabbālāh* 'what is received; tradition'. It is popularly believed, however, that the word cabal originated with the initials of the names of King Charles II's ministers from 1667 to 1673: *Sir Thomas Clifford* (1630–73), *Lord Ashley* (later 1st Earl of Shaftesbury) (1621–83), the *2nd Duke of Buckingham* (1628–87), the *1st Earl of Arlington* (1618–85), and the *Duke of Lauderdale* (1616–82). The political group's powerful scheming and intriguing met with great unpopularity. It was noticed that the ministers' initials made up the word cabal and it seems certain that the existence of this faction made the use of the word more current, adding to it pejorative connotations of reproach.

Cadmean victory see PYRRHIC VICTORY

Caesarean section

A Caesarean section (or Caesarean) is a surgical incision through the walls of the abdomen and womb in order to deliver a baby. The expression is commonly thought to allude to the popular belief that *Julius Caesar* was born in this manner.

An alternative theory is that Caesarean comes from Latin *caesus*, the past participle of the verb *caedera* 'to cut'.

Caesar's wife must be above suspicion

The expression *Caesar's wife must be above suspicion* referred originally to Caesar's second wife *Pompeia*. According to rumours circulating in about 62 BC, it seems that her name was linked with Publius Clodius, a notorious dissolute man of the time. Caesar did not believe such rumours but he made it clear, when divorcing her, that even Caesar's wife must be above suspicion. The expression *like Caesar's wife* also comes from this account, to refer to someone who is pure and honest in morals.

calamine

Calamine, the pink powder of zinc oxide and ferric oxide that is used in soothing lotions for the skin is an alteration of the Latin *cadmia*. This Latin word derives ultimately from the Greek word *Cadmus*, the legendary founder of Thebes, *kadmeia* meaning 'Theban (earth)'. For further discussion of Cadmus and the expression *Cadmean victory*, see PYRRHIC VICTORY.

Calvinist

The name of the theological system known as *Calvinism* comes from the French theologian *John Calvin* (1509–64), whose original name was Jean Cauvin (sometimes also spelt Chauvin). Converted in about 1532, Calvin's most famous work is his *Institutes*, first published in Latin (*Christianae Religionis Institutio*) in 1536.

Calvin has generally been held in low esteem. He himself wrote in 1559 that 'never was a man more assailed, stung, and torn by calumny' than he was. He is known chiefly for his teaching on predestination, yet this was taught earlier by Augustine and is found in the Bible. Calvin himself was careful to keep this teaching in a healthy tension with other biblical doctrines and it is some of his followers who have upset Calvin's balance.

Calvin also sought to reform the behaviour of people in the city of Geneva, to make the whole of Genevan society a model community where every citizen came under a strict religious discipline. A wide range of laws regulated the people's dress and morals. It is this rigorous and austere aspect of Calvin's work that is recalled in the present-day connotation of the word Calvinist, seen for example in the phrase *a strict Calvinist upbringing*.

camellia

Camellia refers to a genus of ornamental shrubs, of which perhaps the best known is *Camellia japonica*. This has shiny evergreen leaves and showy, rose-like flowers. The word camellia comes from the name of the Moravian Jesuit missionary *George Josef Kamel* (1661–1706), also known by the Latinized form of his name *Camellus*. Kamel lived in Manila in the Philippine Islands and there he ran a pharmacy, which was supplied by his herb garden. He published reports on the plants he grew in the *Philosophical Transactions* of the Royal Society. He was certainly the first to describe the shrub and some sources suggest that he may also have been the first to send specimens of it to Europe. In any event, it was the Swedish botanist Linnaeus who read of Kamel's accounts in *Philosophical Transactions* and later named the plant in his honour.

cannibal

A cannibal, referring to someone who eats the flesh of other human beings, comes from the Spanish *Canibales*. This was the name given by Christopher Columbus to the *Caribs*, the American Indian people of the Lesser Antilles and northern South America. Before the conquest by the Spaniards, the Caribs expelled the Arawak Indians from the Lesser Antilles, enslaving the women and killing and eating the men. The Spanish word *Canibal* is derived from the Arawak term *Caniba* for the Caribs. The Caribbean Sea is also named after the Carib people.

cant

The word cant, meaning 'insincere or hypocritical talk; repeated or specialized language' comes from the verb *cant* 'to talk whiningly like a beggar', ultimately from Latin *cantare* 'to sing or chant'. It is quite possible, however, that the meaning of the word and the frequency of its usage were influenced by the name of a Scottish minister *Andrew Cant* (1590–1663). Cant was a Presbyterian minister in Aberdeen; it was said of him that he talked 'in the pulpit in such a dialect that ... he was understood by none but his own Congregation, and not by all of them', though how true this was is uncertain since many churches have said the same of their preachers! Andrew Cant and his brother Alexander were zealous leaders of the Covenanters – the Scottish Presbyterians who bound themselves on oath to defend their church. Some authorities describe the bigotry and hypocrisy of the Cant brothers, persecuting their religious opponents, yet also praying for them. So while the ultimate derivation of cant certainly is Latin *cantare*, it appears that the actions of the Cant brothers may well have supported the meaning of the word.

cardigan

The cardigan, the knitted jacket or sweater fastened with buttons, is named after the British cavalry officer *James Thomas Brudenell, 7th Earl of Cardigan* (1797–1868). The garment was first worn by British soldiers in the intense cold of the Crimean winter. (See also RAGLAN.)

It was the Earl of Cardigan who led the Charge of the Light Brigade in the most famous battle of the Crimean War, near the village of Balaclava on 25 October 1854. (Interestingly, the word for the woollen hood-like head-covering takes its name from this village.)

43

Casanova

A Casanova is a man noted for his amorous, often unscrupulous adventures. The word comes from the name of the Italian adventurer *Giovanni Jacopo Casanova* (1725–98). Born in Venice, the son of an actor, Casanova was expelled at the age of 16 from a seminary for monks for his immoral behaviour. He went on to live in many European cities, working at different times as, amongst other things, a preacher, a philosopher, a diplomat, a gambler, and a violinist. He mixed with the wealthy aristocracy, engaging in many romantic liaisons, making and losing riches and friends wherever he went. He finally settled as librarian to the Count von Waldstein in Bohemia, and it was here that he wrote his memoirs – about $1\frac{1}{2}$ million words in 12 volumes – which were published posthumously 1826–38.

Cassandra

A Cassandra is a person whose prophecies of misfortune are ignored. The original *Cassandra* was a daughter of King Priam, King of Troy in Greek mythology. She was endowed with the gift of prophecy, but after she rejected the advances of Apollo, she suffered the punishment of her prophecies being eternally disbelieved.

Cassandra prophesied the fall of Troy. When Troy was captured, she fell by lot to Agamemnon, who took her back to Greece and to whom she prophesied the doom that awaited him. Cassandra and Agamemnon were later murdered by Clytemnestra. Thus it is that a modern-day Cassandra is someone whose predictions of doom are fated to go unheeded.

Castor and Pollux

Castor and Pollux, meaning 'two faithful friends' were originally twin brothers in Greek mythology, known jointly as the *Dioscuri*.

44

Pollux was immortal, the son of Leda and Zeus; Castor was mortal, the son of Leda and Tyndareus. After Castor's death, Pollux asked Zeus that he might be allowed to die too, in order that the two should be together, and this wish was granted.

The twins' names are used for two stars. The brightest star in the Gemini constellation is Pollux, and the second brightest, Castor.

Catherine wheel

The kind of spinning, burning, firework known as a Catherine wheel is named after the princess *St Catherine of Alexandria*.

A martyr for her Christian faith, she is said to have been sentenced to death in about AD 307 by being broken on a spiked wheel. Legend has it that she survived this torture, as it was the wheel, not her body, that was miraculously broken. Catherine was then beheaded, her body, it is thought, being carried by angels to Mount Sinai where it was found in about the year 800 and on which site a monastery was built to honour her resting-place. In 1969 the Roman Catholic Church ceased to recognize St Catherine because of doubts about her existence.

St Catherine's symbol is a spiked wheel; and a Catherine wheel is the name given also to a circular window that has spokes radiating from its centre, and to the sideways handspring more commonly known as a cartwheel.

cattleya

Cattleya is the name of a genus of tropical American orchids that are grown for their showy hooded flowers. The orchids are named after the English botanist and horticultural patron *William Cattley* (d. 1832). The *Cattleya fly* and the subtropical fruit *Cattley guava* also honour this patron of botany.

HUYOT.

Celsius

Celsius is the name of the temperature scale for which 0° is the freezing point of water and 100° the boiling point. The scale is named after the Swedish astronomer and scientist *Anders Celsius* (1701–44), who devised it in 1742. The new scale simplified the earlier FAHRENHEIT scale by dividing the temperature between boiling point and freezing point into a hundred equal parts.

Originally, Celsius set 0° as the boiling point of water, and 100° as the freezing-point; later the designations were reversed.

The Celsius scale was formerly called centigrade, but this name was officially changed in 1948 to avoid confusion with centigrade meaning 'a hundredth part of a grade'. Centigrade is, however, still used in a few non-technical contexts.

cereal

It may seem unlikely, but the origin of cereal, for many people a familiar sight on the breakfast table, lies ultimately in the name of a Roman goddess. Originally an adjective meaning 'of edible grain', cereal comes from Latin *cerealis*, 'relating to the cultivation of grain', which in turn derives from *Ceres* the goddess of grain and agriculture. Originally a Roman goddess, Ceres, became identified with the Greek goddess Demeter.

Charles's law

Charles's law states that the volume of a gas at constant pressure expands by 1/273 of its volume at 0 °C for each degree Celsius increase in temperature. The law is named after the French scientist *Jacques Alexandre César Charles* (1746–1823). His law was the result of experiments that began in about 1787.

Catherine wheel

Charles's law is sometimes known as *Gay-Lussac's law* after the French scientist *Joseph Louis Gay-Lussac* (1778–1850). In 1802 Gay-Lussac published findings that were more accurate than Charles's.

Charles is also famous as the inventor of the hydrogen balloon, in which he made the first ascent in 1783.

charlotte *(apple charlotte; charlotte russe)*

A charlotte, the baked dessert made of fruit (commonly, apples) that is layered with bread, sponge, etc., is thought to come originally from the name of *Princess Charlotte* (1796–1817), the only daughter of King George IV. The French chef Marc-Antoine Carême (1784–1833) is said to have created a sumptuous pastry in honour of the Princess.

Carême's culinary preparations were so highly regarded that it is said they were taken from the table of the King's court to the marketplace where they were sold for a lot of money.

While serving Tsar Alexander I in Russia, Carême created the charlotte russe (*russe* being French for 'Russian'): the dessert of a mixture of whipped cream and custard set in a crown of sponge fingers.

chateaubriand

The large, thick, fillet steak known as a chateaubriand comes from the name of the French writer and statesman *François René Vicomte de Chateaubriand* (1768–1848).

Chateaubriand fought in the Royalist army in France, living in exile in England from 1793 to 1800. On returning to France in 1800, he achieved great fame with his writings, notably *Le Génie du Christianisme* (1802), and is generally considered as one of the significant leaders of early French Romanticism. Under Louis XVIII, he was French ambassador in London.

It is probable that the steak named in Chateaubriand's honour was created by his chef, Montmirel, and was first prepared at the French embassy in London.

chauvinism

The word chauvinism, referring to an excessive unthinking devotion to one's country, comes from the name of the French soldier *Nicolas Chauvin of Rochefort*.

A soldier in Napoleon's army and wounded many times, Chauvin was ridiculed by his fellow-soldiers for his fanatical devotion to Napoleon. Even when Chauvin was pensioned off with a medal, a ceremonial sabre, and a meagre pension of 200 francs a year, his patriotic zeal continued unabated.

It was the dramatists Charles and Jean Cogniard who made the name Chauvin famous in their comedy *Le Cocarde Tricolore* (1831). In this, Chauvin is a young recruit who sings several songs with the chorus that includes the lines, '*Je suis français, je suis Chauvin*'. The character of Chauvin later featured in a number of other French comedies and as a result became widely known. The word chauvinism soon became familiar in English to describe fanatical patriotism. In more recent years, the sense of the word has widened to include an unreasoned and prejudiced belief in the superiority of one's group or cause, as in the expression *male chauvinism*.

Chesterfield

Chesterfield is used to refer to two items: a padded, often leather, sofa with upright armrests which are the same height as the back, and a man's overcoat with concealed buttons and a velvet collar. Both the sofa and the coat are generally thought to be named after a nineteenth-century *Earl of Chesterfield* (probably not the famous eighteenth-century 4th Earl of Chesterfield, Philip Dormer Stanhope), but it is uncertain which.

Chippendale

The gracefully decorative English furniture style known as Chippendale takes its name from its originator, the English cabinet-maker and furniture designer *Thomas Chippendale* (*c.* 1718–79).

The son of a Yorkshire picture-frame maker Chippendale set up a furniture factory in London in 1749, five years later publishing *The Gentleman and Cabinet Maker's Director*. Illustrating in Louis XV, Chinese, and Gothic styles some 160 designs, this was the first extensive furniture catalogue and was significant in furniture design in both England and America. Chippendale's son, also Thomas (d. *c.* 1822), continued his father's business.

Christian; Christmas; christen

The word Christian occurs in the New Testament in Acts 11:26: '*And the disciples were called Christians first in Antioch*'. From this, its two other occurrences in the New Testament, and a reference in the writings of the Roman historian Tacitus it can be inferred that Christian was a generally recognized title for a follower of Jesus Christ in the time of the New Testament.

The word Christ itself comes from Greek *christos* meaning 'the anointed one', translating Hebrew *Māshīah* 'Messiah'. The name of Christ is also used in other words such as christen, Christianity, and Christendom. The name of the festival of Christmas comes from Old English *Crīstes mæsse*, 'Christ's mass'.

Christopher Columbus

Christopher Columbus is an expression used to show great surprise: *Christopher Columbus! What on earth are you doing here? I thought you were still in Germany!* The name is of course that of the Italian navigator and explorer (1451–1506), who landed on what he named San Salvador island on 12 October 1492.

Also named after Columbus is the Republic of Columbia and numerous cities in the USA.

churrigueresque

The word churrigueresque (pronounced chure-rig-a-resk) is used to describe a Spanish style of baroque architecture of the late seventeenth and early eighteenth centuries. Marked by highly detailed ornate surface features, this style takes its name from the Spanish architect and sculptor *José Churriguera* (1650–1725).

cicerone

A person who acts as a guide to sightseers is sometimes called a cicerone. The word comes from the name of the Roman orator and statesman *Marcus Tullius Cicero* (106–43 B C). The guides take their name from Cicero because he typified the eloquence and knowledge that was expected of these men. They were to be the ones who would point out items of local interest to visitors in the style of the orator Cicero.

cinchona

Cinchona is the name of a genus of South American trees and shrubs that contains some 40 species. One of the most important species is *calisaya*, as its bark produces a drug that can be used in the treatment of malaria.

Cinchona is named after the Spanish vicereine of Peru, *Countess Ana de Chinchón* (1576–1641). In about 1638 the countess was afflicted by a tropical fever that could not be cured by European doctors. The powdered bark of a native Peruvian tree restored her to health, however. The bark was taken back to Spain where it was called Peruvian bark or Countess bark. The modern name Cinchona was given by Linnaeus in honour of the Countess, but it seems that he possibly inadvertently misspelled her name: what should really have been Chinchona was called Cinchona.

Cinderella

A person or thing described as a Cinderella is one that is regarded as being unjustifiably neglected: *For too long distribution has been the Cinderella of the publishing industry.*

The expression comes from the well-known fairytale in which the heroine *Cinderella* is cruelly treated by her stepmother and her two stepsisters but with the help of a fairy godmother finally marries a prince.

clarence

A clarence was a closed, four-wheeled, horse-drawn carriage for four passengers, the driver's seat being outside the carriage. It was named after the *Duke of Clarence*, later to become King William IV (1765–1837).

See also SILLY-BILLY.

clerihew

A clerihew is a witty four-line verse that consists of two rhymed couplets, usually biographical in content. The clerihew was invented by the English writer *Edmund Clerihew Bentley* (1875–1956).

The first clerihew was composed (according to Bentley's friend G. K. Chesterton) while Bentley was at school, 'listening to a chemical exposition, with his rather bored air and a blank sheet of blotting-paper before him'. On this he wrote:

> Sir Humphrey Davy
> Abominated gravy.
> He lived in the odium
> Of having discovered sodium.

Under the name E. Clerihew, Bentley published his first clerihews in 1905. He is also known for his journalistic writings and his detective novel *Trent's Last Case* (1913), but it is for his clerihews he is chiefly remembered. Perhaps the best known is:

> Sir Christopher Wren
> Said, 'I am going to dine with some men.
> If anybody calls
> Say I am designing St Paul's.'

clever Dick see SMART ALEC

Cocker (according to Cocker)

The phrase *according to Cocker* means 'in a manner that is correct, accurate, or reliable'. The expression honours the English arithmetician *Edward Cocker* (1631–75). He is the reputed author of a popular book on mathematics titled *Arithmetick*, which was published in more than 100 editions.

The expression was popularized when introduced into the play *The Apprentice* (1756) by the actor and playwright Arthur Murphy (1727–1805).

The American equivalent of according to Cocker is *according to Hoyle*. This expression honours the British clubman and expert on games *Sir Edmund Hoyle* (1672–1769). At that time the game of whist was very popular and Hoyle was the first person to prepare an authoritative guide to its rules, *A Short Treatise on the Game of Whist*, published in 1742. He also compiled *Hoyle's Standard Games*, the authoritative book of rules of card games. The expert reputation of Hoyle meant that the expression *according to Hoyle* was applied not only to a method of play in accordance with the rules but also more generally to correct or honourable behaviour.

Colt

Colt is the trademark for a type of pistol with a revolving magazine. It has a single barrel with a revolving breech for six bullets. The pistol is named after its inventor, the American engineer *Samuel Colt* (1814–62). Born in Connecticut, Colt ran away to sea at the age of 16. While aboard ship he carved a wooden model of the revolver. On his return home, he established an arms factory, patenting his invention in 1835. The pistols were used notably in the Mexican War (1846–48). In 1854 they were used by the Royal Navy, and a modified .45 calibre version was used by the US army and navy until 1945.

comstockery

Comstockery is strict censorship of literary works on the grounds of immorality or obscenity. The term comes from the name of the American moral crusader *Anthony Comstock* (1844–1915).

Comstock devoted most of his life to suppressing plays and books that he considered immoral. He founded a number of moralistic causes, notably the New York Society for the Suppression of Vice in 1873, the year in which he also secured the passing of the so-called Comstock Laws through Congress to prevent objectionable books and magazines from being sent by the post. As a guardian of the post, he is said to have arrested about 3000 people and destroyed some 50 tons of books that he regarded as immoral. Comstock objected greatly to *Mrs Warren's Profession*, the play by George Bernard Shaw, and it was Shaw who in 1905 coined the word comstockery to describe a narrow moralistic censorship.

Confucianism; Confucius say

Confucianism is the ethical system of the Chinese philosopher *Confucius* (Chinese, Kong Zi) (551–479 BC). Born in Lu, a small state in what is now Shandong province, Confucius became a minor official, later rising to Prime Minister of Lu, when he was well known for his wise, just government. After his advice was ignored, however, he left Lu, returning only in the last years of his life.

From an early age he gathered a group of disciples round him and continued to teach his ethical ideas. (His name means 'Kong, the Master'.) In his final years he edited the books now known as the *Classics*. After his death, his disciples collected his sayings, which became known as the *Analects*. Confucius's ethical system is sometimes summed up in the rule, 'What you do not want others to do to you, do not do to them'.

'*Confucius, he say* . . .' is a humorous expression sometimes used to introduce a maxim or thought that is considered wise.

cordoba

The cordoba is the basic money unit of Nicaragua. The word derives ultimately from the name of the Spanish soldier and explorer *Francisco Fernández de Córdoba* (*c.*1475–1526). It was Córdoba who in 1522 took possession of Nicaragua for the Spanish.

Couéism

'Every day, in every way, I am getting better and better.' This was the formula advocated by the French psychologist and chemist *Emil Coué* (1857–1926) in the treatment of his patients. Establishing a clinic at Nancy in 1910, Coué practised his system of psychotherapy. He believed that by means of autosuggestion – summed up in the formula mentioned above – ideas that lead to illness could be removed from the realm of the will.

coulomb

A coulomb is the basic metric unit of electric charge. The term honours the name of the French physicist *Charles Augustin de Coulomb* (1736–1806).

Originally a French military engineer, Coulomb was forced

because of bad health to retire from the army; subsequently he developed his interests in electricity and magnetism. Coulomb is remembered for his invention of the torsion balance to measure the force between two charged particles and his formulation of what is now known as *Coulomb's law*.

cravat

A cravat is a silk or fine wool scarf worn by men round the neck, often tucked into a shirt. The first cravats were scarves worn by Croatian mercenaries serving in France in the Thirty Years' War (1618–48). Some of French fashionable society were so impressed with the cravats that they adopted the style, calling the scarf after the name of the people, *Hrvat* (pronounced roughly with an initial k-sound), which means 'native of Croatia'.

cretin

A cretin is someone afflicted with cretinism, the condition that arises from a deficiency of thyroid hormone and leads to retarded growth and mental deficiency. The word was originally applied to people who lived in the Swiss Alps. The Swiss called such a person *crestin*, meaning 'Christian, a Christian being, one who is not an animal', this word deriving from the name *Christ*.

crisscross

The word crisscross, referring to a pattern of intersecting lines, comes from *Christ's cross*, the cross of Christ. This word derives in part from the mark of a cross in a children's sixteenth-century hornbook primer, which was a sheet of paper mounted on a wooden tablet and protected by a thin plate of horn. The paper listed the alphabet, the Lord's Prayer, and some numbers. The alphabet that was printed on the top line of the paper was preceded by a small Maltese cross known as the Christ-cross or Christ's cross. The row of letters in the alphabet became known as Christ-cross row, this in time becoming changed to crisscross.

The word crisscross is also usually considered to be a re-duplication of sounds based on the word cross, with the vowel changing (other examples of reduplication being dilly-dally and ding-dong).

Crockford

Crockford is the name often used to refer to *Crockford's Clerical Directory*, the reference book giving facts about the Church of England and its clergy, first published in 1860. It is called Crockford after *John Crockford* (1823–65), managing clerk to serjeant at law Edward Cox, who first published the directory. It seems that Cox preferred to use his clerk's name because of his own official position.

Croesus (as rich as Croesus)

Croesus was the last King of Lydia, a region of Asia Minor, who reigned from 560 to 546 B C. As a result of his conquests, Croesus became extremely rich. Indeed, he was considered by the Greeks to be the wealthiest person on earth, hence the contemporary expression as rich as Croesus meaning 'very rich'.

Legend has it that the Athenian statesman Solon once told Croesus that no man should be considered happy, despite his riches, till he died. Later, when Cyrus the Great defeated Croesus, he condemned Croesus to be burnt alive. It is said that Croesus shouted out Solon's words from the stake, Cyrus intervened, demanding an explanation of Croesus' words, and, being so moved by what his prisoner said, reprieved him and became his friend.

Cruft's

Cruft's is the name of the annual British dog show. It takes its name from the British dog breeder and showman *Charles Cruft* (1852–1938), who in 1886 organized the first dog show.

Cuisenaire rod

Cuisenaire rods is the trademark of a set of rods that have different colours and lengths. The rods are named after the Belgian educationalist *Emil-Georges Cuisenaire* (*c*.1891–1976). Standing for various numbers, the rods are used to teach arithmetic to young children.

Cupid (*to play Cupid; Cupid's bow*)

The expression *to play Cupid*, meaning 'to play the role of matchmaker', alludes to the Roman god of love. Identified with the Greek god Eros, *Cupid* is usually represented as a winged naked boy holding a bow and arrow.

The shape of the bow that Cupid is traditionally shown as carrying is referred to in the expression *Cupid's bow*, used to describe the shape of the upper human lip.

curie see BECQUEREL

curry favour

The expression *curry favour*, meaning 'to try to gain favour by flattery or attention' has nothing to do with the spicy oriental dish.

The phrase is a corruption of the Middle English expression to curry Favel. To curry means 'to groom or stroke down a horse'; *Favel* (or *Fauvel*) was the name of a chestnut horse in a fourteenth-century French satirical poem, the 'Roman de Favel'. Favel symbolized cunning or hypocrisy, so to curry favel was to try to ingratiate oneself through insincere means.

Curzon line

The Curzon line, marking the border between Poland and the Soviet Union, was confirmed at the Yalta Conference of 1945. The boundary is named after the British politician *George Nathaniel, 1st Marquis Curzon of Kedleston* (1859–1925). Curzon served the British government in many capacities including Viceroy of India (1899–1905), Lord Privy Seal (1815–16), and Foreign Secretary (1919–24).

The name Curzon line was first suggested in the Russo-Polish War (1919–20); Lord Curzon suggested that the Poles – who had invaded Russia – should retreat to this line while awaiting a peace conference.

Cushing's disease

Cushing's disease is a condition caused by excessive secretion of certain steroid hormones such as cortisone; its symptoms include obesity, muscular weakness, and high blood pressure. The disease is named after the American neurosurgeon *Harvey Williams Cushing* (1869–1939), who was the first to identify and describe the condition.

Custer's last stand

The expression *Custer's last stand*, referring to a great effort that ends in utter defeat, refers to the American cavalry general *George Armstrong Custer* (1839–76). After distinctive service in the Civil War, Custer commanded the Seventh Cavalry against the Sioux Indian chief Sitting Bull. Custer and his men were massacred by the Indians at the Battle of Little Bighorn, Montana (25 June 1876) in what became known as Custer's Last Stand.

cynic

The followers of the Greek philosopher Antisthenes (*c*.445–*c*.360 BC), especially his later disciples such as Diogenes (411–322 BC) were known as *Cynics*. There are two theories of the origin of this word. One is that the members of the sect were rude and churlish in manner, hence *kunikos*, Greek for 'dog-like'. The other theory is that the sect met in a school called Kunosarges, Greek for 'white dog', as it was supposed that a white dog had once carried off part of a sacrifice being offered to the gods.

Whatever the precise origin of their name, the Cynics were scornful of the accepted values of the rest of society. They tended to live unconventional lives, believing in the self-sufficiency of the individual and that virtue was the highest good, the way to goodness being through self-control. It was, however, the negative aspects of the Cynics' beliefs that came to be emphasized, leading to the contemporary sense of the word, someone who sarcastically doubts others' sincerity, believing that all acts are motivated by selfishness.

Cyrillic

Cyrillic is the name of the alphabet used in writing Slavonic languages such as Russian and Bulgarian. The alphabet is traditionally thought to have been developed by two Greek brothers

St Cyril (hence Cyrillic) (826–69) and St Methodius (*c.*815–85) during the course of translation of the Bible and liturgy into Slavonic. The Cyrillic alphabet is derived from the Greek alphabet and is supplemented by Hebrew letters for non-Greek sounds.

czar see TSAR

D

daguerrotype

One of the earliest practicable photographic processes was the daguerrotype, named after its inventor, the French painter and inventor *Louis Jaques Mandé Daguerre* (1789–1851). In the daguerrotype process, an image is produced on iodine-sensitized silver and developed in mercury vapour.

Daguerre, an officer for the French inland revenue and a landscape and theatrical scenery painter, had been involved in producing the diorama, a method of exhibiting pictures by using special lighting effects. In 1829 Daguerre met the physicist Joseph Niepce (1765–1833), who had been experimenting with different photography methods for some years. Daguerre continued the work after Niepce's death, producing his results in 1839, for which he was awarded the French Legion of Honour.

At about the same time the British botanist and physicist William Henry Fox Talbot (1800–77) was perfecting a photographic process using negatives. Although Fox's system became the basis of modern photography, it was Daguerre's invention that aroused widespread public interest in photography.

dahlia

Dahlia is a genus of herbaceous perennial plants that have showy brightly coloured flowers and tuberous roots. Originally cultivated as a food crop, dahlias are now grown commonly as ornamental plants.

The dahlia was discovered by the German explorer and naturalist Alexander von Humboldt (1769–1859) in Mexico in 1789. It was sent to the Botanic Garden in Madrid, where Professor Cavanilles named it in honour of the Swedish botanist *Anders Dahl* (1751–89), who had died that same year.

daltonism; Dalton's law

Daltonism is another word for colour blindness, especially the inability to distinguish red and green. It is named after the English scientist *John Dalton* (1766–1844), who himself suffered from this disability. He was the first person to give a detailed description of this condition, in *Extraordinary Facts Relating to the Vision of Colours* (1794).

It is for his work in physics and chemistry that Dalton is better known. He is regarded as the originator of the modern atomic theory of matter and he formulated the law relating to the pressure of gases that is known as Dalton's Law.

Dandie Dinmont terrier

Dandi Dinmont terrier is the name of a breed of dog characterized by short legs, a long coat, and drooping ears. The breed is named after *Dandie Dinmont*, a character in the novel *Guy Mannering* (1815) by the Scottish writer Sir Walter Scott (1771–1832). Dinmont was a sturdy farmer who lived in Liddesdale in the Scottish Lowlands and owned a pack of such terriers.

dandy

There are two theories of the origin of the word dandy, 'a man who takes excessive care over his dress and appearance'. One is that the word is short for *Jack-a-dandy*, meaning 'a beau'; the other sees dandy as a nickname for *Andrew*, this name being, it seems, arbitrarily chosen.

Daniel come to judgment; Daniel in the lions' den

The expression *a Daniel come to judgment* refers to someone who makes a wise decision about something that has puzzled others. It alludes to the biblical *Daniel* (Daniel 5:14–16, and especially the devout and upright young man of the apocryphal book of Susanna), but the source of the actual quotation is Shakespeare's *Merchant of Venice* (Act 4, Scene 1):

> A Daniel come to judgment! yea a Daniel!
> O wise young judge, how I do honour thee!

The phrase *Daniel in the lions' den*, referring to someone who is in a place where he or she is exposed to intense personal danger, alludes to Daniel, chapter 6.

darbies

The word darbies, slang for handcuffs, is a shortening of the phrase Father Derby's (or Darby's) bands. This was a sixteenth-century expression alluding to the rigid agreement binding a debtor to a money-lender. *Derby* (or *Darby*) may well have been the name of a notorious usurer of the period.

Darby and Joan

A happily married elderly couple are sometimes known as Darby and Joan: *One summer afternoon we drove to my aunt and uncle's home for tea. They were a real old Darby and Joan – as much in love at 80 as they were at 18.* These names first appeared in a song by Henry Woodfall published in *The Gentleman's Magazine* (1735).

The original Darby and Joan are thought to have been the London printer *John Darby* (d. 1730), to whom Woodfall served as an apprentice, and his wife *Joan*.

The names are further remembered in *Darby and Joan club*, a club for elderly people.

davenport

A davenport is a small compact writing desk with a vertically folding writing surface and side drawers. The word derives from the name *Davenport* between 1820 and 1840, but sources differ as to whether Davenport was a furniture maker or a captain who first commissioned its manufacture. The sense of the word common in America, 'a large sofa, especially one that can be converted into a bed', came later.

David and Goliath; David and Jonathan

David in the expressions David and Goliath and David and Jonathan is the Old Testament King of Israel (*c.* 1000–962 BC). The youngest son of Jesse, David was anointed by Samuel as the successor to Saul as King of Israel. David's successes against the Philistines included the slaying of Goliath. *Goliath*, as is well known, was the Philistine giant who was slain by the seemingly insignificant David: Goliath, the armoured champion bearing a javelin and a spear, David the mere shepherd boy bearing a staff, five smooth stones in his shepherd's bag and a sling. Yet it was David who slung a stone that killed the giant (1 Samuel 17). The expression David and Goliath is used, therefore, to refer to a contest between someone who is apparently weak and someone who seems to possess overwhelmingly superior strength.

David became a close friend of *Jonathan*, Saul's eldest son, and the Bible records their mutual loyalty and affection (1 Samuel 20) hence the expression David and Jonathan to refer to close friends of the same sex.

Davis Cup

The Davis Cup is the annual international lawn tennis championship for men. It is named after the American statesman and sportsman *Dwight Filley Davis* (1879–1945), who instituted the competition in 1900 and donated the trophy that was to be presented to the winners.

An excellent tennis player himself – he was one-time US national doubles champion – Davis was also a respected statesman: he served as Secretary of War (1925–9) and Governor-General of the Philippines (1929–32).

See also WIGHTMAN CUP.

Davy Crockett hat

The American frontiersman, politician, and soldier *Davy Crockett* (1786–1836) is one of the most popular of American heroes. His fearless deeds have been widely described, and his name is still remembered for the Davy Crockett hat, the style of fur hat with a characteristic extended tailpiece that he is said to have worn. Crockett died defending the Alamo during the war for Texan independence.

Davy lamp

The Davy lamp (also known as the safety lamp) takes its name from the British chemist *Sir Humphry Davy* (1778–1829). Davy invented the safety lamp for miners in 1816; it consists of a flame that is enclosed in a metal gauze to prevent its escape and the possible subsequent ignition of explosive gas. His other notable achievements included the isolation of the elements potassium, sodium, calcium, and magnesium.

Davy Jones' locker

The bottom of the sea, thought of as the grave of those drowned or buried at sea is known as *Davy Jones' locker*. Davy Jones is seen as a personification of the devil who rules over the evil spirits of the sea. Being part of sailor slang for over 200 years, there are several different theories of how the expression originated.

Some suggest that Jones is a corruption of the name of the biblical *Jonah*, thrown overboard from a ship and swallowed by a great fish. The name *Davy* is said to have been added by Welsh sailors, *David* being the patron saint of Wales.

Other sources say that Davy is an anglicization of the West Indian word *duffy* or *duppy* meaning 'a malevolent ghost'.

Still others hold that *Davy Jones* was originally the owner of a sixteenth-century London public house that was popular with sailors. The pub is said to have also served as a place for press-ganging unwary seamen into service: Davy Jones was thought to store more than just ale in the lockers at the back of the pub. The sailors would be drugged, transferred to a ship, to awaken only when the ship had put to sea. Thus Davy Jones' locker came to be feared.

Debrett

Debrett – in full *Debrett's Peerage* – is the name of a directory of the British aristocracy. The listing bears the name of the London publisher who first issued it, *John Debrett* (*c.* 1752–1822). The original compilation, published in 1802, was titled *A Peerage of England, Scotland, and Ireland*; it was followed six years later by *A Baronetage of England*.

decibel

The decibel is the unit that is used to compare two power levels, especially of the intensity of sound, on a logarithmic scale. The decibel is one-tenth of a bel, the latter is only rarely used. Both units are named after the Scottish-born American scientist *Alexander Graham Bell* (1847–1922).

Bell is famous for his invention of the telephone (1876) – the first, historic, words that Bell spoke to his assistant Thomas Watson on the telephone were 'Watson, come here, I want you'.

Delilah

A Delilah is a treacherous and seductive woman, especially a mistress or wife. The use of this name alludes to the story of the biblical character *Delilah* who was bribed by the Philistine rulers to discover the secret of Samson's great strength (Judges 16:4–22). Samson lied to her on three occasions, but when she continued to ask him, he grew so weary of her nagging that he told her the truth – that the source of his power lay in his long hair. Delilah then betrayed this secret to the Philistines, and while Samson slept upon her lap, his hair was shaved off, so depriving him of his strength.

See also SAMSON.

demijohn

A demijohn is a large narrow-necked bottle that is made of glass or stoneware. Usually having small handles at the neck, demijohns are often encased in wickerwork. The word demijohn probably derives from the French *dame-jeanne*, 'Lady Jane', from the resemblance between the shape of the large bulging bottle and that of a particular buxom French housewife, or more likely, with portly women in general.

Derby

The Derby is the name of the annual flat race for three-year-old horses run at Epsom Downs, Surrey. It is probably named after *Edward Stanley, 12th Earl of Derby* (1752–1834), who founded the horse race in 1780. The American counterpart is the Kentucky Derby, founded in 1875.

Derby is also the American and Canadian word for a bowler hat, (its first syllable being pronounced to rhyme with *fur*). It is said that some Americans, noticing the distinctive shape of the style of hat worn by English sportsmen, took some of the hats back to American manufacturers, asking them to make such felt, narrow-brimmed hats with a rounded crown that were later sold as 'hats like the English wear at the Derby'.

derrick

The word derrick, now referring to a hoisting apparatus or crane, formerly described a gallows. The word derives from the seventeenth-century English hangman surnamed *Derrick*.

Derrick served under the command of Robert Devereux, 2nd Earl of Essex in the sacking of Cádiz (1596), where he was charged with rape and found guilty. He was sentenced to death by hanging but was pardoned by Essex when he agreed to become executioner at Tyburn gallows, London, near what is now Marble Arch. A few years later, Essex was found guilty of treason after instigating a riot in London (1601) and was sentenced to death, it being Derrick who was to execute him. On this occasion Derrick used an axe, requiring three attempts to cut off Essex's head. In all, Derrick is said to have carried out more than 3000 executions in his service as hangman, his name being applied to the gallows itself and then to the crane which the gallows resembled.

derringer

A derringer is a small, short-barrelled pistol of large calibre. It is named after its inventor, the American gunsmith *Henry Deringer* (1786–1868). Deringer's invention meant that he became one of America's largest manufacturers of arms. There were, however, many imitations of his gun, one of which was the European make of Derringer – i.e. Deringer's name adapted with an additional 'r' to avoid patent laws – and it is the spelling Derringer that has become generally accepted.

deutzia

Deutzia is the name of a genus of ornamental shrubs of the saxifrage family that bear white or pink bell-like flowers. It is named after the Dutch patron of botany *Jean Deutz* (c. 1743–c. 1784).

Dewar flask

A Dewar flask is the name given to a kind of vacuum flask used in scientific experiments to store a liquid or gas at a constant temperature. It is also known by the trademark Thermos flask or, non-technically, as a vacuum flask. A Dewar flask has two thin glass walls that are separated by a vacuum to reduce loss of heat by conduction. The inner surface is silvered to reduce loss of heat by radiation, and the vessel has a tight stopper to prevent evaporation.

The Dewar flask takes its name from the Scottish chemist and physicist *Sir James Dewar* (1842–1923) who invented this prototype of the modern vacuum flask in about 1872. Dewar is known for his research into gases – he was the first person to produce liquid hydrogen – and, with the British chemist Sir Frederick Augustus Abel (1827–1902), he invented the explosive cordite.

Dewey Decimal System

The book classification system known as the Dewey Decimal System is named after the American librarian *Melvil Dewey* (1851–1931). Dewey devised his book-classification system in 1876, while working as acting librarian at Amherst College, Massachusetts. In Dewey's system, books are classified according to their subject matter by a three-digit number showing the main class, followed by numbers after a decimal point, to show subdivisions. The Dewey system is widely used by libraries throughout the world, the classification being constantly revised.

Dickensian

The adjective Dickensian has a number of meanings: 'suggesting poverty, misery, and the squalor of urban or industrial life of Victorian England', 'suggesting conviviality' (*They enjoyed a real old-fashioned Dickensian Christmas*), and 'vividly caricatured', used to describe the figures he created. The word Dickensian comes of course from the name of the English novelist *Charles (John Huffman) Dickens* (1812–70). It was memories of his painful childhood – he himself had to go to work in a blacking warehouse at the age of 12 – that inspired a great deal of his writing. Some of the characters in his writings have also become eponymous, for example SCROOGE from *A Christmas Carol* and GAMP, an umbrella, from *Mrs Sarah Gamp* in *Martin Chuzzlewit*.

It is a mistake, however, to consider that 'the dickens', in expressions such as *what the dickens* and *the dickens only knows* comes from the name of Charles Dickens. The dickens referred to here is a euphemism for the devil. In fact the expression was used centuries before Dickens; Shakespeare used it in *The Merry Wives of Windsor* (Act 3, Scene 2); 'I cannot tell what the dickens his name is'.

diddle

The word diddle, meaning informally 'to cheat or swindle' comes from the name of the character *Jeremy Diddler* in the farce *Raising the Wind* (1803) by the Irish-born English dramatist James Kenney (1780–1849). Diddler, the chief character of the play, has the habit of constantly borrowing small sums of money that he never pays back. The play's success led to the quick acceptance of the verb diddle into the language.

diesel

A diesel engine is an internal-combustion engine in which fuel is ignited by highly compressed air. The word diesel comes from the name of the German mechanical engineer *Rudolf Diesel* (1858–1913), who invented the diesel engine in 1892. Diesel's design followed up earlier ideas of the French scientist Sadi Carnot (1796–1832). Diesel developed the engine at the Krupp factory in Essen; and he not only invented a new kind of engine, he also found the best kind of fuel, the relatively cheap semi-refined crude oil, to power the engine. Today the diesel engine is widely used in industry and road, rail, and maritime transport.

Dionysian

Dionysus was the Greek god of wine, also of fruitfulness and vegetation; he is identified with the Roman god Bacchus. He was worshipped in five annual dramatic festivals (the Dionysia) by the people of Athens. Dionysian feastings were scenes of wild, orgiastic licentiousness and it is with allusion to such ecstatic frenzy that the words Dionysian (or Dionysiac) are sometimes used today.

Dioscorea

Dioscorea is the botanical name of the genus of plants in the yam family. This name was given by Linnaeus in honour of the Greek physician *Dioscorides Pedanius* (*c.* 40–*c.* 90 AD). As a surgeon in the Roman army, Discorides travelled widely and he collected information about nearly 600 plants and their medicinal properties which he recorded in *De materia medica* (*c.* 77 AD). He is commonly regarded as one of the founders of the science of botany.

Dives

Dives is the name given to the rich man in the story about the rich man and Lazarus told by Jesus (Luke 16:19–31). In the story, Dives pays no attention to the plight of Lazarus, the beggar at his gate. After death Lazarus is carried to 'Abraham's side' and Dives to Hades, but it is not possible for there to be any contact between them.

It is interesting to note that the rich man is not actually named in the English Bible text. It is in the Latin version of the New Testament that he is called dives, meaning 'rich', hence 'a rich man', and the word has come to be thought of as a proper noun.

The names of Dives has thus become proverbial for a very rich person, especially one who is unconcerned and hardened to others' needs.

Doberman pinscher

A Doberman pinscher is a breed of short-haired, medium-sized dog with a short tail. The name of the dog derives from the German *Ludwig Dobermann* (1834–94) and the German word *Pinscher*, a breed of hunting dog. A tax collector as well as a dog breeder, Dobermann developed in the 1880s a particularly ferocious breed of dog to help him in his duties. Nowadays Dobermans are widely used as guard dogs.

dolomite

Dolomite is the name given to the mineral calcium magnesium carbonate, which has a hexagonal crystal structure and is used in the manufacture of cement and as a building stone. The term is also used to refer to a rock containing a high ratio of magnesium carbonate that is used as a building material. The word dolomite comes from the name of the French geologist *Déodat de Dolomieu* (1750–1801) who discovered the mineral.

doily

The word doily, for a small ornamental openwork mat made of paper, cloth, or plastic that is laid under dishes of food, comes from the name of a London draper. His name is variously spelt – *Doily, Doiley,* or *Doyley* – and he owned a London shop around the year 1700 in the Strand, where fabrics trimmed with embroidery or crochet work were sold. The decorative cloths were originally known as Doily napkins, then doilies.

Don Juan

A Don Juan is a man who tries to seduce many women, a man with an insatiable desire for women. The name is based on the legendary fourteenth-century Spanish aristocrat and womanizer, *Don Juan Tenorio*. According to the traditional Spanish story, Don

Juan Tenorio of Seville kills the father of Doña, the young girl he is attempting to seduce. On visiting the tomb, Don Juan scornfully invites the statue to a feast, the statue accepts, but seizes Don Juan and delivers him to hell.

Don Juan is the subject of numerous plays and operas: Molière's *Don Juan* (1665), Mozart's *Don Giovanni* (1787), Byron's *Don Juan* (1819–24), and Shaw's *Man and Superman* (1903).

Don Quixote see QUIXOTIC

Doppler effect

The Doppler effect is the technical name for the change in the apparent frequency of the waves of sound, light, etc., when there is relative motion between the source and the observer. For instance, the sound of a low-flying aeroplane seems to drop in pitch as the plane passes the observer, although it in fact remains constant.

The phenomenon is named after the Austrian physicist *Christian Johann Doppler* (1803–53), who first explained it in 1842. Doppler originally tried to apply his principle to explain the coloration of stars.

doubting Thomas

A doubting Thomas is someone who is sceptical, particularly someone who refuses to believe until he has seen proof of something or has been otherwise satisfied as to its truth. The expression alludes to one of Jesus' apostles, *Thomas*, who refused to believe in Christ's resurrection until he had seen and felt Christ's body for himself (John 20:24–29).

Douglas fir

The Douglas fir is a very tall evergreen American tree that is grown both for ornament and for its high-quality timber. With needle-like leaves and large cylindrical hanging cones, the Douglas fir is named after the Scottish botanist *David Douglas* (1798–1834).

Sent to North America at the age of 23, Douglas crossed Canada on foot and travelled as far south as California. When he came across the tall trees (which are second in height only to the giant sequoias and redwoods) Douglas had to shoot his seeds down with a gun – and in the process was chased by American Indians. In all, Douglas collected over 200 plants and seeds that were unknown in Europe. He suffered an unusual death: he was gored by a wild bull while working in Hawaii.

Dow–Jones average

The Dow–Jones average (or index) is a daily index of the relative prices of shares on the New York Stock Exchange. Based on the prices of a representative number of shares, the index takes its name from two American financial statisticians, *Charles Henry Dow* (1851–1902) and *Edward D. Jones* (1856–1920). Dow and Jones founded Dow, Jones and Co. in 1882 to provide information to Wall Street finance houses. Since 1884 indexes of movements of selected stocks and shares have been calculated.

Downing Street

Downing Street is the name of the road in Westminster, London, that houses the official residences of the British Prime Minister (No. 10) and the chancellor of the exchequer (No. 11). The street is named after the English stateman *Sir George Downing* (1623–84). A nephew of a Massachusetts governor, Downing graduated

Douglas Fir
(*Pseudotsuga menziesii*)

David Douglas
-1798-1834-

from Harvard and returned to England where he served under both Cromwell and King Charles II. His warning to Charles II in 1657 that Cromwell wanted to capture him saved Charles' life. Downing was later given a grant of land in what is now Downing Street.

Down's syndrome

Down's syndrome is a congenital disease typically marked by mental retardation and the physical features of staring eyes, a broad short skull, and short fingers. Associated with the presence of one extra chromosome in each cell, the condition is named after the English physician *John Langdon-Down* (1828–96) who first adequately described it in 1866. The disease was formerly called mongolism because the characteristic facial appearance of the affected children was commonly thought to resemble that of the people of Mongolia.

draconian

Draconian means 'very harsh or severe' and is used to describe laws, measures, or regulations. The word comes from *Draco*, the seventh-century BC Athenian law-giver. In 621 BC he drew up what was probably the first comprehensive code of laws in Athens; before that time the laws had been interpreted arbitrarily by members of the city's governing body.

Draco's code of laws was so severe – almost every named crime carried the death sentence – that draconian came to be used to describe laws of unreasonable cruelty. In 590 BC the Athenian statesman Solon issued a more lenient legal code.

Druse

The Druses (or Druzes) are members of a religious sect centred on the mountains of Syria and Lebanon. The name probably derives from the name of one of the sect's founders, *Ismail al-Darazi*, Ismail the tailor (died 1019). The Druses' scriptures are based on the Bible, the Koran, and Sufi writings. Druses believe in the deity of Al-Hakim, a caliph of Egypt.

dryasdust

A boring pedantic person is sometimes called a dryasdust. The name is that of the fictitious character *Rev. Dr Jonas Dryasdust*, to whom the Scottish writer Sir Walter Scott (1771–1832) addressed the prefaces of some of his novels.

dunce

The word dunce, 'a person who is stupid or slow to learn', derives originally from the name of the Scottish theologian *John Duns Scotus* (c. 1265–1308). (The Duns in his name comes from his supposed birthplace near Roxburgh, Scotland.) A Franciscan, his teaching combined elements of Aristotle's and Augustine's doctrines, but he was opposed to the theology of St Thomas Aquinas, he being nicknamed 'the Subtle Doctor' and Aquinas 'the Angelic Doctor'. His teachings ('Scotism') were accepted by the Franciscans and were influential in the Middle Ages but were ridiculed in the sixteenth century by humanists and reformers who considered his followers (called Dunsmen or Dunses) reluctant to accept new theological ideas. The word dunce then came to refer to a person resistant to new ideas, hence to someone who is dull or stupid.

E

Eiffel Tower

The Eiffel Tower in Paris is named after its designer, the French engineer *Alexandre Gustave Eiffel* (1832–1923). Built for the Paris Universal Exposition of 1889, the 300-metre (984-foot) structure was the world's highest building until 1930, when it was displaced by the Chrysler Building in New York.

Eiffel also designed the interior structure of the Statue of Liberty, although the structure itself was designed by the French architect Frédéric August Bartholdi (1834–1904).

einsteinium

Einsteinium is the name of a radioactive chemical element that is produced artificially; its atomic number is 99. The element, originally identified by the American physicist Albert Ghiorso and others in 1952 in fall-out from the first hydrogen bomb explosion, is named after the German-born American physicist *Albert Einstein* (1879–1955). Einstein is most famous for his formulation of the special theory of relativity (1905) and the general theory of relativity (1916) and was awarded the NOBEL PRIZE for physics in 1921.

Eiffel Tower

Paris

LA TOUR
14^F
A 2EME ÉTA

Electra complex see OEDIPUS COMPLEX

Elgin Marbles

The Elgin Marbles is the name given to the collection of ancient Greek marble sculptures that between 1803 and 1812 were removed from the Parthenon in Athens by *Thomas Bruce, the 7th Earl of Elgin* (1766–1841). Elgin was British ambassador to Turkey at the time and he obtained them from the Turks who were then occupying Athens. Elgin sold the sculptures to the British government in 1816 for £35,500 and they are currently on display at the British Museum. Efforts are continuing on the part of the Greek government to have this part of their cultural heritage restored to them.

Elizabethan

The reign of *Queen Elizabeth I* (1533–1603; reigned 1558–1603) was marked by great achievements in literature, exploration, and many other areas, including the life and work of poets such as Shakespeare and Spenser, the discoverers Raleigh and Drake, and musicians such as William Byrd. It is this spirit of outstanding creativity and bold adventure that is evoked by use of the term Elizabethan. The adjective may also be applied to *Queen Elizabeth II* (born 1926), alluding to the possibility of a similarly great and imaginative age.

éminence grise

An *éminence grise* refers to someone who exercises power unofficially by influencing another person or group who appear to have authority. *Éminence grise* (French for 'grey eminence') was originally the nickname given to the French friar and diplomat *Père Joseph* (*François Le Clerc du Tremblay* 1577–1638), private secretary and confidant to the French statesman Cardinal Richelieu. The nickname referred to the colour of Père Joseph's garments and also to the authority he wielded over the unsuspecting Richelieu.

epicure; Epicurean

A person who cultivates a discriminating taste in food or wine is known as an epicure. The word derives from the name of the Greek philosopher *Epicurus* (341–270 BC). Epicurus taught that the highest good was pleasure, but because every joy entailed some pain, he taught his disciples (Epicureans) to exercise moderation in all things. Epicurus also taught that pleasure was gained not through sensual indulgence but by self-control and achieving tranquillity of mind. His teachings have been misunderstood at times, however, and some have seen them as defending the unashamed pursuit of bodily pleasure.

Erastianism

The theory that the state should have authority over the church in ecclesiastical matters is known as Erastianism. This term comes from the name of the Swiss theologian *Thomas Erastus* (1524–83), to whom such a theory was attributed. In fact, however, Erastus limited his argument only to 'the case of a State where but one religion is permitted'.

erotic

The word erotic, 'of or tending to arouse sexual desire', derives from *Eros*, the Greek god of love and the Greek word *erōs*, 'love; (sexual) desire'. The god Eros (Roman counterpart: CUPID) was

the son of Aphrodite and was usually portrayed as a winged
blindfolded youth with a bow and arrows.

eschscholtzia

Eschscholtzia is the name of a genus of plants in the poppy family
and is applied particularly to the California poppy (*Eschscholtzia
californica*) grown for its yellow and orange flowers. The term
Eschscholtzia honours the name of the Russian-born German
naturalist *Johann Friedrich von Eschscholtz* (1793–1834), who accompanied the German navigator and explorer Otto von Kotzebue on
his expeditions (1815–18, 1823).

Esperanto

Esperanto is the name of the artificial language invented by the
Polish doctor and linguist Lazarus Ludwig Zamenhof (1859–1917)
in 1887. The language takes its name from the pseudonym chosen
by its inventor when he wrote his first book on the subject *Linguo
Internacia de la Doktoro Esperanto*. The word Esperanto itself comes
from Latin *sperare* 'to hope'; thus his pseudonym means 'the hoping
doctor'. The language's grammar is completely regular and each
letter represents only one sound. It is the world's most successful
artificial language.

Euclidean geometry

Euclidean geometry is a system of geometry based on the axioms
of the third century B C Greek mathematician *Euclid*. These axioms
are recorded in Euclid's books, *Stoicheia* (*Elements*), which remained
the standard work on geometry for over 2000 years. It was not
until the nineteenth century that the possibility of a non-Euclidean
geometry was seriously contemplated.

Euclid defined a line as 'length without breath'; and he is also said to have warned King Ptolemy I that 'there is no Royal road to geometry' when asked if there was a quicker and easier way to learn the subject. Besides referring to geometry, the adjective Euclidean is also sometimes used to mean 'clear and orderly in presentation and explanation'.

euhemerism

Euhemerism is the theory that the gods described in mythology are in fact historical heroes who have been regarded as divine. The word euhemerism derives from the name of the fourth-century Silician Greek philosopher *Euhemerus* who advanced this theory in his philosophical romance *Sacred History*. Euhemerus asserted that he had come across an inscription that supported his theory on a gold pillar in a temple on an island in the Indian Ocean.

euphorbia

Euphorbia is the name of the genus of plants of the spurge family that have a milky sap and small flowers surrounded by conspicuous bracts. As well as being used for ornamentation, some of the species have been used medicinally. The description euphorbia derives ultimately from the name of the first-century A D Greek physician *Euphorbus*. Euphorbus was physician to King Juba II of Mauritania, who is said to have named the plant after him.

euphuism

Euphuism – not to be confused with euphemism – is used to describe an artificial and highly ornate style of writing or speaking. Fashionable in the late sixteenth and early seventeenth centuries, euphuism derives from *Euphues*, a character in the prose romance in two parts *Euphues: The Anatomy of Wit* (1578) and *Euphues and his England* (1580) by the English writer John Lyly (*c.* 1554–1606). Euphues is Greek for 'well-endowed by nature' and Lyly's prose romance, marked by excessive use of antithesis, alliteration, historical or mythological allusion, and other figures of speech, has given the word euphuism to describe this elaborately embellished style.

Eustachian tube

The Eustachian tube is the name of the canal connecting the pharynx (throat) to the middle ear. Known also as the pharyngotympanic tube, it had already been discovered by the fifth-century BC Greek physician Alcmaeon of Croton, but it was the Italian physician *Bartolommeo Eustachio* (*c.* 1520–74) who first adequately described it. As well as undertaking anatomical research into the ear, Eustachio studied the heart, kidney, and nervous system.

Everest

The name of the world's highest mountain, Mount Everest on the Nepal–Tibet border (8848 m; 29,028 ft), honours the surveyor-general of India, *Sir George Everest* (1790–1866). Everest was the first to undertake detailed mapping of the subcontinent, including the Himalayas.

Since 1920–1 expeditions to climb Mount Everest have been undertaken, the first successful one being the expedition led by Colonel John Hunt when the New Zealander Edmund Hillary and the Sherpa Tensing Norkay became the first to reach the summit on 29 May 1953.

In a derived application of the word, Everest is sometimes used to refer to the highest point of achievement.

everyman

Everyman is the name sometimes given to the typical or average person, 'the man in the street'. The description comes from the allegorical character *Everyman* in the sixteenth-century morality play of the same title. In the play, which is based on a slightly earlier Dutch counterpart *Elckerlijc*, Everyman is summoned by death, but he finds that none of his friends will go with him except Good Deeds. The lines of Knowledge in the play have become legendary:

> Everyman, I will go with thee and be thy guide,
> In thy most need to go by thy side.

F

Fabian

The adjective Fabian is sometimes used to mean 'cautious in politics; avoiding direct confrontation'. This sense derives from the policies of the Roman general *Quintus Fabius Maximus* (also known as Cunctator, the delayer; died 203 B C). As a commander against Hannibal in the second Punic War, Fabius continually harassed Hannibal's armies without ever risking a pitched battle. Fabius' cautious tactics contributed to Hannibal's eventual defeat.

The *Fabian Society*, an association of British socialists, took its name from Quintus Fabius Maximus. Founded in 1884 to establish democratic socialist principles gradually rather than by adopting revolutionary methods, its prominent personalities included George Bernard Shaw.

fagin

The name Fagin is sometimes used to describe an adult who teaches others, especially children, to steal goods, and also to describe a person who receives stolen goods. The allusions are to the fictional character *Fagin*, the head of a gang of thieves in the novel *Oliver Twist* (published 1837–8) by Charles Dickens.

Fahrenheit

Fahrenheit is the scale of temperatures in which 32° represents the freezing point of water and 212° the boiling point of water. It is named after its inventor, the German scientist *Gabriel Daniel Fahrenheit* (1686–1736), who set 0° as the lowest temperature he could scientifically derive, by mixing ice and common salt. The Fahrenheit scale is no longer in general use, having been replaced by the CELSIUS scale.

Fahrenheit was born in Danzig and lived most of his life in Holland and England. His father wanted him to be a merchant, but after a brief and unsuccessful attempt at this career, he turned to physics. Before he was 20, Fahrenheit manufactured meteorological instruments. He initially used alcohol in his thermometers, but he soon used mercury, inventing the first mercury thermometer. He was elected to the Royal Society in 1724.

Falkland Islands

The British name of the Falkland islands, the islands in the South Atlantic, are named in memory of *Lucius Cary, 2nd Viscount Falkland* (c. 1610–43), Secretary of State (1642). The name Falklands was given by an English sailor, Captain John Strong, who in 1690 named the sound between the two main islands Falkland Sound.

The Argentine name for the islands, *Islas Malvinas*, does not come from Spanish, but French. Many of the sailors who went there in the early eighteenth century were from *St Malo* in Brittany, so the French called the islands Îles Malouines, which became the existing Argentine name in Spanish.

Fallopian tube

The Fallopian tubes are the two tubes that connect the uterus to the ovaries in female mammals. They are named after the Italian anatomist *Gabriel Fallopius* (1523–62) who first described them. A pupil of the Flemish anatomist Andreas Vesalius (1514–64), Fallopius was professor of anatomy at Pisa (1548–51) after which he taught at Padua University. He described features of the ear as well as the reproductive system in his *Observationes anatomicae* (1561).

Falstaffian

The adjective Falstaffian is sometimes used to describe someone who is plump, witty, and self-indulgent. The word derives from the character *Sir John Falstaff* in Shakespeare's *Henry IV, Parts I and II* (1597) and *The Merry Wives of Windsor* (1597).

farad; faraday; faradic; faradism

The English physicist and chemist *Michael Faraday* (1791–1867) was born into a poor London family and was apprenticed at an early age to a bookbinder, where he came across books that aroused his interest in science. He attended lectures at the Royal Institution and persuaded Sir Humphry Davy to engage him as his assistant (1813), eventually succeeding Davy as professor of chemistry there (1833).

Faraday made many notable discoveries in different areas of the physical sciences, but it is particularly with electricity and electrochemistry that his name is perpetually linked. A farad is the basic metric unit of electrical capacitance; a faraday is a quantity of electricity used in electrolysis. He is known for his laws of electrolysis (1813–14) and his pioneering work on electromagnetic induction, hence the terms faradic and faradism.

Farmer Giles

Farmer Giles is sometimes used in a mildly humorous way as a generic name for a farmer. The name implies not only a rural simplicity but also a capacity for common sense. The name may be derived from *Giles*, the orphan farm labourer in the poem 'The Farmer's Boy' (1800) by Robert Bloomfield (1766–1823).

faro

Faro, a gambling game in which the players bet on the value of the cards the dealer will turn up, probably derives via French ultimately from *Pharaoh*, the title of ancient Egyptian rulers. It is possible that at one time in the history of the game a picture of one of the ruling pharaohs featured on the cards.

Fata Morgana

Fata Morgana is the name given to a mirage that traditionally is seen in the Strait of Messina from the Calabrian coast. In a derived sense the term may be applied to any mirage and to a figment of the imagination. The name Fata Morgana (English, Morgan le Fay' comes from Italian *fata*, 'fairy' and *Morgana* who was the Queen of Avalon, half-sister of King Arthur, and evil sorceress of Arthurian legend. It was believed by the Norman settlers in England that she lived in Calabria, hence the application of the name to the apparition.

faun; fauna

A faun is a figure in Roman mythology that has the body of a human and the horns and legs of a goat. The word derives from

Faunus, the Roman god of pastures and forests who was later identified with the Greek god Pan.

The name fauna, referring to animal life in general or that of a particular area or period (and often complementing FLORA), was adopted by Linnaeus in 1746, *Fauna* being the sister of the god Faunus.

Faustian

Faust is the name of the semi-legendary medieval German scholar and magician who allegedly sold his soul to the Devil in exchange for knowledge and power. Stories of conjurors working with the Devil, linked with the historical figure of the wandering conjuror *John Faust* (*c.* 1488–1540), have inspired many literary works including Marlowe's *Dr Faustus* (1604) and Goethe's *Faust* (1808, 1832). The adjective Faustian has thus come to describe different characteristics of Faust and Faustus, including the abandonment of spiritual values in order to gain material benefits, the relentless pursuit of knowledge and enjoyment, and spiritual disillusionment and dissatisfaction.

fermium

Fermium is an artificially produced radioactive element. Like EINSTEINIUM, it was first detected by the American physicist Albert Ghiorso in fall-out after the first hydrogen-bomb explosion (1952). It was named after the Italian-born American physicist *Enrico Fermi* (1901–54).

Fermi's early work in Italy was concerned with quantum statistics – the Fermi–Dirac statistics, named after himself and the British physicist Paul Adrien Maurice Dirac (1902–84). Fermi is best known for his work on nuclear physics: he was awarded the NOBEL PRIZE for physics in Stockholm in 1938. Owing to his antifascism and because his wife was Jewish, Fermi sailed directly from Stockholm with his family to the United States. In Chicago he led the group that produced the first controlled nuclear chain reaction (1942). As well as being known for a chemical element, Fermi's name is also honoured by the *fermi* (a former unit of length in nuclear physics), the so-called *Fermi level*, and *fermion* (an elementary particle).

Ferris wheel

A Ferris wheel is a large upright fairground wheel with seats that hang freely from its rim; the seats remain more or less horizontal as the power-driven wheel turns. It is named after the American engineer *George Washington Gale Ferris* (1859–96) and was introduced at the World's Columbian Exposition in Chicago (1893). The first Ferris wheel measured 250 feet (76 m) in diameter, and had 36 cars, each holding up to 40 people. The 'big wheels' of today are more modest attractions, seating six to eight people in each car.

fiacre

A fiacre was a small, four-wheeled, horse-drawn carriage of the seventeenth and eighteenth centuries. The name of the cab derives from the town house where they were first hired out in 1648, the *Hotel de St Fiacre* in Paris. Fiacre is the French version of the name of the Irish Prince *Fiachrach* (or *Fiachra*), who founded a monastery at Breuil, near Paris in about 670.

Fibonacci sequence

The Fibonacci sequence is the name given to the sequence of numbers in which each number after the first two numbers is the sum of the previous two in the series. The sequence begins with the numbers (known as Fibonacci numbers) 0, 1, 1, 2, 3, 5, 8, 13, 21, 34. It is named after the Italian mathematician *Leonardo Fibonacci* (*c.* 1170–*c.* 1250), who is said to have invented it in 1225 in order to solve a puzzle about the breeding rate of rabbits. The sequence has been found to occur in nature, such as in the number of leaf buds on a plant stem and the number of spirals of seeds on the head of a sunflower.

Fibonacci is also credited with popularizing the Arabic numerical notation in his *Book of the Abacus* (1202).

filbert

The filbert (*Corylus maxima*) is a tree that is closely related to the hazel. It is named after the Frankish abbot *St Philibert* (died 684), because his feast day (22 August) falls in the nutting season.

fink

The word fink is used chiefly in US and Canadian slang for a strikebreaker, informer, or a contemptible or unpleasant person. There are a number of different theories of the word's origin. One possible suggestion is that fink is an altered form of pink, which is short for *Pinkerton*, the name of the strikebreakers in the Homestead steel strike of 1892.

flora

The word flora refers to plant life in general or that of a particular area or period; it often complements FAUNA. The term derives from *Flora*, the Roman goddess of flowers, youth, and spring, whose name comes from Latin *flōs* 'flower'. The spring festival (Floralia) in her honour, was established in 283 BC and provided the scene of wild, uninhibited conduct.

Flora

94

Florence Nightingale

The English nurse Florence Nightingale (1820–1910) is known for her work during the Crimean War. She led a party of nurses to work in the military hospital at Scutari (1854), where she sought to improve the living conditions of the patients, who dubbed her 'the Lady with the Lamp'. After the war, Florence Nightingale devoted herself to raising the status of the nursing profession. She was the first woman to receive the Order of Merit (1907). Her name is sometimes used when referring to a devoted and highly efficient nurse.

Fokker

The Fokker was the famous German fighter plane of the First World War, noted for its speed and climbing power. It is named after its designer and manufacturer the Dutch-born *Anthony Herman Gerard Fokker* (1890–1939). In 1912 Fokker set up an aircraft factory in Germany. He later became an American citizen.

forsythia

Forsythia is the name given to a genus of ornamental shrubs of the olive family that have bright yellow bell-shaped flowers which appear before the leaves in early spring. The name honours the British botanist *William Forsyth* (1737–1804). A Scottish gardener and horticulturist, Forsyth became superintendent of the Royal Garden of St James's and Kensington. He may have personally brought the forsythia shrub from its native China and introduced it to Britain.

Fowler

Fowler is sometimes used to refer to the style manual *A Dictionary of Modern English Usage*, compiled by the British lexicographer *Henry Watson Fowler* (1858–1933).

Fowler began his career as a teacher at Sedburgh school, but after 17 years resigned from the school, objecting to the compulsory preparation of boys for confirmation. He then sought to make a living as a writer. With his brother Frank George Fowler (1870–1918) he translated Lucian (1905), and wrote *The King's English* (1906), and *The Concise English Dictionary of Current English* (1911). By lying about his age, Fowler saw active service in the First World War, but was invalided out. After the war he wrote *A Dictionary of Modern English Usage* (1926), the book that was to make him 'a household word in all English-speaking countries' (Sir Ernest Gowers).

Fowler is today seen as a classic, prescriptive guide to usage; its success is generally considered to lie as much in its idiosyncratic style as in its detailed and discursive stylistic commentary.

Franciscan

Franciscans are members of the Orders of Friars Minor founded by *St Francis of Assisi* in 1209. In its original form, the distinctive feature of this order was its insistence on complete poverty of individual friars and corporately of the whole order.

St Francis of Assisi (original name Giovanni di Bernardone; 1182–1226) was the son of a wealthy merchant, who renounced his worldly possessions in 1205, turning to a life of prayer. By 1209 he had gathered a band of disciples around him. He composed for himself and his associates a Primitive Rule – now lost, but it seems to have been composed mainly of passages from the Gospels. In 1212 he presented this rule to Pope Innocent III, who gave his approval to the new order. St Francis later travelled widely, retiring in 1220 from leadership of his order, and, according to tradition, receiving the stigmata of Christ in 1224. He is remembered for his deep humility and generosity, his simple faith, and his love for God, fellow-men and nature.

The Franciscan order has known decline and division since St Francis's time, but has remained a missionary and charitable part of the church.

frangipane

Frangipane is a pastry filled with cream and almonds. The name (often spelt frangipani) is also applied to the shrub *Plumeria rubra* of the periwinkle family (red jasmine) and to a perfume prepared from this plant or resembling the odour of its flowers.

The origin of frangipane is uncertain. It seems that the word came via French from Italian and it was the sixteenth-century Italian nobleman, the *Marquis Muzio Frangipani*, who first invented a perfume for scenting gloves. It may well have been the marquis or a relative of his who originally prepared the pastry named in his honour.

Frankenstein

Frankenstein's monster is the product of an inventor that then destroys its creator. The expression comes originally from the name *Baron Frankenstein* in the novel *Frankenstein or the Modern Prometheus* (1818) by the English novelist Mary Wollstonecraft Shelley (1797–1851). The novel describes how the hero, the philosopher Baron Frankenstein, creates the immense and repulsive monster out of inanimate matter; the monster gets out of control and eventually murders its creator. In contemporary usage, the name Frankenstein is often applied to the monster itself rather than its creator.

Fraunhofer lines

Joseph von Fraunhofer (1787–1826) was a German physicist and optician. In 1814 he observed numerous dark lines in the sun's spectrum, now known as the Fraunhofer lines. He also made significant improvements to the design of telescopes and other optical instruments.

Fraunhofer's success was due in part to a great misfortune. The son of a lens-maker, he was orphaned as a boy and apprenticed to an apothecary in Munich: but he was to be the only survivor when the dilapidated tenement in which he lived collapsed. Watching the rescue was the Elector of Bavaria, Charles Theodore, who was so moved by the boy's predicament that he bought him out of the apprenticeship, so enabling him to develop his knowledge and skills.

freesia

Freesia is the name of a genus of ornamental sweet-scented South African plants of the iris family, grown for their yellow, pink, or white flowers. The plants are named after the German physician *Friedrich Heinrich Theodor Freese* (died 1876).

Freudian slip

A Freudian slip is a slip of the tongue that is considered to reveal an unconscious thought of the speaker's mind. The expression is often used to describe a statement that is uttered unintentionally but which is thought nearer to the truth than the word the speaker originally had in mind.

The expression Freudian slip comes from the teachings of the Austrian psychiatrist *Sigmund Freud* (1856–1939), who pioneered psychoanalysis. Freud developed the method of free association – he encouraged his patients to pursue verbally a particular train of thought. His *Interpretation of Dreams* (1899) analysed dreams in terms of unconscious childhood experiences and desires. His insistence that mental disorders had sexual causes that originated in childhood led to his estrangement with many of his colleagues.

In basic psychoanalytic terms, a Freudian slip is seen as a momentary lapse in a person's defensive position; thoughts or feelings that have been repressed are then unintentionally expressed.

Friday

The name of the sixth day of the week comes from Old English *Frigedæg*, the day of the Norse goddess *Frig* (or *Frigga*), the wife of Woden and goddess of married love. In some legends she is identified with Freya, the Norse goddess of love and fertility and the counterpart of the Roman goddess Venus. It is said that as WEDNESDAY and THURSDAY had been named after Frig's husband Woden and her son Thor, Friday was assigned to her in order to appease her.

A man Friday is a trustworthy, loyal male employed for general duties. The expression comes from the name of the native servant in the novel *Robinson Crusoe* (published 1719) by the English writer Daniel Defoe (*c.* 1660–1731). The expression girl Friday is formed on the analogy of man Friday, for female general assistant, particularly in an office.

fuchsia

Fuchsia is the name of a genus of ornamental shrubs and herbs native to Central and South America; they have showy drooping deep red, purple, pink, or white flowers. The name honours the German botanist and physician *Leonhard Fuchs* (1501–66). Fuchs' book on medicinal plants *De historia stirpium* (1503) was widely known at the time; he was professor of medicine at the University of Tübingen from 1535. The plant was named in honour of Fuchs in 1703 by the French monk and botanist Charles Plumier (1646–1704).

furphy

In informal, chiefly Australian, usage a furphy is an unlikely or ridiculous rumour or story. The word probably derives from the name *Furphy*, a supplier of water and sanitation carts in Australia in the First World War. The name was printed on the water tanks and the latrine buckets used by the Australian troops; they there-fore came to describe news of the war obtained at these centres of gossip as furphies. An alternative, less likely, theory suggests that the origin lies with the name of the Australian writer *Joseph Furphy* (1843–1913), who wrote stories under the pseudonym of Tom Collins.

G

gadolinite; gadolinium

The black or brown mineral known as gadolinite is a silicate of the metallic elements iron, beryllum, and yttrium. It is named after the Finnish chemist *Johann Gadolin* (1760–1852), who discovered and analysed it at Stockholm in 1794.

The metallic element gadolinium, which occurs in gadolinite, is also named after Gadolin. The element was discovered by the Swiss chemist J. C. G. Marignac in 1880.

Galahad

In Arthurian legend, *Sir Galahad* is the most virtuous knight of the Round Table. He is the son of Lancelot and Elaine and is, in many romances, the only knight who succeeds in the quest for the Holy Grail. As one tradition has it, Galahad was added by Walter Map (*c*.1140–*c*.1209) to the Arthurian legends. The name of Galahad has come to stand for chivalrous male purity and nobility.

galenical

The ideas of the Greek physician *Galen* (AD 129–199) dominated medicine for well over a thousand years after his death. He wrote numerous treatises on medical theory and practice; and although some of his views are now known to have been mistaken, his experiments and findings – for example that the spinal cord is important in muscle activity – proved significant in the study of medicine. His name is still remembered in the word galenical, a medicine that is prepared from plant or animal tissue rather than being chemically synthesized.

gallium

The metallic element known as gallium was first identified in 1875 by the French chemist *Paul Lecoq de Boisbaudran* (d. 1912). It is said that the name derives from the Latin translation (*gallus*) of the French *coq* 'cock' in the name of its discoverer.

Gallup poll

A Gallup poll is a survey of the views of a representative sample of the population on a particular issue; it is used especially as a means of forecasting election results. The poll is named after the American statistician *George Horace Gallup* (1901–84), who originally devised the method for assessing public opinion in advertising. Following his successful prediction of the result of the 1936 American presidential election, his techniques have been widely used, and developed, by different organizations, not only to forecast voting patterns but also to provide the basis of many other statistical surveys.

galvanize; galvanometer

Galvanize means 'to cover iron or steel with a protective zinc coating' and in a derived sense 'to stimulate into sudden action'. The word comes from the name of the Italian physician *Luigi Galvani* (1737–98).

Galvani observed that the muscles of a frog twitched when they were touched by metal contacts. He thought this effect was caused by 'animal electricity', and it was his fellow-countryman Volta who later provided the correct explanation, that the current was produced by the contacts of the metals themselves. Nevertheless, Galvani undertook a great deal of research in the development of electricity, and his name is linked both with the verb galvanize and the noun galvanometer, an instrument used to measure small electric currents.

gamp

Gamp is sometimes used in informal British usage for a large umbrella, especially one that is loosely tied. The word comes from the name of the nurse *Mrs Sarah Gamp* – who is known for her large, untidily tied umbrella – in the novel *Martin Chuzzlewit* (1843–4) by Charles Dickens.

Garamond see BASKERVILLE

gardenia

Gardenia is the name of a genus of ornamental tropical shrubs and trees cultivated for their large fragrant, often white, flowers. The name does not come from the word garden, as might be thought, but from the Scottish-American botanist *Alexander Garden* (1730–91). Dr Garden was a physician who spent much of his life in

Charleston, South Carolina. He not only practised medicine but devoted a great deal of his time collecting specimens of different plants and animals. He is said to have discovered the conger eel and several snakes and herbs. He pursued a vigorous correspondence with Linnaeus and other European naturalists, even seeking to persuade Linnaeus to name a plant after him. Dr Garden's wishes were fulfilled: in 1760 Linnaeus named the genus in his honour.

gargantuan

The word gargantuan means 'enormous or colossal'; it derives from the name *Gargantua*, the gigantic king in the novel *Gargantua* (1534) by the French satirist François Rabelais (*c.*1494–1553). Gargantua's appetite was so enormous that he once ate six pilgrims in a salad and it is to food and appetites that the adjective gargantuan is most often applied.

garibaldi

A garibaldi is a woman's loose, long-sleeved blouse or, alternatively, a kind of biscuit containing a layer of currants. The word derives from the name of the Italian patriot and soldier *Giuseppe Garibaldi* (1807–82). The blouse was so named because it resembled the red shirt worn by Garibaldi and his 1000 Redshirt followers in the Risorgimento – the nineteenth-century Italian nationalist movement. Garibaldi led his thousand volunteers to conquer Sicily and Naples, so enabling South Italy to be reunited with the North (1860–1). It is said that the red shirts worn by Garibaldi and his men were presented to him by the government in Uruguay, while he was gathering troops there.

It is uncertain how the biscuit came to be named after him, although it may be that he was fond of such delicacies.

Gatling gun

A Gatling gun was an early type of machine-gun. Mounted on wheels, it had a revolving cluster of barrels, the gunner controlling its rate of fire by means of a hand crank. The gun is named after its inventor, the American *Richard Jordan Gatling* (1818–1903). Patented in 1862, the Gatling was used in the later stages of the American Civil War (1861–5); it was discarded before the beginning of the First World War.

The name survives in the word *gat*, slang for a revolver or pistol.

Gaullism; Gaullist

Gaullism refers to the French political movement devoted to supporting the principles and policies of *General*, later *President*, *Charles (André Joseph Marie) de Gaulle* (1890–1970). Promoted to general in the Second World War (1940), he became leader of the French forces organized in London and a symbol of French patriotism. After the war he was president of a provisional government (1945–6), and later, of the Fifth Republic (1958–69). As President of the Fifth Republic, de Gaulle emphasized the status of the presidency and the supremacy of national interest; his independent foreign policy was aimed at re-establishing France as a world power. Gaullist principles continue to be a dominant influence in contemporary French politics.

gauss

The gauss is the unit of magnetic flux density in the centimetre–gram–second system of measurement. The unit is named after the German mathematician *Karl Friedrich Gauss* (1777–1855). Gauss – who is regarded as one of the greatest mathematicians of all time – is known for significant mathematical work in the fields of probability theory and number theory; he also applied mathematics to electricity, magnetism, and astronomy.

Gauss's name is also remembered in the word *degauss*, meaning 'to demagnetize'. During the Second World War, Germany developed a magnetic mine for use at sea, the mine being detonated by the magnetism of an approaching ship. Equipment was then designed to degauss the ship: to neutralize the magnetic field of the ship's hull.

Gay-Lussac's Law see CHARLES' LAW

Geiger counter

A Geiger counter is an electronic instrument that is used to measure the presence and intensity of radiation. The instrument is named after the German physicist *Hans Geiger* (1882–1945), who developed it with the help of the German scientist Walter M. Müller (born 1905). Research by Geiger and Müller built on investigations undertaken by the British physicist Ernest Rutherford (1871–1937). Geiger later became professor of physics at the universities of Kiel (1925–29), and Tübingen (1929–36), and the Technische Hochschule, Berlin (from 1936).

gentian

Gentian is the name of a group of plants (genus: *Gentiana*) with showy, mainly blue, flowers; many alpine perennials are gentians. The name of the plant is said to derive from *Gentius*, the second century BC King of Illyria, an ancient region on the Adriatic. Gentius is believed to have discovered the medicinal properties of the plant now known as yellow gentian (*Gentiana lutea*).

Geordie; George

The word Geordie, for someone who comes from or lives in Tyneside, in north-east England, derives from the name *George*. This name is also used in the rather old-fashioned exclamation of surprise or disbelief '*By George!*' By George! You're right – how amazing! – and in the language of air crews to refer to the automatic pilot in military and civil aircraft: *Let George do it!* This latter comes from George, originally slang for an airman.

georgette

Georgette (or georgette crepe) is a fine, thin, strong, silk crepe used in clothing, especially for blouses and gowns. The fabric is named after the late-nineteenth-century Parisian dressmaker *Madam Georgette de la Plante*.

Georgia; Georgian

The American state of Georgia, on the south-east coast of the USA, is named after King George II (1683–1760). Founded in 1732, it was the last of the 13 original states.

The Georgian style of architecture is that which was dominant in the reigns of the kings *George I* to *George IV* (1714–1830). The style is marked by well-proportioned gracefulness.

Georgian is also a term applied in a literary sense to the writers, especially poets, during the reign of *King George V* (1910–36).

Geronimo

Geronimo, an exclamation of delight or surprise, was originally the cry of American airborne paratroopers as they jumped from their planes into battle. The name shouted is that of the American Apache Indian chief *Geronimo* (1829–1909), but there are different theories as to how the expression was adopted. One suggestion is that the cry was inspired by paratroopers in training seeing a film featuring the Apache Indian chief. Others suggest that Geronimo, being hotly pursued by the cavalry, shouted out his name as he plunged on horseback down an almost vertical cliff into a river below.

Geronimo, finally captured in 1886, became something of a celebrity when he visited the St Louis World's Fair and other expositions.

gerrymander

To gerrymander means to divide an area into new electoral districts in order to give one party an unfair advantage. It is also used in a derived sense to mean to manipulate to obtain an unfair advantage for oneself. The word comes from the name of the American politician *Elbridge Gerry* (1744–1814). While Governor of Massachusetts (1810), Gerry sought to rearrange the electoral boundaries in favour of his own party in the forthcoming elections. It is said that one day the painter Gilbert Stuart came into the offices of the *Boston Sentinel* newspaper, and, seeing the newly re-drawn district on a map, proceeded to draw a head, wings, and claws round the district that was already in the shape of a sala-mander. 'That will do for a salamander,' declared the artist. 'A Gerry-mander, you mean,' replied the editor Benjamin Russell, and so the word was born.

Gerry later went on to become Vice-President of the USA (1813–14).

gib

A gib is a male cat, especially one that has been castrated. The word is probably originally a nickname for *Gilbert*. See also TOM.

Gideons

The Gideons are an interdenominational Christian group who have the aim of making the Bible freely available. Originally founded in Wisconsin, USA, in 1899, the organization places Bibles in hotel rooms, hospital wards, etc. The name *Gideon* derives from the Old Testament judge noted for his leadership of a small army who triumphed over the Midianites (Judges 6–7).

gilbert

A gilbert is the unit of magnetomotive force in the centimetre–gram–second system of measurement. It is named after *William Gilbert* (1544–1603), English physicist and physician to Queen Elizabeth I. Gilbert is noted for his pioneering work on magnetism, especially his treatise *De Magnete* (1600) and he has come to be known as 'The Father of Electricity'. Gilbert was responsible for introducing many new terms into the language, including electricity, electric force, and magnetic pole.

Gilbertian

Gilbertian is used to refer to the satirical light humour of the English comic dramatist *Sir William Schwenk Gilbert* (1836–1911). Originally a barrister, in 1869 Gilbert met the composer Arthur Sullivan (1842–1900), for whom he wrote the librettos of 14 operettas for D'Oyly Carte, including *Trial by Jury* (1873), *HMS Pinafore* (1878), *The Pirates of Penzance* (1879), *Iolanthe* (1882), *The Mikado* (1885), *Rudigore* (1887), *The Yeoman of the Guard* (1888), and *The Gondoliers* (1889). Thus the adjective Gilbertian has come to mean 'fanciful, wittily humorous', in the style of these ever-popular Savoy Operas.

Gill see BASKERVILLE

girl Friday see FRIDAY

Gladstone bag

A Gladstone bag is an article of hand luggage – a bag that has flexible sides set on a rigid frame, it opens into two equal-sized compartments. The bag is named after the British statesman and Prime Minister *William Ewart Gladstone*, known as the Grand Old Man (1809–98), but he did not invent it. It seems that the article of hand luggage was named in Gladstone's honour because he undertook so much travelling in the course of his public career. The bag was designed for the purpose of being particularly convenient for travellers.

Goethian; goethite

The German *Johann Wolfgang von Goethe* (1749–1832) was not only a great poet and writer; he was also a scholar and scientist. His powerful writings, notably *Götz von Berlichingen* (1773), *The Sorrows of Young Werther* (1774), *Iphigenie auf Tauris* (1787), and *Faust* (1808; 1832), have inspired the adjective Goethian, 'intellectual, yet kind and benevolent'.

His scientific work, for example *The Theory of Colours* (1810) and *Metamorphosis of Plants* (1817–24), led to a mineral being named after him: goethite, the yellow–brown mineral that is formed as a result of the oxidation and hydration of iron minerals.

golliwog

A golliwog is a soft children's doll made of cloths that has a black face and black hair that sticks our around its head. The word golliwog comes from the name *Golliwog*, an animated doll in children's books by the American writer Bertha Upton (d. 1912), and the American illustrator and portrait painter Florence Upton (d. 1922).

Gongorism

Gongorism is used to refer to an artificial literary style whose chief characteristics include elaborate constructions and obscure allusions and comparisons. It is named after the Spanish priest and lyric poet *Luis de Góngora y Argote* (1561–1627). Góngora's earlier works are not written in such a style, but his later works, including notably *Soledades* (1613), show many Gongoristic elements. The style resembles EUPHUISM.

Good Samaritan

A Good Samaritan is a kind person who selflessly helps people in distress. The allusion is to the biblical story told by Jesus (Luke 10:25–37); the *Good Samaritan* has come to stand for a helpful person who assists others, often to the point of inconvenience and without the slightest thought of personal gain.

Samaritans, the people of Samaria (now in Israel), are remembered not only in the expression the Good Samaritan, but also in the name of the voluntary telephone service to help those in need. Established in Britain in 1953, the Samaritans provide a confidential and anonymous service to anyone in despair.

goodbye

Goodbye, the conventional expression said as two people part, was originally a contraction of the phrase 'God be with you'. The word good was substituted for the name God by analogy with the expressions good day and good night.

Gordian (cut the Gordian knot)

The expression *cut the Gordian knot* means to solve a complex problem by a single decisive, brilliant action. The phrase alludes to the story of *Gordius*, the peasant King of Phrygia in Asia Minor. Gordius dedicated his chariot to Jupiter, fastening the yoke to the beam of his chariot with such an intricate knot that no one could untie it. The legend developed that whoever could untie the knot would reign over the whole empire of Asia. When Alexander the Great passed through the town (333 BC) he is said to have simply cut the knot with his sword and so claimed fulfilment of the legend in himself.

Gordon Bennett

The name Gordon Bennett is used as an exclamation to express great surprise: *Gordon Bennett! It's Jack – how are you? It must have been years since I've seen you!* The expression comes from the name *Gordon Bennett* (1841–1918), the proprietor of the *New York Herald*. He is famous for his sponsorship of balloon races at the beginning of the twentieth century. Like the slang expression gorblimey, Gordon (Bennett) was originally used as a euphemism to avoid using the name of God directly.

Gordon setter

The black and tan breed of dog known as the Gordon setter originated in Scotland. The breed was developed by the Scottish nobleman *Alexander Gordon* (1743–1827). Gordon was also a sportsman and a writer of folk ballads.

gorgon

A gorgon is sometimes used informally to refer to an ugly or repulsive woman. The word derives from the *Gorgons* of Greek mythology, the three winged females that had snakes for hair, claws, and enormous teeth. Medusa was the only mortal of the three Gorgons: she was so hideous that anyone who looked at her was instantly turned into stone.

gossip

The Old English word from which gossip derives is *godsibb* which originally meant a godparent, from *God* plus *sibb* 'relation'. Gossips were the sponsors for children at baptism – Shakespeare in *Two Gentlemen of Verona* wrote: ''Tis not a maid, for she hath had gossips' (Act 3, Scene 1). Gradually the word came to be applied to familiar friends and acquaintances, and then to the contemporary sense of someone fond of idle talk. Interestingly, the Old English *sibb* is preserved in the modern word sibling 'a person's brother or sister'.

Gothic

The word Gothic is used to describe a style of art or architecture used in Western Europe from the twelfth to the sixteenth centuries and imitated later in the so-called Gothic Revival of the eighteenth and nineteenth centuries. Features of Gothic architecture include the pointed arch, slender tall pillars, and flying buttresses. The description Gothic was originally used as a term of ridicule by Renaissance artists and architects: they considered the medieval style to be crude and barbarous, blaming the destruction of the superior classical art on the *Goths*. The Goths were a Germanic people who originated in Scandinavia and invaded many parts of the Roman Empire from the third to the fifth centuries A D. Although the Goths' artistic styles were certainly not 'Gothic', it is the name of this people that is remembered in the Gothic style of architecture.

Graafian follicle

A Graafian follicle is one of the small liquid-filled sacs in the ovary of a mammal that contains the developing egg. The name Graafian follicle honours their discoverer, the Dutch physician and anatomist *Regnier de Graaf* (1641–73).

gradgrind

A hard, utilitarian person who remorselessly pursues facts and statistics is sometimes known as a gradgrind. The word derives from *Thomas Gradgrind*, a character in the novel *Hard Times* (1854) by Charles Dickens. Gradgrind is a hardware merchant in Coketown, a drab northern industrial centre. Considering himself to be an 'eminently practical man', he suppresses the imaginative and spiritual aspects of the education of his children Tom and Louisa.

graham flour

Graham flour is a Northern American term for wholemeal flour. The name derives from the American dietary reformer *Sylvester Graham* (1794–1851). Originally a Presbyterian minister, Graham advocated temperance and also campaigned widely for changes in Americans' diets, especially the use of unbolted wheat flour. His efforts were rewarded by the emergence in the 1830s of *Graham food stores* and *Graham Societies*. He is still remembered in America by *graham crackers*, *graham bread*, and *graham flour*.

grangerize

The verb grangerize means to illustrate a book with pictures taken from other books or publications. The word comes from the name of the English writer and clergyman *James Granger* (1723–76), who in 1769 published a book entitled *Biographical History of England from Egbert the Great to the Revolution, Consisting of Characters Dispersed in Different Classes, and Adapted to a Methodical Catalogue of Engraved British Heads*. The book contained blank pages that were to be filled by cutting illustrations out of other books. A craze (*Grangerism*) developed, leading to the mutilation of many other valuable books.

Granny Smith

Granny Smith is the name of a variety of hard green apple that can be cooked or eaten raw. It is named after the Australian gardener *Maria Ann Smith*, known as *Granny Smith* (d. 1870). Granny Smith first grew the apple at Eastwood, Sydney in the 1860s.

Graves' disease

Graves' disease (exophthalmic goitre) is a disorder of the thyroid gland accompanied by protrusion of the eyballs. It is named after the Irish physician *Robert James Graves* (1796–1853) who first identified it in 1835.

Great Scott

The expression of great surprise *Great Scott!* probably alludes to *General Winfield Scott* (1786–1866). Scott was a hero of the Mexican

War (1846–48) and candidate for the US presidential election in 1852. The exclamation may originally have been applied in praise of the hero's achievements.

greengage

The variety of greenish or greenish-yellow plums known as greengage comes from a combination of the word green and the name Gage. It was the English botanist *Sir William Gage* (1777–1864) who introduced the variety of plum to England from France about 1725.

Interestingly, the French word for a greengage is also eponymous. This variety of plum was brought in the early sixteenth century from Italy to France, where it was named *reine-claude*, ('queen Claude') in honour of *Queen Claudia*, wife of King Francis I of France, the reigning monarch of the time.

Gregorian calendar

The old-style *Julian calendar* was the name given to the system introduced by *Julius Caesar* in 46 BC in which three years, each of 365 days, were followed by a leap year of 366 days. The average length of the year was therefore 365¼ days. This was approximately 11 minutes longer than its actual length as derived from astronomical and seasonal data. In order to rectify this error *Pope Gregory XIII* introduced a new system in 1582 which became law in Britain and the colonies in 1752, and is now used throughout most of the world. To allow for the alteration to the new system, 11 days were omitted, 2 September in 1752 being followed by 14 September. Under the new-style Gregorian system, named in the Pope's honour, leap years are every year that is divisible by four and century years divisible by 400 (thus 2000, but not 1900).

Gregorian chant

The Gregorian chant is the official liturgical plainsong of the Roman Catholic Church. The term derives from the name of *Pope Gregory I* (*c.* AD 540–604). It was under his papacy (590–604) that the whole subject of plainsong was reviewed, and the vocal, unaccompanied chant now known as the Gregorian chant was introduced.

Gresham's law

Sir Thomas Gresham (*c.*1519–79) was the English financier who founded the Royal Exchange (1568). He is perhaps better known for the so-called Gresham's law, attributed to him in the midnineteenth century. Gresham's law, usually formulated as 'Bad money drives out good money', means that if two different types of coin are in circulation, the less valuable will remain in circulation, while the more valuable will be hoarded and will eventually disappear from circulation.

Grimm's law

Grimm's law is a rule that describes the change of consonants in the Germanic and Indo-European languages. Named after its formulator, the German philologist *Jakob Ludwig Karl Grimm* (1785–1863), Grimm's law explains, for example, the change from Latin p-sounds to English f-sounds, as in the progression from Latin *piscis* to English fish.

Jakob Grimm is also known with his brother Wilhelm Karl (1786–1859) for their *Kinder- under Hausmärchen*, a collection of German folk tales, published 1812–14, which came to be known in English as *Grimm's Fairy Tales*.

gringo

The derogatory term gringo, used by Latin Americans to refer to an English-speaking foreigner probably comes from Spanish *gringo* 'gibberish', from *griego*, meaning 'Greek' or 'stranger' (compare the expression 'It's all Greek to me' meaning 'it's all strange; I find it utterly incomprehensible').

An alternative, more picturesque, suggestion is that the word gringo derives from the singing of the American soldiers in the Mexican War (1846–48). The soldiers are said to have sung the song 'Green grow the Lilacs' so much that the natives described the singers as green-grows or gringos.

grog

Grog is the term for diluted spirits, usually rum, as formerly given to sailors. The word comes from *Old Grog*, the nickname of the British admiral *Sir Edward Vernon* (1684–1757). Old Grog began the issue of diluted alcoholic spirits in 1740, in order to put an end to drunken brawling aboard his ship, and soon the sailors were calling the drink grog. The nickname Old Grog arose from the fact that in rough weather the admiral wore a cloak made of grogram – a coarse fabric, usually of wool and mohair or silk.

Grundy, Mrs

A Mrs Grundy is a narrow-minded person noted for prudish conventionality in personal behaviour. The name comes from a character in the play *Speed The Plough* (1798) by the English dramatist Thomas Morton (*c*.1764–1838). From the name Mrs Grundy the word *grundyism* is derived, referring to a disapproving or censorious, prudish attitude.

guillemot

A guillemot is a kind of narrow-billed sea-bird, an auk, that is found in coastal regions of the northern hemisphere. The name of the bird derives from the French *Guillemot*, an affectionate form of *Guillaume*, which is the English name William.

guillotine

The device for beheading people known as a guillotine consists of a heavy blade that slides down between two grooved upright posts. The name of the machine derives from the French physician *Joseph Ignace Guillotin* (1738–1814). Contrary to popular belief, Guillotin did not invent the device; it was designed as a development of similar instruments in use elsewhere in Europe by a colleague of Guillotin, Dr Antoine Louis (1723–92). Guillotin advocated the use of this machine on humanitarian grounds: it was a speedier and more efficient method than the former practice of putting common criminals to death by means of a clumsy sword. Guillotin therefore proposed to the French National Assembly that this device should be used as a means of capital punishment. The first person to be decapitated by the guillotine was a highwayman in April 1792.

gun

The word gun, first recorded in the fourteenth century, may come originally from the Old Norse female name *Gunhildr*, both elements of which mean 'war'. The list of weapons in the Engish Exchequer Accounts of 1330–1 records '*a large ballista* [a catapult used to hurl stones] *called Lady Gunhilda*', a name derived from Scandinavian Gunhildr. With the passage of time, the name became shortened to gunne and then to gun, the word's application also changing, on the invention of the cannon, from a weapon that threw missiles to one that discharged missiles by explosion.

Gunter's chain; gunter rig

A Gunter's chain is a measuring device 66 feet (20 m) long used, especially formerly, in surveying. The term derives from the name of the English mathematician and astronomer *Edmund Gunter* (1581–1626). Gunter's name is also honoured in the gunter rig, a kind of ship's rig with a sliding topmast, so called because it resembled a slide-rule invented by Gunter that was used in solving navigational problems.

guppy

A guppy is the name of a kind of freshwater fish that is popular in aquaria. The fish is named after the Trinidadian naturalist and clergyman *Robert John Lechmere Guppy* (1836–1916). Guppy sent specimens of the fish to the British Museum in 1868. The male guppy is brightly coloured – hence the alternative name rainbow fish; the female is a prolific breeder – hence the name millions – and produces live young, rather than eggs, every four weeks.

guy

The word guy referring in informal use to a man or fellow (or in recent American usage, in the plural, any group of people) comes from the first name of the English conspirator *Guy Fawkes* (1570–1606). Fawkes served as a mercenary in the Spanish army in the Netherlands and when he returned to England in 1604 became involved in the Gunpowder Plot. A convert to Roman Catholicism, Fawkes was outraged by the harshness of the anti-Catholic laws imposed by King James I. Together with a group of other Catholics, Fawkes plotted to blow up James I and parliament on 5 November 1605. The conspirators were informed on and Fawkes was caught red-handed, with the gunpowder in a cellar of the Palace of Westminster. Guy Fawkes and six of the other conspirators were executed the following year. The anniversary of 5

November continues to be remembered in Britain, with firework displays and guys, stuffed effigies of Fawkes, being burnt on bonfires.

Gypsy

The wandering people known as Gypsies (or Gipsies) were thought at one time to have come from Egypt, and so were called *Egyptians*. In time, this came to be shortened to Gyptians, from which came the present word Gypsy. In fact, it seems that the people probably originally came from north-west India.

H

Hadrian's Wall

The fortified Roman wall across northern England known as Hadrian's Wall is named after the *Emperor Hadrian* (AD 76–138). The wall was built under Emperor Hadrian's orders about AD 122–130, in order, as Hadrian's biographer comments, 'to separate the Romans from the barbarians'. The wall extends 120 km (85 miles) from the Solway Firth in the west to the mouth of the River Tyne in the east. Substantial parts of Hadrian's Wall still stand and it is one of the largest Roman remains in the United Kingdom.

Hadrian (Latin name Publius Aelius Hadrianus) was the adopted son of Trajan. On his father's death in 117, Hadrian became Emperor. From then onwards Hadrian travelled throughout the Roman Empire, consolidating the gains made by his predecessor, though some of Trajan's conquests including Mesopotamia, had to be abandoned.

Halley's comet

The British astronomer *Edmund Halley* (1656–1742) was the first to realize that comets do not appear haphazardly but have orbital periods. Following his observations in 1682 of the comet that has been named after him, he correctly predicted it would reappear in 1758. Halley was a friend of Sir Isaac Newton and had financed the publication of Newton's *Principia* (1686–87). Halley was appointed to the post of Astronomer Royal in 1720. The last appearance of Halley's comet was in 1985–6.

Hansard

Hansard is the official verbatim report of debates in the Houses of Parliament in the United Kingdom. The reports are so called after the name of the London printer *Luke Hansard* (1752–1828), who printed the *Journal of the House of Commons* from 1774 onwards. His eldest son, Thomas Curson Hansard (1776–1883) printed the first reports of parliamentary debates in 1803, and the Hansard family continued to print parliamentary reports up to the end of the nineteenth century. Now printed by HM Stationary Office, the official record of the debates is still known as *Hansard*.

hansom

The hansom cab, a light two-wheeled covered carriage, in which the driver sits high up at the back, is named after its designer, the English architect *Joseph Aloysius Hansom* (1803–82). Noted for his designs of public buildings and churches, Hansom designed the town hall of Birmingham in 1833. A year later he registered a 'Patent Safety Cab'. These hansom cabs – or hansoms – quickly became popular and were manufactured in various designs. Disraeli called them 'the gondolas of London'.

It seems that he was not so skilled at handling financial arrangements as designing buildings and vehicles. He is said to have sold his patent rights for a mere £300, while the manufacturers of his designs made fat profits.

See also BROUGHAM.

Harlequin

Harlequin

The stock character of pantomime, Harlequin, has a shaved head, a mask over his face, and diamond-patterned multicoloured tights. The name may come from Old French *Hellequin*, the name of a devil-horseman riding by night, which in turn may derive ultimately from old English *Herla cynnig*, King Herle, a legendary king who is identified with the god Odin (Woden).

The Harlequin has its origins in the Italian *commedia dell'arte*. In traditional English pantomime, Harlequin is the mute character who is the foppish lover of the beautiful Colombine. He is supposedly invisible to both the clown and pantaloon and rivals the clown in the affections of Columbine.

havelock

A havelock is the cloth cover for a soldier's cap with a long flap that extends down the back, designed to protect the wearer's head and neck from the heat of the sun. The word comes from the name of the English general *Sir Henry Havelock* (1795–1857).

Havelock served for over 34 years with the British army in India, taking only one period of home leave during that time. He is noted for his recapture of Kanpur (Cawnpore) and his holding of Lucknow until relieved by troops under Campbell (1857). It seems unlikely that Havelock actually invented the cloth cover named in his honour, a similar covering having been known for centuries before, but it was the havelock which he devised for his brigades that became known. Nowadays it may be seen in films depicting desert hostilities.

Heath Robinson

A Heath Robinson device or contraption is one that is absurdly complex in design. The description comes from the name of the English artist *William Heath Robinson* (1872–1944). Known for his drawings that depict ingenious devices used to perform trivial tasks, Robinson was also a serious artist whose illustrations accompanied poems in several books of verse. He also designed stage scenery.

Heaviside layer

The Heaviside layer is a former name of the E-layer of the earth's atmosphere – the charged level of the upper atmosphere that reflects medium-frequency radio waves. This layer is 90–150 km above the earth's surface. The Heaviside layer was so called because it was predicted and then discovered by the British physicist *Oliver Heaviside* (1850–1925).

The American electrical engineer *Arthur Edwin Kennelly* (1861–1939), working independently of Heaviside, made a similar prediction in 1902, the same year as Heaviside's prediction, and so the layer was also known as the *Heaviside–Kennelly* layer.

Heaviside is also noted for his development of the mathematical study of electric circuits and his work in vector analysis. See also APPLETON LAYER.

Heaviside lived the life of an eccentric hermit in Devon. Even after gaining public recognition for his scientific achievements, he was still so poor that at times he could not even afford to pay his gas bills.

hector

The word hector may be used as a noun to refer to a bully or as a verb to mean 'to bully or torment'. The word alludes to the Greek legendary character *Hector*, the son of Priam and Hecuba and the Trojan hero of Homer's Iliad who was killed by Achilles.

Homer, and English literature up to the seventeenth century, depicted Hector as a gallant warrior. It seems that the derogatory meaning derives from a gang of disorderly youths in London at the end of the seventeenth century. This band of young men took the name Hectors, fancying themselves as models of bravery. In reality, however, their bullying, terrorizing behaviour became infamous and the unfavourable meaning of the word hector became predominant.

henry

The henry is the derived metric unit of electric inductance; it is named after the American physicist *Joseph Henry* (1797–1878). Henry is famous for his contributions to electromagnetism, inventing the first electromagnetic motor; he discovered electromagnetic induction independently of the English scientist Michael Faraday.

The US Weather Bureau was established as a result of Henry's meteorological work while he was the first director of the Smithsonian Institute, Washington DC. He is considered the founder of weather forecasting from scientific data in the USA.

Hepplewhite

Hepplewhite is used to describe an eighteenth century style of English furniture. The style is noted for its graceful elegant curves, and in chairs, for straight tapering legs and oval or heart-shaped chairbacks with openwork designs. The name of the style honours the English cabinet-maker *George Hepplewhite* (d. 1786). Probably originally a Lancastrian, Hepplewhite worked from a shop in St Giles', Cripplegate, London.

herculean

A herculean task is one that requires immense effort or strength. The word comes from *Hercules* (Greek, *Heracles*), the son of Zeus and Alcmena, and the greatest and strongest of the Greek demigods. While in the service of his rival Eurystheus, Hercules completed twelve supposedly impossible labours: he killed the Nemean lion and the Lernean water-snake Hydra; he captured the Arcadian stag and the Erymanthian boar; cleaned the Augean stables (see AUGEAN), killed the ferocious Stymphalian birds; captured the white Cretan bull; caught the man-eating mares of Diomedes; stole the girdle of the Amazon Queen Hippolyte; captured the oxen of Geryon; took the golden apples of Hesperides; and finally brought the three-headed dog Cerberus (see SOP TO CERBERUS) to its master, Hades. This last task was seen as representing the victory over death itself.

hermaphrodite

A hermaphrodite is an animal or plant that has both female and male reproductive organs. The word comes from *Hermaphroditos*, the Greek mythical son of Hermes and Aphrodite, goddess of love. Hermaphroditos refused the love offered by the nymph Salmacis, in whose pool he was bathing. She embraced him, however, and prayed to the gods to make them indissolubly one. The gods answered her prayer and the body of both the nymph and Hermaphroditos grew together as one. From this story of the union of these two beings comes the word hermaphrodite.

hermetic

A hermetic seal is one that is airtight, the word hermetic deriving ultimately from the name *Hermes Trismegistus* ('Hermes, thrice-greatest'). This is the Greek name given to the Egyptian god of learning, Thoth, and also the name given after the third century AD to the author of certain writings on alchemy and mysticism. Hermes Trismegistus is traditionally believed to have invented a seal to keep containers airtight by using magical powers.

hertz

A hertz is the derived metric unit of frequency, equal to one cycle per second. (The term may be more familiar in the word kilohertz, meaning one thousand hertz or one thousand cycles per second.) The terms honour the German physicist *Heinrich Rudolph Hertz* (1857–94). Developing the work of the Scottish scientist James Clerk Maxwell, Hertz was the first person to detect radio waves (1888). The type of electromagnetic wave known as the *herzian wave* is also named after him.

Hilary term

The term that begins in January at Oxford University and certain other educational institutions is known as the Hilary term. The name is chosen because the feast day of *St Hilary* falls on 13 January. St Hilary of Poitiers (*c.* AD 315–*c.* 367) was converted to Christianity from Neoplatonism and became bishop of Poitiers in about 353. The most highly regarded Latin theologian of his time, he was a leading critic of Arianism. His defence of orthodox beliefs led to his exile for four years. St Hilary's works include *De Trinitate* (a criticism of Arianism) and *De Synodis*.

Hindenburg line

The Hindenburg line was the German western line of fortifications in the First World War. It is named after the German general *Paul von Beneckendorff und von Hindenburg* (1847–1934). Recalled from retirement at the outbreak of the First World War, Hindenburg, together with Erich von Ludendorff (1865–1937) led Germany to a decisive victory over Russia at Tannenburg (August 1914). In 1915 Hindenburg and Ludendorff were given command of the western front. Together they directed the construction of the line of fortifications known as the Hindenburg line near the border between France and Belgium in 1916–17. It was breached by the Allies in 1918 by troops under the direction of Douglas Haig.

After Germany's defeat in 1918, Hindenburg again retired, but became President of the Weimar Republic in 1925. He was re-elected President in 1932, but with the growing prominence of Hitler was compelled to appoint Hitler as Chancellor in January 1933.

Hippocratic oath

The Greek physician *Hippocrates* (*c*. 460–*c*. 377 BC) is commonly regarded as the father of medicine. He has given his name to the Hippocratic oath traditionally believed to be taken by a doctor before commencing medical practice. The oath comprises a code of medical ethics probably taken by members of the school of Hippocrates.

Born on the island of Cos, Hippocrates was the most famous physician of the ancient world. Some of his writings still survive, including his *Aphorisms*, of which the most famous reads in Chaucer's translation, 'The life so short, the craft so long to learn'.

Hitler

A person showing ruthless dictatorial characteristics may be described as a Hitler, with reference to the German dictator *Adolf Hitler* (1889–1945). Born in Austria, Hitler served in the First World War and became President of the National Socialist German Workers' (Nazi) Party in 1921. After an abortive coup (the Munich Putsch, 1923), Hitler spent several months in prison, during which time he wrote *Mein Kampf*, which expressed his political philosophy based on the innate superiority of the Aryan race and the inferiority of the Jews.

Hitler was appointed Chancellor of Germany in 1933 and a year later assumed the title of Führer (leader). Germany became a totalitarian state, with Hitler establishing concentration camps to exterminate the Jews. The Second World War was precipitated by his invasion of Austria (1938), and Czechoslovakia and Poland (1939). He narrowly escaped assassination in 1944 and, in the face of an Allied victory in April 1945, committed suicide.

Ho Chi Minh City

Ho Chi Minh City (former name, Saigon) is a port in Vietnam, inland from the South China Sea. It is named after the Vietnamese statesman *Ho Chi Minh* (original name Nguyen That Thanh; 1890–1969).

In 1941 Ho Chi Minh founded the Viet Minh, the Vietnamese organization that fought against the Japanese and then the French in an attempt to create an independent Vietnamese republic. He was the first President of the Democratic Republic of Vietnam (1945–54) and of North Vietnam (1954–69). In 1959 he supported the Viet Cong guerrilla movement in the South, although he was not actively involved in the work of government. When Saigon yielded to the communists in 1975, it was renamed Ho Chi Minh City in his honour.

Hobson's choice

If you were in seventeenth-century England and wanted to hire a horse from *Thomas Hobson* of Cambridge, you would have had no choice at all over which horse you could take. The liveryman Thomas Hobson (1544–1631) is said not to have allowed his customers any right to pick one particular horse, insisting that they always choose the horse nearest the door. Hence the expression Hobson's choice, a situation in which there appear to be alternatives but, in fact, no real alternative is offered and there is only one thing you can do.

Hodgkin's disease

Hodgkin's disease (also known as lymphoma, lymphadenoma) is a cancerous disease marked by an enlargement of the lymph nodes, liver, etc. The disease is named after the English physician *Thomas Hodgkin* (1798–1866), who first described it in 1832. A physician at Guy's Hospital, London, Hodgkin was one of the most distinguished pathologists of his time.

Homer sometimes nods; Homeric

The expression *Homer sometimes nods* means that even the wisest of people make mistakes. Homer is the presumed author of the great epic poems the *Iliad* and *Odyssey*, but little is in fact known about his life. He is believed to have lived in the eighth century BC and, according to legend, was blind.

The source of the expressions *Homer sometimes nods* and *even Homer nodded* are Horace: '*If Homer, usually good, nods for a moment, I think it shame*' (*Ars Poetica*) and Byron (*Don Juan*): '*We learn from Horace, "Homer sometimes sleeps";/We feel without him, Wordsworth sometimes wakes*'.

The adjective Homeric is used to mean 'heroic; majestic or imposing'.

hooker

Hooker is slang for a female prostitute. While it is possible that the word was popularized during the American Civil War – *General Joseph Hooker* (known as 'Fighting Joe'; 1814–79) is said to have associated with prostitutes – earlier usages of the word have been recorded. For example, 1845, in N. E. Eliason *Tarheel Talk* (1956) 'If he comes by way of Norfolk he will find any number of pretty Hookers in the Brick row not far from French's hotel'. (Oxford English Dictionary, Supplement).

hooligan

The origin of the word hooligan, meaning a rough lawless young person, seems to lie with the name *Patrick Hooligan*, an Irish criminal who was active in London in the 1890s. It is said that Pat Hooligan and his family – their real name may have been Houlihan – attracted a gang of rowdy followers, basing themselves at the Lamb and Flag, a public house in south London.

Hoover

Hoover is a trademark used to describe a type of vacuum cleaner. The name comes from the American *William Henry Hoover* (1849–1932). Hoover, however, did not invent this cleaner; he was a perceptive businessman who saw the possible sales of a new kind of cleaner that had been made by a J. Murray Spangler, a caretaker in an Ohio department store. Hoover persuaded Spangler to sell his rights to the invention and so, in 1908, it was the Hoover Suction Company that produced the first Hoover – selling for $70. Four years later vacuum cleaners made by Hoover were exported to Britain, where, in fact, the vacuum cleaner had been invented in 1901 by the Scotsman Hubert Cecil Booth (1871–1955). However, it is neither Booth's nor Spangler's name that is remembered today; Hoover now often being used not only generically as a noun to refer to a vacuum cleaner but also as a verb to mean 'to clean with a vacuum cleaner'.

hotspur

The word hotspur, meaning a rash or fiery person, was originally applied to the English rebel *Sir Henry Percy* (1364–1403), known as *Harry Hotspur*. Together with his father, also Sir Henry Percy, 1st Earl of Northumberland, he led a revolt against King Henry IV, whom earlier he and his father had supported. Impetuous and headstrong – hence his nickname – he was killed at the battle of Shrewsbury. Shakespeare featured the rash, fearless character of Hotspur in *Richard II* and *Henry IV*.

Houdini (*do a houdini*)

Someone who does a houdini succeeds in performing an astonishing act of escape or disappearance. The expression honours *Harry*

Hoover

Houdini, the stage name of the American magician and escapologist *Ehrich Weiss* (1874–1926). Of Hungarian–Jewish descent, Weiss assumed the name of Harry Houdini to echo the name of the great French magician *Jean Eugene Robert Houdin* (1805–71). Houdini became world famous for his ability to escape from handcuffs, straitjackets, locked chests, even when under water.

Hoyle (*according to Hoyle*) see COCKER

Huguenot

The Huguenots were Calvinist French Protestants, especially in the sixteenth and seventeenth centuries. The name of this religious movement comes from the Middle French dialect word *huguenot*, which is an alteration of Swiss–German *Eidgnoss*, 'confederate', influenced by the name of the Swiss political leader *Besançon Hugues* (d. 1532). Hugues was a Protestant syndic and party leader in Geneva.

Huntingdon's chorea

Huntingdon's chorea is a rare hereditary disorder of the brain in which there is progressive involuntary spasmodic movement (chorea) and gradual mental deterioration. It is named after the American neurologist *George S. Huntingdon* (1851–1916) who described it.

husky

A husky – also called an Eskimo dog – is a breed of very strong sledge dog that has a double-layered coat. The word husky is probably an alteration and shortening of the Tinneh Indian (one of the Athapascan – American Indian – languages) *uskimi*, an Eskimo, or of *Esky*, English slang for Eskimo, or the English word *Eskimo*. The word Eskimo itself is of Algonquian origin, and is related to a Cree Indian word meaning 'eaters of raw flesh'.

See also SAMOYED.

hyacinth

The hyacinth, the fragrant plant of the lily family that bears clusters of typically blue, pink, or white flowers takes its name from *Hyacinthus*, a youth in Greek mythology. Hyacinthus was so attractive that he was loved by both Apollo, god of the sun, and by Zephyrus, god of the west wind. Hyacinthus' preference for Apollo made Zephyrus intensely jealous, and while the three of them were playing games one day, Zephyrus hurled Apollo's quoit of iron at Hyacinthus, hitting him on the head and killing him. It is said that a flower grew from the blood of the wound, 'that sanguine flower inscribed with woe', as Milton describes it.

hygiene

The word hygiene, the science of maintaining good health, and the clean conditions that lead to good health, comes from *Hygeia*, the Greek goddess of health. Hygeia was worshipped with Aesculapius, the god of medicine, and is sometimes identified as his wife or daughter. Hygeia was typically depicted as feeding a serpent from a dish in her hand.

I

iris

Iris is the name of a genus of plants that have sword-shaped leaves and large showy flowers made up of three upright petals and three drooping petals. The name of the plant comes from *Iris*, the Greek goddess of the rainbow, because of the flower's bright and varied colours. Messenger of Hera (the queen of the Olympian gods), Iris travelled along the colours of the rainbow to bring her messages to earth.

The name of iris is also used for the coloured part of the eye surrounding the pupil.

isabelline

The adjective isabelline meaning 'greyish-yellow', comes from the name of the colour isabel or isabella. It is said that these words are derived from the colour of the underwear of *Isabel Clara Eugenia*, daughter of King Philip II of Spain, who in 1598 married Albert, Archduke of Austria. Tradition has it that at the siege of Ostend, she vowed not to change her underwear until the city was captured. The siege lasted for three years, so the colour of her under-garments must have been truly isabelline when the city was finally taken.

Other sources relate a similar story about *Queen Isabella of Castile* (1451–1504) and the siege of Granada.

Ishmael

An Ishmael is a social outcast. The expression comes from the Bible figure of *Ishmael*, the son of Abraham and Hagar, the Egyptian maidservant of Sarah. According to the biblical narrative (Genesis 16–25), when Sarah realized that she could not conceive children, she gave her maidservant to Abraham to conceive by her. When Hagar became pregnant, she began to despise her mistress who then drove her out of her home. An angel of Jehovah met Hagar and told her to return and submit to Sarah, also saying that her descendants through Ishmael would be innumerable – God assured Abraham that Ishmael would be the father of 12 rulers and ultimately a great nation. When in due course Sarah bore a son, Isaac, by Abraham, she insisted that Ishmael and Hagar be expelled from the home. In the desert, the outcasts nearly perished for lack of water, but God showed Hagar his provision of a well of water. Ishmael grew up to become an archer, and Hagar found a wife for Ishmael, who then indeed became the father of 12 sons.

J

Jack

Jack is the commonest pet-form of the name John and is used in a large number of expressions, in many of which it stands simply for 'man', for example *lumberjack* and *steeplejack*, sometimes with derogatory connotations, as in *cheapjack*. It is also used to refer to a mechanical appliance used to lift a heavy weight such as a car, and as a verb to lift a car, etc., using such a device.

The generic use of the name Jack features in other expressions, including *Jack Frost*, a personification of frost, the surname Frost being chosen probably because it was well known; *a jack in office*, meaning a pretentious petty official; *a jack in the box*, the toy consisting of a small box out of which a figure springs when the lid is opened; *Jack* and *Jack Tar* referring to a sailor, tar probably being a shortening of tarpaulin; and the *Union Jack*, the national flag of the United Kingdom. *I'm all right Jack*, the slogan of the smug, complacent opportunist out to satisfy his or her own interest, was popularized by the film *I'm All Right, Jack* (1960). *A Jack of all trades (and a master of none)* refers to a person who can undertake various kinds of work, and is sometimes used to imply that the person has no great ability in any of the different trades. The informal expression *every man Jack* is an idiom meaning 'everyone of a large number of people, with no exceptions': *He thinks that all politicians – every man Jack of them – are in it just for the power they have.* Finally, the phrase *before you can say Jack Robinson* means 'very quickly' – *I'll be back before you can say Jack Robinson* – but it is not known who Jack Robinson actually was.

Jack Ketch

Jack Ketch was a seventeenth-century English public executioner who was notorious for his barbarism. He was appointed hangman in 1663 and was particularly infamous for his executions of Lord William Russell, a conspirator in the Rye House Plot against King Charles II (1683) and the Duke of Monmouth (1685).

Ketch was known for his bungling, cruel, work – he is said to have required several blows to sever Russell's head. The Duke of Monmouth's last words are reputed to be, 'Do not hack me as you did my Lord Russell!', but it seems that he was slaughtered as ineptly or even more clumsily than the earlier victim.

After his death in 1668, the name of Jack Ketch came into common use to refer to a public executioner, and it was later used for the hangman of the Punch and Judy puppet shows.

Jack Russell terrier

A Jack Russell terrier is a breed of dog with a stocky body, small drooping ears, short legs and a short white, black, and tan coat. The breed of terrier is named after the English clergyman *John (Jack) Russell* (1795–1883) who developed the breed from the fox terrier. Russell was curate of Swimbridge, near Barnstaple, and was also master of the local foxhounds.

jackanapes

The word jackanapes is sometimes used to refer to an impudent or conceited person or a mischievous child. There are two theories of the origin of the word. Some suggest that it is an alteration of *Jack Ape*, a term of endearment for a pet monkey. Other sources suggest that it derives from *Jack Napes*, the nickname of *William de la Pole, 1st Duke of Suffolk* (1396–1450), whose symbol showed an ape with a ball and chain. In 1450 de la Pole was arrested and beheaded at sea, while being sent into exile for conspiring against King Henry VI. He was later nicknamed Jack Napes or Jackanapes.

Jacky Howe

The expression Jacky Howe is used in Australian English for a sleeveless shirt, as worn by sheep-shearers. It is named after *John (Jacky) Howe* (1855–1922). Howe was the world sheep-shearing champion for many years; in 1892 he shore 321 merinos in one day.

Jacobean

Jacobean refers to the styles of furniture and architecture current at the time of *King James I* of England, from New Latin *Jacōbaeus*, from *Jacōbus*, 'James'. He was the first Stuart King of England and Ireland (1603–25), and, as King James VI, ruled Scotland (1567–1625). The Jacobean style of furniture is particularly noted for its use of dark brown carved oak. In architecture, the Jacobean style stands between the Elizabethan and the classical Palladian style of the English architect and designer Inigo Jones (1573–1652). It is marked by a combination of Renaissance forms, e.g. ornamental gables, and the late Gothic preference for mullioned windows.

Jacobin

The *Jacobins* were an extremist group during the French Revolution. Founded in 1789, they were responsible, under the leadership of the French revolutionary Robespierre (1758–94), for the Reign of Terror, in which over a quarter of a million people were arrested, and nearly 1500 guillotined. The name of the society comes from the group's original meeting place – a Dominican convent in Paris, near the church of *St Jacques* (St James). The word Jacobin has since passed into general use for a member of an extremist, radical, or terrorist political group.

Jacobite

The Jacobites were followers of the Stuart *King James II* (New Latin, *Jacōbus*) after his overthrow in 1688 (the Glorious Revolution), or of his descendants. The Jacobites made several attempts to enable the House of Stuart to regain the throne. Two Jacobite rebellions, in 1715, led by James Edward Stuart (James II's son, known as the Old Pretender) and in 1745, led by Charles Edward Stuart (the son of James Edward Stuart, known as the Young Pretender or romantically as Bonnie Prince Charlie), were suppressed. At the battle of Culloden (April 1746), Bonnie Prince Charlie was defeated by the Duke of Cumberland, so concluding the Jacobite rebellion.

Jacob's ladder

Jacob's ladder is the name given to two items – a ladder used on board ship and a plant. The Jacob's ladder that is used on board ship is made of rope or cable; it has wooden or metal rungs and is dropped over the side of a ship to allow people to ascend from or descend to small boats positioned alongside. The plant known as Jacob's ladder (*Polemonium caeruleum*) has blue or white flowers and a ladder-like arrangement of its light-green leaves.

The origin of the expression Jacob's ladder is to be found in the Bible (Genesis 28:12); it is the ladder, which rested on the earth and reached to heaven, that *Jacob* saw in a dream.

Jacquard loom

The Jacquard loom was a loom for weaving patterned fabrics. It is named after the French weaver and inventor *Joseph Marie Jacquard*

(1752–1834), who completed its design in 1801. When first introduced in France, it was very unpopular, because it was so efficient that it made thousands of people redundant. Within 11 years of its introduction, however, over 10,000 Jacquard looms were in use in France. Napoleon bought the loom for the state, declaring it to be public property; he payed Jacquard a yearly pension of 3000 francs and also a small sum for each machine sold. The revolutionary loom was the first automatic machine that could weave patterns into fabrics. It was controlled by punched cards – a method that was later applied by the British mathematician Charles Babbage (1792–1871) in his development of the calculator and subsequently in the development of computers.

Jacquerie

Jacquerie is the name given to a peasants' revolt, particularly the revolt of the peasants of north-east France against the nobility in 1358. During the period of the Hundred Years' War between England and France, the rebellion had its roots in famine and plague and was quickly suppressed. The name Jacquerie derives from the contemptuous name given by the nobles to the typical French peasant *Jacques Bonhomme*, which, as Eric Partridge suggests, might be translated into English as 'goodman James' or 'simple, easy-going James'.

Jacuzzi

Jacuzzi is a trademark used to describe a system of underwater jets of water that massage the body. The name derives from its creator, the Italian-born *Candido Jacuzzi* (*c*. 1903–86). Candido was born the youngest of seven brothers and six sisters. When the family emigrated to California early in the twentieth century, it seemed that they would prosper from aviation engineering. But in 1921, when the first Jacuzzi monoplane crashed on its first flight, the Jacuzzi boys were forbidden by their mother to develop these skills.

The brothers also worked in the field of fluid dynamics, patenting a jet pump, originally for use in ornamental gardens. When one of the children of the family was stricken by rheumatoid arthritis, they developed a pump that could be used to produce the therapeutic effects of swirling bubbly water in a home bath tub. In 1968, Roy Jacuzzi, a third-generation member of the Jacuzzi family, saw the commercial potential of the whirlpool bath: a pump was fixed to the bath's outer walls to force the water and air through four jets and so the modern Jacuzzi came into being.

Jansenism

Jansenism was a Roman Catholic movement in the seventeenth and eighteenth centuries based on the teaching of the Dutch theologian *Cornelius Otto Jansen* (1585–1638). First director of the episcopal college in Louvain, and consecrated Bishop of Ypres (1636), Jansen is noted for his treatise *Augustinus* (1640), which he wrote after reading St Augustine's works many times. The teaching of Jansenism, as expressed in *Augustinus*, emphasized the more strictly predestinarian points of St Augustine's doctrines. The teaching brought the followers of Jansenism into conflict with the Jesuits and was condemned by Pope Innocent X as heretical (1653).

January

January, the first month of the year, comes from the name of the Roman god *Janus*. Janus was the god of doors, thresholds, and bridges. He is usually portrayed as having two faces, one looking forwards and the other backwards. January is therefore seen as providing an opportunity for looking back to take stock and of gazing into the future to wonder what lies ahead. From the representation of Janus as having two faces also comes the expression *Janus-faced*, meaning two-faced or hypocritical.

jay

The word jay, the bird (*Garrulus glandarius*) of the crow family, probably derives ultimately from the Latin name *Gaius*. It seems that this name may well have been used in a similar manner to Jack in English, namely as a familiar way of describing people generally.

JCB

A JCB is the trademark for a type of mechanical earth-mover. At the front of the vehicle is a hydraulically operated shovel and at the back, an excavator arm. The name of the earth-mover comes from the initials of its English manufacturer *Joseph Cyril Bamford* (born 1916).

A skilled welder and fitter, Bamford built a farm trailer using materials surplus to war use in 1945. Various types of trailer were then constructed, and by the late 1940s and the early 1950s hydraulics were introduced in tipping trailers and loaders. The JCB company is currently headed by the eldest son of the original Bamford, Anthony P. Bamford.

Jehovah's Witness

A Jehovah's Witness is a member of a religious movement originally founded in 1872 by Charles Taze Russell (1852–1916). Members of the organization aim to follow the literal sense of the Christian Bible, but they reject some basic tenets of established Christianity, especially the doctrine of the Trinity and the deity of Jesus Christ and the Holy Spirit. Jehovah's Witnesses are known for their zealous door-to-door personal evangelism.

Jehovah's Witnesses use the name *Jehovah* for God, applying the personal name of God, revealed to Moses on Mount Horeb (Exodus 3:13–15). The word Jehovah (also Yahweh) comes from Hebrew *YHVH*. Because this name was regarded as too sacred to be pronounced, Jews from about 300 BC onwards replaced the word by *Adonai* (Hebrew for 'Lord') when reading their Scriptures. The vowel sounds a, o, a, from Adonai were later inserted into the word Y H V H, hence YaHoVaH and Jehovah.

Jekyll and Hyde

The phrase Jekyll and Hyde is used to describe a person who has two separate personalities, one good and the other evil. The expression derives from the name of the main character in the novel *The Strange Case of Dr Jekyll and Mr Hyde*, published 1886, by the Scottish writer Robert Louis Stevenson (1850–94).

In the story Doctor Jekyll discovers a drug that will change him into an evil dwarf, whom he calls Mr Hyde. At first, Doctor Jekyll is able to change from one personality to another at will, but gradually the personality of Mr Hyde begins to predominate, and Hyde later commits murder. In the trial that follows and as the secret is made known, Hyde commits suicide. The expression is often used in front of a noun; for example, *a Jekyll-and-Hyde personality*.

jemmy

A jemmy (American English, jimmy) is a short steel crowbar, as used by burglars to force open doors and windows. The word comes from *Jemmy*, a nickname for James.

jennet

A jennet is the name given to a female donkey or ass or to a small Spanish riding horse. The word comes from Catalan *ginet*, a horse of the tribe used by the Zenete, a member of a Berber people famous for their horsemanship.

jenny

The word jenny – from the name *Jenny*, a nickname of Jane or Janet – has a number of different meanings including a female donkey, a wren, and the early type of spinning frame (*spinning jenny*).

jeremiad; Jeremiah

A jeremiad is a lengthy lamentation or complaint. The word comes via French, from the name *Jeremiah*, the Old Testament prophet. His book contains many prophecies of judgment, particularly against idolatry, immorality, and false prophets, and he is sometimes known as the Prophet of Doom. Thus a Jeremiah has come to be used to refer to a pessimistic person who foresees a gloomy future or one who condemns the society he lives in.

jeroboam

A jeroboam is a very large wine bottle, one that holds the equivalent of four standard bottles. It seems that the expression was first humorously applied to such bottles in the nineteenth century, alluding to *Jeroboam*, the first king of the northern kingdom of Israel, who the biblical text describes as 'a mighty man of valour' (1 Kings 11:28) and who 'did sin, and who made Israel to sin' (1 Kings 14:16). The bottle is without doubt 'mighty' and the alcoholic drink contained in it could certainly lead to 'sin'.

Other Old Testament figures after whom bottles and large drinking vessels are named include: *jorum*, a large drinking bowl, from *Joram*, who brought to King David 'vessels of silver, and vessels of gold, and vessels of brass' (2 Samuel 8:10); *methuselah*, a bottle holding eight times the standard amount from the patriarch *Methuselah* who lived to be 969 years old (Genesis 5:27); *nebuchadnezzar*, a very large bottle holding the equivalent of 20 standard bottles, after *King Nebuchadnezzar* of Babylon; and *rehoboam*, a wine bottle holding the equivalent of six standard bottles, from *Rehoboam*, a son of Solomon, last King of the united Israel and first King of Judah, and whose name means 'may the people expand'.

jerry-built

A building that is jerry-built is one that has been poorly built with cheap, low-quality materials. There are various theories of the origin of the expression. According to some sources jerry could refer to the tumbling walls of *Jericho* in the Bible, (Joshua, chapter 6). An alternative theory states that jerry comes from the name of the prophet *Jeremiah*, who predicted decay and destruction. Still others suggest that jerry is a corruption of *jury-mast*, a makeshift wooden mast in use in English shipbuilding yards in the mid-nineteenth century.

jerry can

A jerry can is a narrow flat-sided container used for storing or carrying liquids, especially petrol. It has a capacity of about 25 litres (about 5 gallons). The expression comes from *Jerry*, the word for a German or German soldier. It was the Germans who designed this metal fuel container in the Second World War; and since its design was superior to the design of the can used by the Allied troops, it was copied, the new container being called a jerry can.

Jesuit

A Jesuit is a member of the Society of Jesus, a Roman Catholic religious order founded by St Ignatius Loyola in 1534. Its original aims were to defend Catholicism in the face of the Reformation and to undertake missionary work amongst the unbelieving world.

The word Jesuit comes from Late Latin *Jesus* (Jesus Christ) and the suffix *-ita* meaning follower or supporter.

Because of a tendency of a few Jesuits, especially in the seventeenth century to be concerned with politics, the word Jesuit and the adjective *Jesuitical* are sometimes used to refer to a person who is involved in subtle intrigue or cunning deception.

Jezebel

A Jezebel is a shameless, scheming, or immoral woman. The word comes from the biblical figure of *Jezebel*, daughter of Ethbaal, King of Tyre and Sidon, who married Ahab, the King of Israel. Jezebel's notorious wickedness is described in 1 and 2 Kings. She worshipped the fertility god Baal and persuaded Ahab and his people to follow her religion. Under her orders, God's prophets were killed, and were replaced by the prophets of Baal. In answer to Elijah's prayer, God defeated Baal at Mount Carmel. Jezebel then resolved to kill Elijah, who was forced to go into hiding. After the incident over Naboth's vineyard, Elijah predicted Jezebel's violent end, and some time later she was thrown down from a high palace window.

jilt

If you jilt a lover, you end your relationship with that person, leaving and rejecting him or her in an unfeeling way and without previous warning. The earlier form of the word, *jillet*, indicated that it comes from the proper name *Jill* – a very common girl's name, used in the same way that Jack is used to refer to any boy or man.

jim crow

The phrase jim crow (or Jim Crow) was used in American English to refer to a Black person, and also to racial segregation imposed by Whites on Blacks. The phrase was very common in the 1880s and 1890s, but has been dated back to 1730, when Black people were first described as crows. In 1828 a White blackface minstrel Thomas D. Rice wrote the song 'Jim Crow', which was widely sung and danced in both Britain and the United States in the 1830s. *Jim Crow* was the Black person of the song-and-dance act. The song popularized the expression Jim Crow to mean 'a Black', a *Jim Crow store* being a shop with provisions that would be sold only to Blacks, and, later, *Jim Crow laws* being discriminatory laws against Black Americans.

Job (patience of Job); Job's comforter

The Old Testament character of *Job* was a man of upright character who lost his wealth, his ten children, and his health. Satan brought these disasters on him with God's permission. The book of Job tells how Job kept his faith in God in the midst of all his afflictions. Thus the *patience of Job* has become proverbial to stand for the enduring of difficulties, misfortunes, or laborious tasks with supreme patience, courage, and tolerance.

Job was visited by three friends who gave him the advice of popular opinion, emphasizing particularly that his misfortunes were brought about by his own disobedience to God. From these friends, whom Job refers to as 'miserable comforters' (Job 16:2), comes the expression *a Job's comforter*, used to describe someone whose attempts to bring encouragement or sympathy have the opposite effects of discouragement and distress in reality.

jockey

The word for a jockey, a person who rides a horse, especially a professional rider in horse-races, comes from the name *Jockey*, originally the Scottish variant (*Jock*) of Jack. It seems that the name was chosen as a nickname for a young man who rode well. In the sixteenth century the word meant simply 'lad'.

Joe; Joe Bloggs; Joe Blow; Joe Public; Joe Soap

In British English, the name Joe Bloggs is used to refer to an average or typical man. Its American and Australian equivalent is Joe Blow. Joe Public is a member of the general public (cf John Citizen – the ordinary person – as in *John Citizen and the Law* (published 1947), by the London lawyer Ronald Rubinstein; 1896–1947). A Joe Soap is someone who is considered stupid or credulous and who can be imposed upon as a dupe or object of ridicule.

In American and Canadian English a Joe is man or fellow (*a good Joe*); in American English a Joe or GI Joe is an American soldier, the equivalent of the British *Tommy Atkins*.

joey

The traditional name of a circus clown, Joey, comes from the famous English clown *Joseph Grimaldi* (1779–1837). He is said to have been only one year old when he made his debut at the Drury Lane Theatre in London. He began as a dancer, and later became well known as a clown and pantomime artist. His memoirs (1838) were edited by Charles Dickens.

Joey, for a young kangaroo, is not a name, but comes from a native Australian language.

john; johnny

Particularly in American English, the word john is an informal term for a toilet. The first appearance of the word in print, according to William and Mary Morris (*Morris Dictionary of Word and Phrase Origins*) was in 1735, in an official rule of Harvard College. The word appeared in the full expression Cousin John: '*No Freshman shall go into the Fellows' Cousin John.*'

A *Dear John letter* is an informal expression used to refer to a letter from a girl who wants to break off a love affair. The expression comes of course from the opening words of such a letter, but the original person named John has not been identified with a particular individual.

Johnny, the nickname for John, is used informally in British English to mean a man or fellow and also to refer to a condom. The word Johnny also occurs in some compounds, including *johnnycake*, 'an American cake or bread made with meal from maize' (possibly originally journeycake or Shawneecake), *Johnny-come-lately*, 'a person who has recently joined a social or working group', and *Johnny-jump-up*, American for a 'violet or wild pansy'.

Long johns are a pair of usually woollen underpants with long legs that extend to the ankles. The garment may be so called because a *long john* – originally a lanky man – looked particularly unusual wearing long johns.

John Barleycorn

John Barleycorn is a personification, usually in humorous usage, of alcoholic drink. The expression may have originated in the early seventeenth century, but it was popularized by the Scottish lyric poet Robert Burns (1759–96) in his narrative poem 'Tam o' Shanter':

> Inspiring bold John Barleycorn
> What dangers thou canst make us scorn!

John Bull

John Bull is a personification of the English nation or a typical Englishman. The expression was first used in the satirical pamphlet by the Scottish writer and physician John Arbuthnot (1667–1735), *Law Is a Bottomless Pit*, published in 1712. The pamphlet was designed to ridicule the Duke of Marlborough and to express disgust at the continuing war against France.

In the pamphlet *John Bull* is an allegorical character representing England. He is straightforward, honest, independent, bold, and quarrelsome. Other characters in the pamphlet are Humphrey Hocus (the Duke of Marlborough), Lewis Baboon (Louis XIV of France), Nicholas Frog (the Dutchman), and Lord Strutt (Philip of Spain). The pamphlet was originally one of a series and later the collection was reissued under the title *The History of John Bull*.

John Doe; Richard Roe

John Doe and Richard Roe are the names sometimes given to the two parties to legal proceedings. It seems unlikely that men by these names actually existed, the forenames being apparently chosen randomly because of their frequent occurrence. The surname *Doe* was probably chosen with reference to the gentle and pleasant character of a doe and *Roe* seem to have been chosen because it rhymes with Doe.

The names were used in legal documents since at least the fourteenth century – one source suggests that the names may even date back to Magna Carta (1215). Originally, prosecutors are said to have used these names when they could not find two genuine witnesses or when the true witnesses did not wish to disclose their real names. Later, the names came to be used instead of the real names of the parties to legal proceedings, John Doe usually being the plaintiff and Richard Roe the defendant.

John Dory

A John Dory is a golden yellow food fish, *Zeus faber*, with an oval compressed body, long spiny dorsal fins and a black spot on each side. The name *John* may have been chosen arbitrarily, and *dory* is probably simply derived from Middle French *dorée*, 'gilded one'. An alternative theory suggests that the fish is named after a *John Dory*, an infamous privateer in the sixteenth century and the subject of a popular song, but this seems unlikely.

John Hancock; John Henry

The expressions John Hancock or John Henry are used particularly in American English to refer to a person's signature. *John Hancock* (1737–93) was the Boston merchant and revolutionary patriot who not only was the first to sign the American Declaration of Independence but also was the one who wrote his signature the most prominently and apparently the most aggressively, 'so big no Britisher would have to use his spectacles to read it'. Hancock later became President of the Continental Congress and Governor of Massachusetts.

The alternative expression John Henry came originally from the cowboy slang of the American west.

johnny   see JOHN

Jolly Roger

The Jolly Roger is the traditional flag of pirates, consisting of a white skull and crossbones on a black background. It is said that the earliest flags of pirate ships were plain black cloth sheets, later some pirates adding the decoration of the white skull and crossbones. The expression Jolly Roger seems to have come from thieves' slang, in which a *Roger* meant a beggar or rogue. In time the adjective *jolly*, meaning 'carefree', was added, so Jolly Roger came to stand for the flag of carefree rogues seeking booty.

Blue peter, a blue signal flag with a white square at the centre, is used to show that a vessel is ready to leave port, honours the name Peter. As Partridge comments, 'the choice of the name Peter was probably a matter of caprice'.

Jonah

A Jonah is a person who is believed to bring bad luck. The expression derives from the biblical *Jonah*, the Hebrew prophet who was held responsible for the storm that struck the ship he was travelling on (Jonah 1 : 4–7). Jonah was running away from God, disobeying his command to go to Nineveh to denounce its people.

Joneses (keeping up with the Joneses)

The idiomatic expression *keeping up with the Joneses* means 'to try to maintain the same living standards as one's richer neighbours'. The expression derives from a comic strip by Arthur R. Momand with the title *Keeping Up With the Joneses*. The comic strip, which began in the New York *Globe* in 1913, was based on the experience of the author and his wife trying to maintain the same material standards as those living around them. Originally the author thought of calling the cartoon strip 'Keeping Up With the Smiths' but 'Keeping Up With the Joneses' was eventually chosen 'as being more euphonious'.

jorum see JEROBOAM

joule

A joule is the metric unit of work or energy. The unit is named after the English physicist *James Prescott Joule* (1818–89). Born in Salford and a student of Dalton, Joule performed experiments in the 1840s to determine the mechanical equivalent of heat. He is also known for his work on the heating effects of an electric current (*Joule's law*), his work on the effect on temperature that occurs when a gas expands under certain conditions (*the Joule–Thomson effect* or *Joule–Kelvin effect*), and his research that formed the basis of the theory of the conservation of energy.

Jove (by Jove); jovial

Jove was the Roman god Jupiter and the word is sometimes used in the exclamation *by Jove* to express surprise or agreement, for example, *By Jove, you're right!* Originally a euphemism for by God, the first recorded use of by Jove is 1570.

Jovial, with its contemporary meaning of good-humoured, originally meant '(born) under the influence of the planet Jupiter', which astrologers considered to be the source of good humour.

Judas

A Judas is a traitor, a person who betrays a friend. The word comes from the name of Christ's betrayer, *Judas Iscariot*.

The name Judas occurs in a number of expressions that allude to betrayal or cunning. A *Judas kiss* is a show of affection that conceals treachery. A *Judas slit* is a peep-hole in a door through which guards can observe their prisoners. A *Judas tree* is an ornamental shrub or tree of the genus *Cercis*; its pinkish-purple flowers bloom before the leaves appear. The genus is so called because it is traditionally thought that Judas hanged himself on such a tree.

jug

Jug, a vessel for holding or pouring liquids, usually with a handle and a lip or spout, is probably derived from the name *Jug*, a nickname of Joan. In informal usage, jug can also mean prison, as in *ten years in jug*. This usage may well be influenced by Spanish *juzgado* meaning 'jailed'.

juggernaut

In contemporary English, a juggernaut is a large articulated lorry: *huge juggernauts roaring through country villages*. The original meaning of the word is 'an irresistible, overwhelming force or object': the inexorable juggernaut of government. The word comes from Hinduism: *Jagannath 'Lord of the World'*, is one of the titles of the Hindu god Vishnu. At an annual festival, an idol of this god is carried in an enormous wheeled vehicle; devotees, it was once said, formerly threw themselves under its wheels.

Julian calendar see GREGORIAN CALENDAR

July

The seventh month of the year is named after *Julius Caesar*: see AUGUST

Juggernaut

jumbo

The adjective jumbo means enormous or very large, as for example in a *jumbo packet of washing powder*. Originally, *Jumbo* was the name of a very large, 6½-ton African elephant exhibited at London Zoo 1865–82.

Despite an outcry, which included a personal protest from Queen Victoria, Jumbo was bought by the American showman P. T. Barnum in 1881. In the USA, Jumbo was exhibited in the Barnum and Bailey Greatest Show on Earth. Jumbo lived for 3½ years in America and during this time it is estimated that he carried a million children on his back. He died in 1885, when a railway train hit him while he was trying to rescue Tom Thumb, Barnum's smallest attraction.

There are several different theories of the origin of Jumbo's name. Some believe it comes from *mumbo-jumbo*, others that it is derived from Swahili *jumbe*, meaning 'chief', while still others claim that its origin lies in *Gullah jamba*, meaning 'elephant'.

Whichever theory is correct, P. T. Barnum's showmanship resulted not only in the arrival of an outsize animal, but also in the introduction of a new word into the language, now seen also in the compound *jumbo jet*.

June; Junoesque

The name of the sixth month of the year may come from *Junius*, the Roman family to which the murderers of Julius Caesar belonged. Other sources suggest that June derives from the name of the goddess of the moon, and women and marriage, *Juno*, whose festival fell in this month. She was both the wife and sister of Jupiter.

The adjective Junoesque derives from the name *Juno* and means beautiful in a stately or regal manner.

K

Kafkaesque

The adjective Kafkaesque is used to describe a nightmarish sense of unreality and helplessness in the face of an impersonal and sinister bureaucracy. The word derives from the name of the Czech-born Austrian novelist *Franz Kafka* (1883–1924). Virtually unknown as an author in his own lifetime, Kafka wanted his manuscripts to be destroyed at his death. However, his friend Max Brod undertook to publish his works posthumously. Among his best known writings are *Metamorphosis* (1912), *The Trial* (1925), and *The Castle* (1926).

kaiser see TSAR

keeshond

The keeshond is a breed of small dog with a compact body, fox-like features, and a shaggy grey coat. This breed is traditionally used by the Dutch as barge dogs. The word keeshond comes from Dutch, probably from *Kees*, a nickname for *Cornelius* and *hond*, dog, but it is uncertain why the name Cornelius was chosen.

kelvin

The kelvin is the metric unit of thermodynamic temperature. The kelvin scale is a scale of temperature in which the hypothetically coldest temperature (absolute zero) is 0 K and the freezing-point of water is 273.16 K. It is named after the Scottish physicist *William Thomson Kelvin, 1st Baron Kelvin* (1824–1907), who was a professor at Glasgow University for 53 years.

As well as suggesting the temperature scale, Kelvin is noted for his work on electricity and the conservation of energy, his many inventions of instruments, including the modern compass, and his personal supervision of the laying of the first transatlantic cable in 1866.

King James Bible

The King James Bible is an alternative name for the Authorized Version of the Bible, written under the patronage of *King James I* (1566–1625) and published in 1611.

At a conference at Hampton Court (1604) a suggestion was made by a Dr John Reynolds (1549–1607), a Puritan and President of Corpus Christi College, that a new translation of the Bible be undertaken. The proposal appealed to the King, who wanted a uniform translation written by scholars from Oxford and Cambridge Universities, to be considered by bishops and to be ratified by his authority. The translation was based on the earlier Bishops' Bible (1568), and other versions, especially the Geneva Bible (1560), and work by William Tyndale. The style and wording of the Authorized (King James) Version has had a unique influence on the English language, becoming the familiar version of the Bible for generations of English-speaking people. Many of its phrases have become part of the language, including 'an eye for an eye', 'a fly in the ointment', 'the powers that be', and 'the salt of the earth'.

knickerbockers

Knickerbockers are short, baggy breeches gathered in at the knee. The word comes from the name *Dietrich Knickerbocker*, the pseudonym under which the American author Washington Irving (1783–1859) wrote his *History of New York from the Beginning of the World to the End of the Dutch Dynasty*, published in 1809.

The name Knickerbocker came to stand for the typical, solid Dutch burgher, who was a descendant of the original Dutch settlers in New York. The word knickerbocker is said to have been used for the baggy breeches because they were considered the traditional dress of the Dutch settlers in America. This tradition arose from illustrations by the caricaturist George Cruikshank (1792–1878) in a British edition of Irving's book in the 1850s. Cruikshank portrayed the Dutch settlers as wearing baggy breeches and so the name knickerbockers came to be used.

See also BLOOMERS.

Köchel number

A Köchel number is a serial number in a catalogue of the works of Mozart, for example Mozart's Clarinet Concerto in A major is K.622. Köchel numbers are named after the Austrian botanist and cataloguer Ludwig von Köchel (1800–77), whose catalogue of Mozart's works was first published in 1862. The letter K (or in German KV, for *Köchelverzeichnis*, 'Köchel index') followed by a number, shows the chronological order of Mozart's works.

L

Lady Bountiful

A Lady Bountiful is a woman who is noted for her generous bestowing of charity or favours in a condescending, patronizing manner, as for example in: *We don't need her coming round here to play Lady Bountiful; we can afford to buy our own food and clothes, thank you very much.* The expression comes from the character in the comedy *The Beaux' Stratagem* (1707) by the Irish dramatist George Farquhar (1678–1707). In the play, *Lady Bountiful* gives half her money to charity.

lambert

Born the son of an impoverished tailor, the German scientist *Johann Heinrich Lambert* (1728–77) is noted for his work in several disciplines, such as mathematics, physics, astronomy, and philosophy. Lambert proved that pi was an irrational number; he derived the trigonometric hyperbolic functions; and he measured the amount of light emitted by stars and planets.

It is for his work in physics that Lambert is particularly honoured: the unit of illumination in the centimetre–gram–second system of measurement is named after him.

Larousse

The well-known French Larousse dictionaries are named after the French grammarian, lexicographer, and encyclopedist *Pierre Athanase Larousse* (1817–75). The son of a blacksmith, Larousse founded the reference-book publishing firm that bears his name in 1852. His most important work was the *Grand dictionnaire universel du XIXe siècle* (1866–76), issued originally in fortnightly parts, and finally totalling 15 volumes.

lawrencium

Lawrencium is a short-lived radioactive chemical element that is artificially produced from the element californium. It is named after the American physicist *Ernest Orlando Lawrence* (1901–58). As physics professor at the University of California (1930), Lawrence invented the cyclotron, a type of particle accelerator that produces high-energy particles, for which he was awarded the NOBEL PRIZE for physics in 1939.

lazaret; lazaretto

A lazaret or lazaretto is a hospital for people with contagious diseases, a building or ship used for quarantine, or a ship's store-room. The terms derive from a combination of the words *lazar* and *Nazaret*. Lazar is an archaic word for a poor diseased person, especially a leper, and comes from *Lazarus*, the name of the beggar in Jesus' parable (Luke 16:20; see also DIVES). Nazaret is short for *Santa Maria di Nazaret*, a church in Venice that maintained a hospital.

Leninism; Leningrad

The word Leninism is used to refer to the political, economic, and social theories of communism propounded by the Russian statesman *Vladimir Ilyich Lenin* (1870–1924), whose original surname was Ulyanov. It was the close study of Marxism and the execution of his elder brother Aleksandr that set Lenin on his political career. In exile in Siberia for his revolutionary activities (1897–1900) he wrote his first book, and married a fellow Marxist, Nadezhda Krupskaya. He was one of the leaders of the unsuccessful Russian Revolution of 1905. After the Russian Revolution broke out in 1917, Lenin led the Bolshevik Revolution, overthrowing the provisional government. He made peace with Germany (1918), and fought off opposition in the civil war (1918–21). As Head of State, he founded the Third International (1919), and instituted the New Economic Policy (1921), which allowed a small degree of free enterprise. After a series of strokes, he died in 1924. His body lies embalmed in a tomb in Red Square, Moscow.

The former capital of Russia known as St Petersburg (1703–1914) and Petrograd (1914–24) was renamed Leningrad after Lenin's death.

See also MARXISM, STALINISM, TROTSKYISM.

leotard

A leotard is a close-fitting, one-piece garment worn by acrobats, ballet dancers, and others performing physical exercises. It is named after the French acrobat *Jules Léotard* (1842–70), who designed and introduced the original costume for the circus. Léotard was one of France's most famous acrobats, starring in circuses in Paris and London. He perfected the first aerial somersault and invented the flying trapeze; he was known as 'That Daring Young Man on the Flying Trapeze', from a song (1860) by George Leybourne. At the age of 28 he died of smallpox.

Levis

Levis is a trademark for a kind of jeans, from the name of *Levi Strauss* (1830–1902), a Bavarian immigrant to the USA and a San Francisco clothing merchant at the time of the Gold Rush. Strauss started to make durable jeans in the 1850s. He added rivets to the corners of the pockets in the mid 1870s, so that, it is said, the pockets would not tear when they were loaded with ore samples. As he became more well-known, so these hard-wearing jeans came to be called Levis.

lewisite

The colourless, poisonous liquid known as lewisite causes blistering of the skin. It was developed (1917–18) by the American chemist *Winford Lee Lewis* (1878–1943), after whom it is named, as a gas to be used in chemical warfare.

life of Riley

A person who enjoys an easy, lazy, and luxurious life may be said to be *living the life of Riley*. There are a number of different theories of the origin of this expression. Some sources state that the original Riley was the American poet *James Whitcomb Riley* (1849–1916), whose writings often concerned boys spending summer days in a carefree manner; others suggest that the phrase originates with the song 'The Best In the House is None Too Good for Reilly' by Lawlor and Blake; still others say that the original Riley was an *O'Reilly* of the song 'Are You the O'Reilly?' popularized by Pat Rooney in the 1880s: O'Reilly would one day strike it rich, and everyone would be prosperous.

Linnaean

Carolus Linnaeus (1707–78; original name *Carl von Linné*) was the Swedish botanist who established the system of naming living organisms. In his Linnaean system, all organisms have two names, the first identifies the genus to which the organism belongs, the second its species. For example, Linnaeus classified members of the human race as belonging to *Homo sapiens* ('wise man'), *Homo* being the genus, and *sapiens* the specific species.

The son of a Lutheran clergyman, Linnaeus had an early interest in nature – he was nicknamed 'the little botanist' at the age of eight. He became assistant professor of botany at Uppsala University, studied medicine in Holland, and later became professor of medicine and botany at Uppsala University in 1741.

Linnaeus' system is outlined in his books, especially *Systema naturae* (1735), *Genera plantarum* (1737), and *Species plantarum* (1753). His was the first significant attempt to bring all living beings together in a systematic classification.

It is said that he believed he had been chosen by God to name and classify plants and animals. Not only did he indeed name more living organisms than any other person in history, but also his system of nomenclature formed the basis of modern classification.

lobelia

Lobelia is the name of a genus of flowers bearing showy lipped blue, red, yellow or white flowers. The genus is named after the Flemish botanist and physician *Matthias de Lobel* (1538–1616), who was physician to King James I.

loganberry

The loganberry, the large sweet purplish-red berry of the upright-growing raspberry plant (*Rubus loganobaccus*) takes its name from an American lawyer. It was judge *James Harvey Logan* (1841–1928) who developed the plant in his experimental orchard at his home in California in about 1881.

The *boysenberry* was developed as a hybrid of the loganberry, blackberry, and raspberry by *Rudolph Boysen* (died 1950), an American botanist and horticulturist, in the 1920s or 1930s.

long johns see JOHN

Lonsdale belt

The belt awarded as a trophy to professional boxing champions is known as a Lonsdale belt. It is named after *Hugh Cecil Lowther, 5th Earl of Lonsdale* (1857–1944) who originated the awards. The Earl of Lonsdale was an all-round sportsman; he was president of the National Sporting Club. Not only was he a sparring partner to the heavyweight fighter John Lawrence Sullivan (1858–1918), he was also an expert huntsman, steeplechaser, and yachtsman.

Lucullan

The Roman general *Lucius Licinus Lucullus* (*c.* 110–57 BC) was a Roman general and administrator. He waged war against the Mithridates, gaining both riches and success. He retired to private life in Rome in about 66 BC, to enjoy a life of luxury; and his Lucullan (or Lucullian) feasts became proverbial for their lavishness.

Luddite

A Luddite is a person who is opposed to industrial innovation. It is said that the name derives from a *Ned Ludd*, an eighteenth-century

English labourer who in about 1779 destroyed labour-saving stocking frames at his workplace. The name Luddite was adopted by a group of workers between 1811 and 1816 who tried to destroy new mechanical textile appliances in the Midlands and the north of England. The workers saw the new machines as a threat to their livelihood. The movement was suppressed and some Luddites were hanged or transported. Distrust of innovation continues and the word Luddite is still used to refer to someone who opposes the latest technological changes.

lumber

The word lumber, old disused articles that are stored away, may come from *Lombard*, in the now obsolete sense of a pawnbroker's shop, from the *Lombards*, the merchants of *Lombardy*, a region in north Italy. A Germanic tribe known as *Longobardi* or long-bearded (men), settled in this region about AD 568.

It seems that the sense of disused articles may derive from the fact that the lumber (pawnshop) rooms were filled with evidence of unredeemed pledges – boxes, furniture, and other miscellaneous articles.

The American English use of lumber to mean 'sawn timber' is also a development of this sense.

lush

Lush, slang for intoxicating liquor and also a drunken person, is said to have originally been a shortening of the name of an actors' drinking club in London, the *City of Lushington*. The club, founded in the mid eighteenth century, met in the Harp Tavern in Great Russell Street until the 1890s. The name of the club may possibly have come from a chaplain, *Dr Thomas Lushington* (1590–1661), who was a drinking companion of Bishop Richard Corbet, although a number of alternative theories have been proposed, including the suggestion that the origin is *lush*, 'to eat and drink' in Shelta, the jargon of some Irish vagrants.

lynch

If an angry mob of people lynch someone, they put that person to death without giving him or her a proper trial. The word comes from *lynch law*, the condemning and punishing of a person without a proper trial, but dictionary writers have long argued over which person with the name Lynch originated the expression. Most now agree, however, that lynch law and lynch probably derive from the name of *William Lynch* (1742–1820), an American who organized extra-legal trials in Virginia.

The evidence for this is an editorial on lynching by the American short-story writer Edgar Allen Poe (1809–49) in an issue of the *Southern Literary Messenger*, published in 1836. Poe wrote that the expression lynch law originated in 1780 when Captain William Lynch led a group of his fellow citizens in Pennsylvania County, Virginia, to deal with a group of ruffians who were disturbing public order. Lynch had an agreement with his fellow vigilantes 'to inflict such corporeal punishment . . . as shall seem adequate to the crime committed or the damage sustained'. Thus lynch law came to refer to the administration of mob justice using non-legal means, and on occasions men were hanged for their alleged crimes.

The expressions lynch law and lynch also, no doubt, gained currency because of the practices of another person named Lynch, the planter and justice of the peace, *Charles Lynch* (1736–96), who took the law into his own hands and set up his own trials during the American War of Independence. However, there is no evidence that the administration of rough justice by this Lynch ever led to any hangings.

M

macabre

The adjective macabre, meaning 'grim or gruesome', is derived from Old French *danse macabre*, 'dance of death', a medieval representation of a dance in which living people are taken, in order of their social standing, to their graves, by a personification of death. The origin of the *danse macabre* may lie in a miracle play in which the martyrdom of the seven young *Maccabee* brothers under the Syrian (Seleucid) King Antiochus IV is depicted. This story is told in the apocryphal book 2 Maccabees, Chapter 7.

macadam

A macadamized road is one that has a surface made of macadam: compacted layers of small broken stones bound together with tar, asphalt, etc. The word macadam honours its inventor, the Scottish engineer *John Loudon McAdam* (1756–1836). It is said that as a small boy McAdam laid out model roads in his back garden – but it was years later, after spending some time in America, that he returned to Scotland, to discover that the roads in the estate that he had bought in Ayrshire were, like most roads, in a poor condition. McAdam set to work to improve the state of the roads, experimenting in Ayrshire and later in Falmouth. His efforts led to his appointment in 1815 to construct new roads around Bristol, and in 1827 he was made surveyor general of all British metropolitan roads.

Macadamizing – covering the earth base with a layer of large, tightly packed, broken stones that were covered by a layer of smaller stones – soon became the standard road-surfacing method. The trademark *Tarmac*, is an abbreviation of *Tarmacadam*, a company formed in 1903, describes a technique of using tar and bitumen to bind the stones in the surface together.

McCarthyism

The name of the US Republican senator *Joseph Raymond McCarthy* (1909–57) is remembered for McCarthyism, a kind of political witchhunting in America in the early 1950s. In February 1950, McCarthy claimed he knew of over 200 communists, or communist sympathizers, in the State Department. The investigations that followed marked a witchhunt that personally attacked individuals not only in politics, but also in television and film industries. McCarthy was, however, unable to prove his allegations. Eventually he was censured by the Senate in December 1954 and his witchhunt came to an end.

The term McCarthyism is still used, however, to refer to an obsessive opposition to individuals considered disloyal or who hold views held to be subversive, especially when the charges against the individuals are not substantiated.

McCoy (the real McCoy)

Someone or something that is described as *the real McCoy* (or *the real Mackay*) is certainly genuine; it is not an imitation or a fake. There are, however, many different theories of the origin of this expression.

Some say it comes from *Kid McCoy* (professional name of the American *Norman Selby*, 1873–1940), welterweight boxing champion 1898–1900, who was said to have proved his identity by boxing with his doubters until they conceded he was 'the real McCoy'.

Others suggest a Chicago livestock trader *Joseph McCoy* (born 1838) who changed the town of Abilene, Kansas, into a cow town in 1867, taking cattle via the new railhead at Abilene to the cities of the north and east. It is said that he transported half a million cattle a year and he claimed that he was 'the real McCoy'.

Still further explanations of the origin of the expression include a chief of the *Mackay* clan; a Prohibition rum-runner named *Bill McCoy*; a character in an Irish ballad of the 1880s; the island of *Macao* (hence McCoy), where drug addicts are said to have demanded 'the real Macao' of the island's uncut heroin; and whisky dispatched from Glasgow to the United States by *A. M. MacKay*. This last explanation may well have increased the currency of the expression, since it seems that the phrases McCoy or *the clear McCoy* were originally (1908) used to refer to good whisky.

Mach number

A Mach number is a number that represents the ratio of the speed of a body to the speed of sound in the same medium. Thus Mach 1 corresponds to the speed of sound, a number less than 1 is subsonic, a number greater than 1 is supersonic, and a number greater than 5 is said to be hypersonic. The term Mach number is named after the Austrian physicist and philosopher *Ernst Mach* (1838–1916) for his research into airflow.

Mach was also known as a philosopher, as one who held the theory of sensationalism – that the only things that ultimately exist are sensations. This theory influenced the philosophical movement of logical positivism in the 1920s.

Machiavellian

The adjective Machiavellian has come to refer to cunning, double-dealing, and opportunist methods and to describe a view that in politics the use of any means, however unscrupulous, can be justified in the pursuit/of political ends. The term derives from the Italian political theorist *Niccolò Machiavelli* (1469–1527). Machiavelli served as a statesman and secretary to the Florentine Republic from 1498 to 1512. When the Medici family were restored to power, he was forced into exile, however. His most famous work was *Il Principe* (*The Prince*; published in 1532), in which he argued that all means are acceptable in the securing and maintenance of a stable state. It seems that his views have been unfairly exaggerated in the modern meaning and connotations of unprincipled trickery that are apparent in the word Machiavellian.

mackintosh

The word for a kind of raincoat made of rubberized cloth, a mackintosh (also mac or macintosh), is named after the Scottish chemist *Charles Macintosh* (1760–1843). It was, however, another Scotsman, James Sym (1799–1870), who first invented the process of making waterproof fabrics in 1823. A few months later, the fabric was patented by Macintosh, who went on to found a company in Glasgow, which produced the first mackintoshes in 1830. In Mackintosh's process, a waterproof fabric was produced by sticking two layers of cloth together with rubber dissolved in naphtha. Nowadays, the word mackintosh is applied to any raincoat.

madeleine

A madeleine is a small, rich sponge cake that is baked in a small mould. It is probably named after *Madeleine Paulmier*, the nineteenth-century French pastry-cook who is said to have been the first to have concocted this delicacy.

Mae West

A Mae West is an inflatable life jacket that was issued to airmen in the Second World War. When inflated, the life-jacket resembled a well-developed bust – hence the choice of the name of the American actress *Mae West* (1892–1980), renowned for her full figure.

On learning that she was honoured in the name of the life jacket, she is said to have uttered, 'I've been in *Who's Who* and I know what's what, but it's the first time I ever made the dictionary'.

magdalen

The word magdalen (or magdalene) means 'a reformed prostitute' and 'a house of refuge or of reform for prostitutes'. It comes from the name *Mary Magdalene*, a woman healed by Jesus of evil spirits (Luke 8:2) and the first person to whom the risen Jesus appeared (John 20:1–18). Mary Magdalen is often also traditionally identified with the sinful woman of Luke 7:36–50, and considered to have been a reformed prostitute, though the biblical text does not justify such a conclusion.

Maginot line

The original Maginot line was a line of fortifications built by France to defend its north-east frontier with Germany before the outbreak of the Second World War from 1929 onwards. The Maginot line is named after the French Minister of War (1922–24, 1929–32) *André Maginot* (1877–1932). In the event, their blind confidence in the defences lulled the French into a false sense of security, and when in 1940 Germany invaded France, the Maginot line (which was not even continued to the coast) was easily by-passed by the flanking manoeuvres of the Germans through Belgium. Nowadays, a Maginot line is any defensive position in which blind confidence is placed.

Mae West

magnolia

Magnolia is the name of a genus of evergreen or deciduous shrubs or trees with showy white, yellow, rose, or purple flowers. The genus is named after the French botanist *Pierre Magnol* (1638–1715). Magnol, professor of botany at Montpellier University, is known for his systematic classification of plants.

malapropism

A malapropism is an instance of the unintentional confusion of words that produces a ridiculous effect. The word comes from the name of the character *Mrs Malaprop* in the play *The Rivals* (1775), by the Irish dramatist Richard Brinsley Sheridan (1751–1816). In the play, Mrs Malaprop – her name comes from French *mal à propos*, meaning inappropriate – misapplies words on numerous occasion; for example, 'If I reprehend anything in this world, it is the use of my oracular tongue and a nice derangement of epitaphs!' (Act 3, Scene 3).

Other examples of malapropism are: *under the affluence of alcohol* and *teutonic ulcers*.

Malpighian

The name of the Italian physiologist *Marcello Malpighi* (1628–94) is relatively unknown, but he was a pioneer in the field of microscopic anatomy. In 1661 he identified the capillary system, confirming the theory of the English physician and anatomist William Harvey (1578–1657). Malpighi made several studies of organs of the body, and the *Malpighian corpuscle* (or body), part of the kidney, and the *Malpighian layer*, a layer of skin, are named after him. Malpighi held professorships at Bologna, Pisa and Messina; he also served as private physician to Pope Innocent XII.

Malthusian

The adjective Malthusian refers to the population theories of the English economist *Thomas Robert Malthus* (1766–1834). In his *Essay on the Principle of Population*, which aroused great controversy throughout the world when it was published in 1798, Malthus argued that population increases at a faster rate than the means of subsistence. The inevitable result would be that the human race would remain near starvation unless the growth in population was checked by sexual restraint or by natural controls such as disease, famine, or war.

man Friday see FRIDAY

Manichaenism

Manichaenism is the religious movement named after its Persian founder, *Mani* (c.217–c.276 A.D.). It combined elements from Buddhism, Zoroastrianism, and Christianity. According to the teaching, the world and the human race are engaged in the struggle between the good and evil (light and darkness, or God and matter). By strict abstinence and prayer, Manichaeans believed that man could become aware of the light.

The religion spread throughout Asia and the Roman Empire and lasted until the thirteenth century. Mani, its founder, was martyred by the disciples of Zoroastrianism. St Augustine followed Manichaenism for a brief period before his conversion to Christianity.

mansard roof

A mansard roof has two slopes on both sides and ends, the lower slopes being almost vertical and the upper ones nearly horizontal. It is often used to provide a high ceiling to an attic. The roof is named after the French classical architect *François Mansart* (1598–1666). Notable buildings that Mansart designed include the north wing of Blois Château (1635–38) and the Maisons-Laffitte near Paris (1642). It is said that he was chosen to design the Louvre, but since he would not allow his design to be changed during the building, he was not appointed.

Maoism

The theory of Marxism–Leninism was developed in China by *Mao Tse-tung* (Chinese, *Mao Zedong*) (1893–1976). Born into a peasant family in Hunan province, Mao helped establish the Chinese Communist Party in 1921 and founded a Soviet republic in Jiangxi province in south-east China (1931).

He led the Long March, the flight of the Chinese communists from Jiangxi to north-west China (1934–6), and this established him as leader of the Communist Party. He joined forces with the Guomindang (Nationalist Party), to bring about the defeat of Japan in the Sino-Japanese War (1937–45), but he then opposed and defeated the Guomindang in the ensuing civil war.

In 1949, he founded the People's Republic of China and was Chairman of the Communist Party from 1949 until his death. He instigated the ecnomic Great Leap Forward (1958–60) and the Cultural Revolution (1966–9). Mao, one of the most significant revolutionary figures of the twentieth century, is remembered for, amongst other things, his emphasis on revolutionary guerrilla warfare of the peasant armies, his courageous political and social activities in transforming China, and his stress on moral exhortation and indoctrination, typified by 'The Little Red Book' of his sayings.

See also MARXISM, LENINISM.

marcel

A marcel is a deep, soft, continuous wave made in the hair with a curling iron; to *marcel the hair* is to make such a wave in the hair.

The word comes from the name of the French hairdresser *Marcel Grateau* (1852–1936). In 1875, Grateau devised the marcelling process; it is said that the hairstyle became so popular in France that Grateau amassed a great wealth, enabling him to retire even before he was 30.

marigold

A marigold is one of several annual herbaceous plants grown for their yellow or orange flower heads. The word marigold comes from a combination of the name of the *Virgin Mary*, the mother of Jesus, and the word *gold*. The name marigold was probably first applied to the plant now known as a pot marigold (*Calendula officinalis*), once used for healing wounds and as a flavouring for soups and stews.

Mariotte's law see BOYLE'S LAW

Marshall Plan

The Marshall Plan (officially known as the European Recovery Programme) was the programme of US economic aid to Europe after the Second World War. The Marshall Plan is named after the US general and statesman *George Catlett Marshall* (1880–1959), who originally proposed it when he was Secretary of State (1947–9). For this work, he was awarded the NOBEL PRIZE for peace in 1953. Earlier in his career, Marshall had been Army Chief of Staff (1939–45) and was responsible for organizing the expansion of American armed forces during the Second World War.

martin

A martin is a bird of the swallow family that has a square or slightly forked tail. Its name may come from the time of the birds' migration, reckoned to be about the time of *Martinmas*, 11 November, the festival of *St Martin*, the fourth-century Bishop of Tours.

martinet

A martinet is a strict disciplinarian. The word comes from the name of a French army officer during the reign of Louis XIV, *Jean Martinet*. Under Martinet's influence, the French army was transformed from an ill-disciplined group into an efficient military force by a rigorous system of drilling and training that even included punishing his soldiers with the cat-o'-nine tails. Thus Martinet's name became associated with harsh forms of discipline, and the term gradually entered non-military contexts.

Somewhat ironically, Martinet was 'accidentally' killed by his own forces. In the siege of Duisberg (1672), it is said that Martinet over-zealously entered the line of fire of his own rear ranks. But to those who had experienced the severity of Martinet's training methods, it seems quite possible that the event was not an accident.

Marxism

Marxism is the theory of socialism of the German political philosophers *Karl Marx* (1818–83) and Friedrich Engels (1820–95).

Born in Prussia, Marx was educated at the universities of Bonn and Berlin. He edited the radical Cologne newspaper, the *Rheinische Zeitung* (1842–3), but after its suppression, he left Germany. At first he stayed in Paris, where he met Engels; later in Brussels the communist manifesto (1848) was written. Marx settled in London in 1849, where he spent the rest of his life. He assumed leadership of the International Working Men's Association, (the First International) in 1864. His theories of the class struggle and the economics of capitalism were developed in *Das Kapital* (first volume, 1867; the remaining two volumes published posthumously).

Marxism has come to stand for the theory that capitalism and the class struggle will give way to the dictatorship of the proletariat and then to the establishing of the classless society.

See also LENINISM, STALINISM, TROTSKYISM.

masochism

The word masochism is used to describe the mental disorder that causes a person to derive pleasure (especially sexual) from the experience of self-inflicted pain, humiliation, etc. The word derives from the name of the Austrian novelist *Leopold von Sacher-Masoch* (1836–95), whose writings depicted this condition.

This form of obsession was reflected not only in the novels of Sacher-Masoch; it was also evident in his bizarre life – he was the self-appointed 'slave' of a number of mistresses and two wives in his lifetime. It was probably the German psychiatrist Richard von Krafft-Ebing (1840–1902) who coined the word masochism after studying Sacher-Masoch's works.

Mason–Dixon line

The Mason–Dixon line (originally Mason and Dixon's line) was the name given to the boundary between the states of Maryland and Pennsylvania, set in 1763–7. It is named after its English surveyors *Charles Mason* (*c.*1730–87) and *Jeremiah Dixon*. Before the American Civil War the line came to be regarded as the demarcation line between the North and South, the free states and the slave states.

maudlin

The word maudlin is sometimes used to refer to someone who is tearfully sentimental, or foolishly drunk. The word comes originally from the name *Mary Magdalene*, traditionally portrayed in paintings as a weeping penitent. The biblical text relates that Mary weeps when she discovers the empty tomb after the resurrection of Jesus (John 20:1–18).

On the identity of Mary Magdalene, see MAGDALEN.

Mauser

Mauser is the trademark used to describe a type of pistol. The word comes from the name of the German firearms inventors *Peter Paul von Mauser* (1838–1914) and his older brother *Wilhelm* (1834–82). The Mauser rifle (or pistol) was used by the Germany army for many years from 1871; modified versions were used in both World Wars. The younger brother also invented the Mauser magazine rifle, in 1897.

mausoleum

A mausoleum, a grand stately tomb, comes from the name of *King Mausolus*, ruler of Cari in ancient Greece. When he died in 353 BC, his widow, Artemisia, built a huge magnificent tomb at Halicarnassus in his honour. The monument was probably a raised temple with decorative statues and a pyramid-like roof; it was considered one of the seven wonders of the ancient world. It is believed that the monument was destroyed by earthquake in the Middle Ages.

maverick

A person who is independent and who does not wish to conform or be identified with a group is sometimes called a maverick. The word comes from the name of the American pioneer *Samuel Augustus Maverick* (1803–70). Also known as a fighter for Texan independence and originally a lawyer, Maverick became a rancher when he gained a herd of cattle in settlement of a debt. He failed, however, to ensure that all his calves were branded, perhaps so that he could claim all unbranded calves as his own or so that neighbouring ranchers could put their own brands on them. In the course of time the word came to be used to refer not only to unbranded cattle but also to people who do not 'go with the herd', who do not give allegiance to a particular group, especially a political one.

Maxim gun

The Maxim gun is the name of the first fully automatic machine-gun, a water-cooled, single-barrelled weapon that used the recoil force of each shot to keep up the automatic firing. The machine gun is named after the US-born British inventor *Sir Hiram Stevens Maxim* (1840–1916), who developed it in 1884.

Maxim originally served as chief engineer for America's first electric company, the United States Electric Lighting Company. He later applied his engineering skills to inventing his machine-gun, and also to other items such as a kind of mousetrap and a fire sprinkler.

maxwell

The maxwell is the unit of magnetic flux in the centimetre–gram–second system of measurement. The unit is named after the Scottish physicist *James Clerk Maxwell* (1831–79).

Maxwell wrote his first scientific paper at the age of 15; he later became professor of physics at the University of Aberdeen and then London. In 1871 he became the first professor of experimental physics at Cambridge. Maxwell made significant advances to the study of physics, notably in his unifying of electricity, magnetism, and light into one set of equations (*Maxwell's equations*; published 1873 in his *Treatise on Electricity and Magnetism*), which form the basis of electrodynamics. Maxwell also made important contributions to the kinetic theory of gases, and to the understanding of colour vision.

March

The name of the third month of the year comes from the name of the Roman god *Mars*, the god of war. Before the time of Julius Caesar, the Roman year began in March. This month was considered the beginning of not only a new year but also a new season of waging war; so the month was committed to Mars and named in his honour.

May

The fifth month of the year takes its name from the Roman goddess *Maia*, the goddess of spring and fertility, and daughter of Faunus and wife of Vulcan.

The Old English name for the month is said to have been of a more practical nature: *Thrimilce*, because in the longer days of spring, the cows could be milked three times between sunrise and sunset.

Medes (laws of the Medes and Persians)

The laws of the Medes and Persians are unchangeable laws that are to be strictly followed: *She need not be so inflexible – after all, it's not a law of the Medes and Persians that lunch has to be eaten at 1 o'clock every day*. The expression comes from the Bible (Daniel 6:8), 'Now, O King, establish the decree, and sign the writing, that it be not changed, according to the law of the Medes and Persians, which altereth not'.

The Medes were inhabitants of Media, north-east of Mesopotamia, between the Black Sea and the Caspian Sea. In 550 BC the Persian King Cyrus the Great defeated his overlord and father-in-law Astyages to gain control of the Median empire. Many Medes were then granted high positions in the Persian court and the Medes' customs and laws were amalgamated with those of the Persians – hence the expression the laws of the Medes and the Persians.

medusa

A medusa is the name given to a type of jellyfish and also to the free-swimming form in the lifecycle of a coelenterate animal. The word comes from the name *Medusa*, one of the Greek mythological GORGONS. When the goddess Athena was incensed by Medusa's favouring of Poseidon, she changed Medusa's locks into serpents and made her face so hideous that everyone who looked at her was turned to stone. The name of the jellyfish comes from the resemblance of its tentacles to the serpent-like curls of the Gorgon.

Melba toast; peach melba

Melba toast (thinly sliced toasted bread) and peach melba (a dessert of peaches, ice-cream, and raspberry–melba–sauce) owe their origin to the stage name of the Australian operatic soprano singer *Dame Nellie Melba* (1861–1931).

Born as Helen Porter Mitchell, and later adopting the name Melba (from Melbourne, near which she was born), the singer made her debut in *Rigoletto* (Brussels, 1887) and went on to star in London, Paris, and New York. It is said that Melba toast

originated at the Savoy Hotel in London when Dame Nellie Melba ordered toast, only to be served with several pieces of crisp burnt toast – which were then named after her. Peach melba is said to have been originally made by the French chef Auguste Escoffier (1846–1935) in her honour.

mendelevium

The artificially produced radioactive metallic chemical element known as mendelevium is named in honour of the Russian chemist *Dmitri Ivanovich Mendeleyev* (1834–1907). Mendeleyev was professor of organic chemistry at St Petersburg (1866–1890). After listening to a lecture on the subject of atomic weights by the Italian chemist Stanislao Cannizzaro (1826–1910), Mendeleyev became interested in a classification of the elements and in 1869 he devised the first version of the periodic table of the chemical elements.

Mendel's laws

Mendel's laws are the basic principles of heredity proposed by the Austrian botanist *Gregor Johann Mendel* (1822–84). Mendel was originally a monk; however, because of his earlier scientific training and interest in botany he began to experiment with the hybrid breeding of pea plants in the monastery garden at Brno, Moravia. His conclusions were formulated in two principles – Mendel's laws – in 1865, but remained unrecognized until 1900, when they were rediscovered by Hugo de Vries and others. Mendel is now recognized as the founder of the science of genetics.

Peach Melba

mentor

Mentor, the word for a wise and trusted adviser, comes from the name *Mentor*, Odysseus' loyal friend who was also the tutor of his son, the young Telemachus, in Homer's *Odyssey*. Mentor's identity is assumed by Athene, the goddess of wisdom; she accompanies Telemachus in his search for his father. The currency of the word in English is probably due to the prominence of the character in *Les Aventures de Télémaque* (1699) by the French theologian and writer, François de Salignac de la Mothe Fénelon (1651–1715).

Mephistopheles; Mephistophelean

A person may be described as a Mephistopheles or as being Mephistophelean if he or she is diabolical or evil in a sinister, persuasive manner. The term comes from the *Mephistopheles* of German legend – the contemptuous, merciless, tempting evil spirit to whom Faust sold his soul. The origin of the word Mephistopheles itself is uncertain; it is said to have been used by magicians and alchemists in spells. The earliest form of the word is *Mephostophiles* (*Faustbuch*, 1587), possibly meaning 'not loving the light'.

Mercator projection

Mercator (or Mercator's) projection is the form of map projection in which lines of latitude and longitude are straight lines that intersect one another at right angles and all lines of latitude are the same length as the equator. The projection is used for navigation charts but it has the disadvantage of distorting outlines and exaggerating sizes at increasing distances from the equator.

This form of map projection is named after the Flemish geographer *Gerardus Mercator* (original name *Gerhard Kremer*; 1512–94) who devised it in 1568. Originally working in Louvain, Mercator had to flee to Protestant Germany in 1552 to escape charges of heresy.

See also ATLAS.

mesmerize

If you are mesmerized by something you are extremely fascinated, spellbound, or even hypnotized by it. The word comes from the name of the Austrian physician and hypnotist *Franz Anton Mesmer* (1734–1815), who induced a hypnotic state in his patients. Born in Austria, Mesmer studied and later practised medicine in Vienna. He considered his medical success was due to his method (so-called 'animal magnetism') of stroking his patients with magnets.

In spite of the support of those he had treated, Mesmer was compelled by the Austrian authorities to leave Vienna, so he moved to Paris in 1778. Here, his healing technique became very fashionable. Wearing purple robes, he would wave his magic wand, and seek to treat individuals in the gathered group.

In 1784 Louis XVI appointed a scientific commission to investigate the practices; they concluded that Mesmer was a charlatan and an imposter. This led him to flee from Paris and he spent the rest of his life in obscurity in Switzerland. Mesmer believed that his success was due to the supernatural; today we would acknowledge that it was due to his hypnotic powers.

Messerschmitt

The Messerschmitt planes (particularly Me-109 and the first mass-produced jet-fighter, Me-262) of the Second World War are named after the German aircraft designer *Willy Messerschmitt* (1898–1978). Messerschmitt built his first aeroplane at the age of 18 and owned his own factory by the time he was 25. In 1927 he was appointed chief designer at the Bayerische Flugzeugwerke; in 1937 he received the Lilienthal prize for research into aviation.

Methuselah (as old as Methuselah)

The expression *as old as Methuselah*, meaning 'very old', refers to the age of the Old Testament patriarch. According to Genesis, chapter 5, Methuselah was the son of Enoch and grandfather of Noah and lived to be 969 years old.

See also JEROBOAM.

Micawber

Someone who is described as a Micawber or as being Micawberish is a person who does not make provision for the future, optimistically trusting that 'something is bound to turn up'. The name comes from the character *Wilkins Micawber* in the novel *David Copperfield* (published 1849–50) by Charles Dickens. By the end of the story, Micawber, relieved of his debts and having emigrated to Australia, appears as a highly regarded colonial magistrate.

Michaelmas

Michaelmas is the feast of *St Michael the Archangel*, 29 September, and is one of the four quarter days when certain business payments become due. The autumnal celebration of St Michael is recalled in the naming of the *Michaelmas daisy*, an autumn-blooming aster, and *Michaelmas term*, another name for the autumn term at some universities.

See also HILARY.

mickey (take the mickey out of); Mickey Finn

If you *take the mickey out of someone*, you make fun of him or her. The origin of the word is not known, but it could derive from the derogatory use of the name *Mick* (from Michael) to refer to an Irishman, Michael being a common Irish first name.

A Mickey Finn is slang for an alcoholic drink containing a drug to render someone unconscious. The expression is said to derive from the Chicago saloon-keeper at the end of the nineteenth century *Mickey Finn*. He would add a knock-out drug to the drinks of his unsuspecting victims, and would rob them once they had passed out. It is possible that the original Mickey Finn was a laxative for horses.

Mickey Mouse

Something may be described as being Mickey Mouse if it is trivial or trite. The expression derives from the name of the simple-minded cartoon character *Mickey Mouse* created by the American film producer and animator Walt Disney (1901–66).

Disney first drew Mickey Mouse in 1928; it seems that the character is based on his former pet mouse known as Mortimer. Mickey Mouse made his debut in the first animated sound cartoon *Steamboat Willie* (November 1928), in which Disney used his own voice for Mickey's high-pitched speech. The mouse became an instant success, and by 1931 Mickey Mouse clubs had a million members throughout the USA.

Midas (*the Midas touch*)

Someone who has the Midas touch makes an easy financial success of all his or her business undertakings. The expression comes from the *King Midas of Phrygia* in Greek legend. In gratitude to King Midas's provison of hospitality to the satyr Silenus, the god Dionysus promised to fulfil any wish King Midas might make. The King told Dionysus that he wanted everything he touched to be turned to gold. Dionysus granted this – but on discovering that even his food and drink turned to gold, Midas asked that this gift be taken away. Dionysus then ordered King Midas to bathe in the River Pactolus and he was washed clean of his power.

mint

The word for the place where money is coined, a mint, comes from the Latin word for money, *monēta*. The Romans coined their money in the temple of the Roman goddess Juno, who was known by the title *Moneta*, 'the admonisher'; so it was that the mint and its product came to be known by this name.

mithridatism

The word mithridatism is used to refer to an immunity to poison that is acquired by a gradual drinking of increasing doses. The expression comes from the name of the King of Pontus, *Mithridates VI*, called the Great (*c.* 132–63 BC), who allegedly produced this condition in himself.

King Mithridates engaged the Romans in many significant battles, but was eventually defeated by Pompey in 66 BC. During his whole lifetime he is said to have guarded himself from being poisoned by gradually drinking increasing amounts of poison, so rendering himself more and more immune to its effect. On his defeat by Pompey he decided to commit suicide, only to discover that he had mithridatized himself too successfully. He was completely immune to poison, and so ordered a mercenary to kill him with his sword.

Möbius strip

A Möbius strip is a one-sided continuous surface that is made by twisting a strip of paper through 180° and joining the ends. It is named after the German mathematician *August Ferdinand Möbius* (1780–1868), who discovered it. The Möbius strip is significant because its unexpected properties are of interest in topology: if it is cut lengthways, it remains in one piece.

mogul

A Mogul was a member of the Muslim dynasty of rulers in India in the sixteenth–eighteenth centuries, and (with a small 'm'), is an important or very rich person: *a film mogul*. The founder of the dynasty was the emperor Barbur (1483–1530). Both usages of the word have their origin in Persian *Mughul*, which in turn comes from Mongolian *Mongol*. The figurative sense probably comes from the Great Moguls, the first six rulers of the dynasty.

Mohammed (if the mountain will not come to Mohammed, Mohammed must go to the mountain)

The idiomatic expression *if the mountain will not come to Mohammed, Mohammed must go to the mountain* means that if a person or set of circumstances will not change or be adapted to suit one's own wishes, then one must oneself change or adapt to suit them. The expression derives from the life of *Mohammed*, the prophet and founder of Islam (*c.* AD 570–632). It is said that when he brought his message of Islam to the Arabs, they demanded a miracle to prove his claims. Mohammed then ordered Mount Safa to come towards him. When it failed to do so, he explained that God had been merciful: if the mountain had moved, it would have fallen on them and destroyed them. Mohammed then proposed that instead he would go to the mountain, and give thanks to God for his mercy.

molly

The molly is a brightly coloured tropical fish that belongs to the genus *Mollienesia*, and is often valued as aquarium fish. The molly takes its name from the French statesman *Comte Nicolas-François*

Mollien (1758–1850). Mollien served as financial adviser to Napoleon, although it seems his advice was often rejected. It is not clear why the fish is named after this French statesman; he was not even a collector of tropical fish.

Molotov cocktail

The Soviet statesman *Vyacheslav Mikhailovich Molotov* (original surname *Scriabin*; 1890–1986) played a substantial role in the growth of the Soviet Union as a superpower. After the Bolshevik Revolution of October 1917, Molotov held a series of posts in the ranks of the Party, becoming (1921) a secretary to the Central Committee; in 1922 he was instrumental in promoting Stalin to General Secretary. He was Prime Minister (1930–41) and Foreign Minister (1939–49; 1953–6). He negotiated the Soviet–German non-aggression treaty (1939), and after the Germans invaded the Soviet Union he negotiated alliances with the Allies. He was also a prominent figure in the Cold War between the USA and the Soviet Union after the Second World War. Disagreements with Khrushchev led, however, to his dismissal from office in 1956 and in 1962 his expulsion from the Communist Party, although he was readmitted to the party in 1984.

The crude petrol bomb known as the Molotov cocktail is named after the Russian statesman. It consists of a bottle filled with a flammable liquid, such as petrol, which is covered by a saturated rag; the rag is ignited as the bottle is thrown. It seems that the device may have been used as early as 1934 but the term Molotov cocktail was not applied to the device until 1940, when the Finns used them against the tanks of the invading Russians.

Monroe doctrine

The US President *James Monroe* (1785–1831) is remembered for his proclamation to Congress on 2 December 1823 that has come to be known as the Monroe doctrine. In this statement he warned the European nations against trying to interfere in or influence the affairs of the Americans; in return the USA would not intervene in Europe. The Monroe doctrine, largely the work of Secretary of State John Quincy Adams, became a fundamental principle in the foreign policy of the USA.

Earlier, Monroe had fought and been wounded in the American Revolution; he had also served as Minister to France (1794–6) and Britain (1803–7). His two terms in office (1817–25) as President are known as the 'era of good feelings'; during this term Florida was acquired and five states were added to the Union.

Monrovia, the capital and main port of the African country of Liberia, is also named in honour of Monroe. The country was founded during Monroe's presidency, in 1822, as a settlement for freed American slaves.

Montbretia

A montbretia is a plant of the Iris family that bears showy orange or yellow flowers. The plant is named after the French botanist *A. F. E. Coquebert de Montbret* (1780–1801).

Montessori method

The Italian physicist and educator *Maria Montessori* (1870–1952) is remembered for the development of an educational method that is named after her. In this method the creative potential of young children is developed; they are provided with different sensory materials in a prepared environment, and they make their own rate of progress through free but guided play.

Born into a noble family, Montessori studied medicine at the University of Rome and became the first woman in Italy to receive a degree in medicine (1896). She then began to work with retarded children, later opening a school for children of normal intelligence in a slum area of Rome (1907). The success of her methods led to the founding of other schools in Europe and Asia. With some refinements, Montessori's ideas have had an important influence on the modern education of children.

Moog synthesizer

Moog is the trademark for a type of synthesizer. *Robert Arthur Moog* (b. 1934) is an American physicist, engineer, and electrician who designed the synthesizer that bears his name. Working with the composer H. A. Deutsch, Moog developed his device that could electronically reproduce the sounds of conventional musical instruments and also produce a variety of artificial tones. The Moog synthesizer was patented in 1965.

Moonie

Moonie is the name given to a member of the Unification Church founded by the Korean industrialist *Sun Myung Moon* (original name *Yong Myung Moon*; b. 1920).

The religious group was established in 1954; its members believe that the 'Reverend' Moon has been given the responsibility, begun by Adam and Jesus, to unite the human race into a perfect family. The movement is also known for its indoctrination of potential recruits and its methods of fund raising.

Mop, Mrs

Mrs Mop is an informal expression for a lady who cleans a house or office. The name, often used in a facetious or derogatory way, derives from the character (*Mrs Mopp*) in the BBC radio programme 'ITMA' broadcast during the years of the Second World War. Mrs Mopp was a Cockney charlady who first featured in the radio show on 10 October 1940. Her original question was, 'Can I do for you now, sir?' This was later shortened by omitting the *for*, to the expression that has become a familiar catch-phrase, 'Can I do you now, sir?'

Mormon

A Mormon is a member of the Church of Jesus Christ of Latter-Day Saints, that was founded in 1830 by Joseph Smith (1805–44) in New York State. Several visions led to Smith's claim that in 1827 he had discovered some gold plates which contained the *Book of Mormon*. This sacred book is named after its compiler, and, according to Mormon belief, was buried in the fifth century A D.

Smith published the book in 1830; Mormons see it as one of a series of scriptures that supplement the Bible. Following Smith's murder in Illinois, the movement was led by Brigham Young (1801–77), and their headquarters were established at Salt Lake City, Utah, in 1847. The Mormons' former practice of polygamy brought them into conflict with the Federal authorities until 1890, when it was disallowed.

morphine

Morphine (or morphia) is an addictive narcotic drug used medicinally to alleviate pain and to induce sleep. The word is derived from the name *Morpheus*, the god of dreams in Greek mythology. He was the son of Somnus, the god of sleep.

Morris chair

The Morris chair, an armchair that has an adjustable back and large loose cushions, is named after its designer, the English poet, artist, and socialist writer *William Morris* (1834–96). Morris founded a firm of designers and decorators in 1861 and he designed furniture, wallpaper and stained glass of a style different from those of the contemporary Victorian era. The work of William Morris and his Pre-Raphaelite associates led to the development of the Arts and Crafts movement in England.

Morris is also noted for his development of the private press with his founding of the Kelmscott Press (1890), for his poetry and prose writings, and for his establishing of the Socialist League in England.

morris dance

A morris dance is a traditional English dance performed in the open air by costumed men, morris men, wearing bells and often carrying sticks. The name morris dance is thought to have originally been *Moorish dance*; it is said that the dances derived from the ancient dances of the Moors and were introduced from Spain into England about 1350. The dances often illustrate a legend or portray an activity.

Morrison shelter see ANDERSON SHELTER

Morse code

Morse code is a telegraphic system of signalling in which letters and numbers are represented by dots and dashes. The code is named after its inventor, the American artist and inventor *Samuel Finley Breese Morse* (1791–1872).

Morse was originally an artist: he exhibited paintings at the Royal Academy in London and enjoyed a good reputation as a portrait painter. He founded and became the first president of the National Academy of Design in New York in 1826, and then was appointed professor of painting and sculpture at New York University.

Morse's interests gradually turned to electric telegraphy. His work was only very slowly recognized, but following financial backing from Congress, the first line, between Washington and Baltimore was built (1843–4). The words 'What hath God wrought?' constituted the first communication in Morse code sent on 24 May 1844. Following a series of legal battles, Morse patented his system in 1854, and the Morse code is still in use today.

mosaic

A mosaic is a decorative design or picture that is made by inlaying different coloured pieces of material, especially glass or stone. The word mosaic comes via French and Italian from Medieval Latin *mōsaicus*, which in turn is derived from Greek *Mousa*, a *Muse*. In Greek mythology, the Muses were nine sister goddesses who were patrons of music and poetry, and the arts and sciences. The English words *museum* and *music* also derive from the same Greek word for a Muse.

Moses basket

A portable shallow wickerwork cradle for a baby is sometimes known as a Moses basket. This expression alludes to the papyrus cradle into which the infant *Moses* was placed, among the reeds by the River Nile (Exodus 2:3).

Mother Carey's chickens

Mother Carey's chickens are storm petrels – small sea-birds with dark plumage and paler underparts. It is not known who the original Mother Carey was; it is possible that the expression is a corruption of the Latin *Mater Cara* ('Beloved Mother'), a name for the Virgin Mary, considered to be the protector of sailors. An alternative suggestion is that the expression is an alteration of a nautical Spanish or Italian name.

Mother Goose

A Mother Goose rhyme is a nursery rhyme. The name derives from the title of the collection of fairytales by the French writer Charles Perrault (1628–1703), *Contes de ma Mère L'Oye*, published in 1697, and translated into English as *Tales of Mother Goose* (1729).

muggins

The word muggins is sometimes used in informal English to refer to someone when he or she has been foolish. Often the person referred to is oneself: *I'm sorry but muggins here has forgotten to bring the tickets!* The expression probably derives from the surname *Muggins*, and is influenced by *mug* in the sense of a fool or someone who can be deceived easily and *juggins*, an old-fashioned informal word for a simple person.

Murphy's Law

'If anything can go wrong, it will' – this is the pithy wisdom of Murphy's (or Sod's) Law. Other humorous rules of thumb that go under the name of Murphy's Law include: 'Nothing is as easy as it looks' and 'Everything takes longer than you think it will'. It is not certain who the original Murphy was; quotations of the 'law' in print date back to the 1950s.

museum; music see MOSAIC

myrmidon

Myrmidons are loyal followers, especially those who carry out orders without questioning. The word derives from the *Myrmidons*, the people of Greek legend from Thessaly. It is said that Zeus made the Myrmidons from a race of ants (Greek *murmēx*, an ant). They were well known for their loyal devotion to Achilles in the Trojan War.

N

namby-pamby

Someone or something that is described as namby-pamby is thought of as being very sentimental in an insipid manner. The word was originally a nickname for the English poet *Ambrose Philips* (1674–1749). His verse about children (such as 'Dimply damsel, sweetly smiling' and 'Timely blossom, infant fair, Fondling of a happy pair') were mocked by writers such as Pope and Carey for their weak sentimentality. It was Henry Carey (*c*.1687–1743) who is credited with the coining of the word namby-pamby: *amby* comes from the poet's first name and the alliterative *P* from his surname.

nancy

The use of the word nancy for an effeminate boy or man or a homosexual dates back to the early twentieth century. The word comes from the girl's name *Nancy*, originally a diminutive of the name *Ann*, derived from a Hebrew word meaning grace. A *nanny* goat, a female goat, comes from Nancy. A *billy* goat, a male goat, takes the name *Billy*, a nickname for *William*.

nap; napoleon; Napoleonic

Nap is a card game that is similar to whist in which the number of
tricks that a player expects to win is declared. The longer version
of the name of the card game is napoleon, which reveals the word's
origin: the French Emperor *Napoleon Bonaparte* (1769–1821). It is,
however, uncertain why the game is named after him.

The adjective Napoleonic is sometimes used with allusion to the
Emperor's masterly tactics or the vastness of his ambitions.

Napierian

The mathematical functions known as logarithms, used in calcu-
lations of multiplication and division, were invented by the Scottish
mathematician *John Napier* (1550–1647). He published his table
of logarithms in 1614; these came to be known as Napierian or
natural logarithms. A modified version of these mathematical
functions (common logarithms) came into use later.

Napier also devised a simple calculating machine that consisted
of a series of graduated rods, known as *Napier's bones*.

narcissism

Extreme interest in or love for oneself is known as narcissism. This
word comes from *Narcissus*, the beautiful young man in Greek
mythology who, after spurning all offers of love, including that of
the nymph Echo, was punished by falling in love with his own
reflection in the waters of a fountain, thinking that it was a
a nymph. His attempts to approach the beautiful object were to no
avail, however. He was driven to despair and pined away, finally
being transformed into the flower that bears his name.

nebuchadnezzar see JEROBOAM

negus

A negus is a drink of wine (usually port or sherry), hot water, lemon juice, sugar, and nutmeg. It is named after the English soldier and politician in the reign of Queen Anne, *Colonel Francis Negus* (d. 1732), who is reputed to have invented it.

The *Dictionary of National Biography* records that on one occasion, Negus averted a fracas between Whigs and Tories 'by recommending the dilution of the wine with hot water and sugar. Attention was diverted from the point of issue to a discussion of the merits of wine and water, which ended in the compound being nicknamed "Negus".'

nemesis

Nemesis means vengeance or something that is thought to be or bring retribution. The word derives from *Nemesis*, the Greek mythological goddess of retribution. Nemesis personified the gods' resentment at, and just punishment of, human arrogance, pride, and insolence. According to the early Greek poet Hesiod, Nemesis was a child of Night.

nestor

A nestor is a wise old man or a sage. The word derives from the King of Pylos, *Nestor*, in Greek legend, particularly the *Iliad*. He was the oldest – he was about 70 – and most experienced of the Greek commanders in the Trojan War, and advised moderation to the quarrelling Greek leaders. He was well known for his wise advice and the narration of his deeds in earlier days, in spite of his wordiness.

newton

Newton, the metric unit of force, comes from the name of the British physicist and mathematician *Sir Isaac Newton* (1642–1727), one of the world's greatest scientists. Newton is particularly noted for his law of gravitation – said, as is well known, to have been inspired by the falling of an apple on his head – his laws of motion, and his studies of calculus and the theory of light.

Newton was also a Member of Parliament (1689–90), and Master of the Mint (1699–1727), during which time he undertook a reform of the coinage. From 1703 he was president of the Royal Society and he was knighted in 1705. His last words are said to have been: 'I don't know what I may seem to the world. But as to myself I seem to have been only like a boy playing on the seashore and diverting myself in now and then finding a smoother pebble or prettier shell than ordinary, whilst the great ocean of truth lay all undiscovered before me.'

nicotine

Nicotine, the chemical compound found in tobacco, comes from the name of the French diplomat *Jean Nicot* (1530–1600). Nicot was ambassador in Lisbon at the time that Portuguese explorers were bringing back seeds of tobacco from the newly discovered continent of America. In 1560, Nicot was given a plant from Florida, which he grew, sending tobacco seeds to the French nobility. When Nicot returned to France in 1561, he took a cargo load of tobacco with him. The powder quickly became so well known that the tobacco plant itself was named after Nicot: *Herba nicotiana*. It was in the early years of the nineteenth century that the liquid nicotine was isolated and named in Nicot's honour.

Nimrod

The name Nimrod is sometimes used to describe a great, skilful hunter. Use of this word derives from the biblical *Nimrod*, the son of Cush, a warrior or hero of Babylon. Genesis 10:9 describes him as 'a mighty hunter before the Lord'.

Nimrod is credited with the founding of the cities of Ninevah and Calah (modern Nimrud) in Assyria.

Nissen hut

A Nissen hut is a prefabricated military shelter that has a semi-circular arched roof of corrugated iron sheeting and a cement floor. The hut was named after its inventor, the British mining engineer *Lt.-Col. Peter Norman Nissen* (1871–1930) and was used in both World Wars.

The American equivalent is the *Quonset hut*, given its trademark name after *Quonset Point*, Rhode Island, where the huts were first made.

Nobel prize; nobelium

The Swedish chemist, manufacturer, and philanthropist *Alfred Bernhard Nobel* (1833–96) is noted for his invention of dynamite (1866). A pacifist, Nobel believed that his explosives would be the foundation of a country's defence system and, acting as a deterrent towards belligerent countries, would bring about peace.

Nobel amassed a great fortune from the manufacture and sale of explosives and also from his exploitation of oil interests. His great wealth went towards the funding of the Nobel prizes – prizes awarded annually for outstanding contributions to the service of humanity in the field of physics, chemistry, medicine, literature, and peace. The first of these annual awards was given in 1901; in 1969 a prize for economics was added.

The artificially produced element nobelium, discovered in 1957, is also named after Nobel.

nosey parker

A nosey (or nosy) parker is someone who pries very inquisitively into other people's affairs. It is said that the origin of the expression lies in the way of life of the Anglican churchman *Matthew Parker* (1504–75).

Having moderate Protestant views, Parker was forced to flee to Germany during the reign of Queen Mary. Later, he was appointed Archbishop of Canterbury (1559–75) and participated in the issue of the Thirty Nine Articles. He also directed the compilation of a new version of the Bible, the Bishops' Bible (published 1568) essentially a revision of the Great Bible.

Various sources point to different aspects of Parker's life in attributing the origin of the expression nosey Parker to him; some note his over-long nose while others describe his intense curiosity in other people's affairs.

O

obsidian

Obsidian is a dark, glassy, volcanic rock that is formed by the fast cooling of molten lava. It has sharp edges and was originally used for weapons. The word obsidian is said to have come from a wrong manuscript reading of Latin *obsiānus lapis*, stone of obsius, a *d* being incorrectly inserted in the spelling. According to Pliny the Elder in his *Natural History*, *Obsius* was the first person to discover the rock, in Ethiopia.

Ockham's razor

The philosophical principle known as Ockham's (or Occam's) razor is usually formulated as 'Entities are not to be multiplied unnecessarily'. This means that an explanation should contain the simplest elements that are necessary, with as little reference as possible to unknown or assumed matters. This statement is attributed to the English philosopher and Franciscan *William of Ockham* (*c.*1285–1349), but these actual words have not been found in his writings.

Ockham was a pupil of Duns Scotus (see DUNCE), but later became his rival. He is known for his nominalist views, holding that general (or universal) terms have no real existence that is independent from the individual things denoted by the terms. The expression Ockham's Razor is therefore to be seen as an attack on the proposed existence of universals by the realists.

odyssey

An odyssey is a long quest or wandering that is full of adventures. The word comes from the *Odyssey*, the ancient Greek epic poem by Homer that describes the many adventures of the Greek king and hero *Odysseus* (Latin name, Ulysses) on his return home from the Trojan War.

Oedipus complex

An Oedipus complex is the unconscious sexual attraction of a child (especially a boy) to the parent of the opposite sex, while having jealous, aggressive feelings towards the parent of the same sex.

The expression derives from *Oedipus*, the character in Greek mythology, who is the son of Laius and Jocasta, the King and Queen of Thebes. When an oracle informed Laius that he was to perish at the hands of his son, he ordered his son to be destroyed, but Oedipus was rescued by a shepherd. Later, unaware of the identity of his parents, Oedipus killed his father, subsequently marrying his mother and having four children by her.

The expression is most commonly used to refer to the attraction of a male child to his mother. In cases when a female child is attracted to her father and shows hostility to her mother, the term *Electra complex* is more commonly used. In Greek mythology, *Electra* was the daughter of Agamemnon and Clytemnestra. She persuaded her brother Orestes to avenge their father's murder by killing her mother Clytemnestra and her lover, Aegisthus.

oersted

The oersted is the unit of magnetic field strength in the centimetre–gram–second system of measurement. The unit honours the Danish physicist *Hans Christian Oersted* (1777–1851) who was a professor at Copenhagen University. Oersted discovered the magnetic effect of an electric current in 1819, thus founding the science of electromagnetism.

ohm

The ohm, the metric unit of electrical resistance, is named after the German physicist *Georg Simon Ohm* (1787–1854). In 1827 he discovered that the electric current that passes through a conductor is directly proportional to the potential difference between its ends; this formulation became known as *Ohm's Law*.

After gaining a doctorate in physics, Ohm prepared to teach but failed to find sufficient financial support. It is said that following the publication of his first book – which included discussion of what is now known as Ohm's Law – he sent copies to several of the ruling European monarchs. It was the King of Prussia who decided to give him financial support. In 1841 he was awarded the Copley Medal of the British Royal Society, and at the International Electrical Congress of 1893 it was decided to honour Ohm by naming the unit of electrical resistance after him. See also SIEMENS.

old Adam see ADAM'S APPLE

Old Bill

Old Bill, the slang expression for a policeman or the police, probably comes from the name of a character in cartoons current at the time of the First World War. In the cartoons by the Indian-born British cartoonist and author Charles Bruce Bairnsfather (1888–1959), *Old Bill* was the name of a grousing old soldier with a large moustache. One particular cartoon depicts two British infantrymen Bert and Bill with water up to their knees in a shell-hole. To Bert's complaint about the inconvenience of their situation, Old Bill answers, 'If you know of a better 'ole, go to it'. During the Second World War, Bairnsfather became an official war cartoonist.

Old Nick

There are several different theories of the origin of the expression Old Nick, the informal or jocular name for the devil. Some suggest that Nick, being the nickname for Nicholas, derives from the name of *St Nicholas*, the fourth-century bishop of Asia Minor. The patron saint of Russia, sailors, and children, he is said to have brought gifts of gold to three poor girls for their dowries. Those who support this view however fail to show the link between the good-natured saint and the 'prince of evil'.

Others propose that Nick refers to the Florentine statesman and philosopher *Niccolò Machiavelli* (1469–1527). His supposed political unscrupulousness is said to have been the origin of the satanic reference to Old Nick. Still others point to non-eponymous sources, such as a shortening of German *nickel*, 'goblin'.

onanism

Onanism is used to refer to two sexual practices: coitus interruptus and masturbation. The word derives from the biblical character *Onan* who 'spilled his seed on the ground' (Genesis 38:9), though it seems that the biblical passage describes coitus interruptus rather than masturbation. When Onan's elder brother, Er, died, Judah commanded Onan to take his brother's wife, Tamar, under the custom of levirate law which said that if a married man died without a child, his brother was expected to take his wife. Onan, however, was not willing to follow this practice and did not fully consummate the union.

Orangeman

An Orangeman is a member of a society (the Orange Order) originally established in 1795 to uphold the Protestant religion and defend the British monarch. The word Orangeman derives from the Protestant King William III of England (1650–1702), known as *William of Orange*. At the Battle of the Boyne, north of Dublin, (July 1690), William defeated the Roman Catholic King James II. On 12 July, Protestants in Northern Ireland still celebrate the anniversary of this battle.

orrery

An orrery is a device that shows the relative positions and movements of planets, stars, and other heavenly bodies round the sun. The first orrery was invented by the mathematician George Graham (1673–1751) in about the year 1700. Graham sent the device to an instrument maker, John Rowley, who built a copy of such an apparatus, presenting it to his patron, *Charles Boyle, the 4th Earl of Orrery* (1676–1731), and naming the device in his honour.

Orwellian

The adjective Orwellian is used to describe aspects of life that are thought to be typical of the writings of the English novelist *George Orwell* (real name, *Eric Arthur Blair*; 1903–50). The adjective is most commonly used with reference to the nightmarish way of life that is experienced in a totalitarian state – for example, an Orwellian vision of total uniformity – particularly as described in Orwell's novel *1984* (published 1949), in which life is controlled by the ever-present Big Brother, the head of the Party.

Oscar

An Oscar is one of several gold statuettes awarded annually by the Academy of Motion Picture Arts and Sciences in the USA for outstanding achievements in the cinema.

The idea for the presentation of trophies came in 1927, the first were awarded in 1929, but they were not called Oscars until 1931, when, so the story goes, the Academy's librarian, Margaret Herrick is alleged to have remarked that the statuettes reminded her of her *Uncle Oscar*. It is said that a newspaper reporter happened to be listening and he passed on the news to his readers that 'Employees of the Academy have affectionately dubbed their famous statuette "Oscar".' It seems that Herrick's uncle was *Oscar Pierce*, a wheat and fruit grower formerly of Texas, who later lived in California.

Otto engine

The German engineer *Nikolaus August Otto* (1832–91) devised in 1876 the four-stroke petrol engine, the Otto engine, which represented the first practical internal-combustion engine. In Otto's engine, with the induction, compression, power, and exhaust strokes, gas was used as a fuel. Subsequently, oil was used and the Otto engine became the source of power for motor cars. A variation of the Otto engine is the DIESEL engine.

ottoman

An ottoman, a heavily padded box used as a seat and usually without a back, originated in Turkey. The word ottoman comes from French *ottomane*, which in turn comes from Arabic and then Turkish *Othman*. This was originally the name of the Turkish sultan *Osman I* (1259–1326) who founded the Ottoman Empire, which ruled in Europe, Asia, and Africa from the fourteenth to the twentieth centuries.

out-herod Herod

The expression *to out-herod Herod* means 'to exceed someone in a particular quality, especially wickedness or cruelty'. The Herod referred to is *Herod the Great* (*c.*73–4 B C), the ruler of Judaea who had all the baby boys of Bethlehem killed (Matthew 2:16). The source of the expression itself is *Hamlet* (Act 3, Scene 2): '*I would have such a fellow whipped for o'erdoing Termagant: it out-herods Herod: pray you, avoid it*'.

P

paean; peony

Nowadays, a paean is a piece of music or writing, or a film that expresses praise, triumph, joy, etc. Originally, a paean was a hymn to Apollo, the god of healing and physician of the gods in Greek mythology. Apollo bore the title *Paion*. Songs or hymns were sung to Apollo to ask or give thanks for his healing favours. From this developed the modern sense of the word.

The herb or shrub known as peony, grown for its large, showy, pink, red, or white flowers, also comes from *Paion*: the plants were once widely used in medicine.

Palladian

The Palladian style of architecture is characterized by symmetry and free-standing classical columns in façades. The style is named after the Italian architect *Andrea Palladio* (1508–80), who based his work on the architecture and principles of the first-century Roman architect Vitruvius. Originally a stonemason, Palladio began his successful career as an architect, commencing with his remodelling of the basilica at his home town of Vicenza (from 1549). He designed many villas, palaces, and chambers, particularly in the vicinity of his home town. His treatise *Four Books on Architecture* (1507) helped spread his ideas. It was the English architect Inigo Jones (1573–1652) who introduced Palladianism into England.

palladium

A palladium, something that gives protection, was originally the wooden statue of the Greek goddess *Pallas Athenas* that was kept in the citadel of Troy. It was believed that the statue was sent from heaven by Zeus and the safety of the city of Troy was believed to depend on the protection of the statue. The word palladium later came to refer to anything, such as the constitution or the freedom of the press, or religion, on which the safety of a country might be thought to depend.

pamphlet

The word for a pamphlet, an unbound printed publication with a paper cover, comes originally from a twelfth-century love poem, 'Pamphilus seu De Amore', (Pamphilus or On Love), *Pamphilus* being a masculine proper name. This short Latin love poem evidently became so popular that it came to be known simply as Pamphilet, later pamflet, and eventually pamphlet. The sense of a brief treatise on a matter of current interest was added in the sixteenth century.

pander

If you pander to someone's wishes, you do everything that he or she wants. This verb sense comes from the rarer noun form of the word, meaning a go-between in love affairs, a procurer, and someone who exploits evil desires. The noun sense derives from the character *Pandarus*, who takes a role devised by the Italian Giovanni Boccaccio in his poem *Filostrato*, and who features in a number of romances, particularly Chaucer's *Troilus and Criseyde* and Shakespeare's *Troilus and Cressida*. Pandarus is the intermediary between the two lovers, procuring Cressida for Troilus.

The Pandarus of Greek legend is a Trojan archer who shot the

Greek commander Menelaus with an arrow and was killed in the battle that followed by Diomedes.

Pandora's box

A Pandora's box is a source of great troubles; if it is opened, then difficulties that were previously unknown or under control are unleashed. The expression derives from the story in Greek mythology of *Pandora*, the first woman. Pandora ('all gifts') is given a box into which all the powers that would eventually bring about the downfall of man had been put; the box was to be given to the man that Pandora married. There are several different conclusions to the story. According to one version, her husband Epimetheus opened the box against her advice, to release all the misfortunes that have beset the human race. Another version has Pandora herself opening the box out of curiosity, letting out all the ills that afflict mankind, leaving only hope inside.

panic

Panic, the state of sudden overwhelming terror or fright, derives ultimately from *Pan*, the name of the Greek god of woods, shepherds, and flocks. He is usually depicted as having a human body and the ears, horns, and legs of a goat. Pan was, it seems, known for the mischievous tricks he would play of suddenly springing out from the undergrowth to inspire panic in those walking by. The god was also considered the source of the weird noises that could be heard in the forests at night, filling lost wanderers with panic.

pantaloon; pants

The fourth-century Venetian physician and saint *San Pantaleone* is remembered for a number of words that do not seem to be

associated with the saint's mild personality. There was the stock character in the Italian *commedia dell'arte*, the lecherous old man known as pantaloon, who wore spectacles, slippers and tight breeches. In time, the word pantaloons came to describe trousers, later being shortened to pants (in American English, trousers; in British English, an undergarment, underpants).

Pap test (or smear)

A Pap test is an examination for the early detection of cancer in which cells in a smear of bodily secretions, especially from the uterus or vagina, are examined. The test takes its name from the Greek-born American anatomist *George Nicholas Papanicolaou* (1883–1962), who devised it.

Pareto principle

Sometimes referred to as the 80/20 rule, the Pareto principle (or law) is seen, for example, in company sales: 80 per cent of the sales may come from 20 per cent of the customers. The expression derives from the name of the Italian economist and sociologist *Vilfredo Frederico Pareto* (1848–1923).

Pareto worked as director of Italian railways and superintendent of mines before being appointed professor of economics in 1892. His studies led him to analyse consumer demand and to formulate a law of the distribution of income within a society.

Pareto's law has since come to be formulated as the 80/20 rule and to apply to spheres outside economics and business, for example one could speak of taking 80 per cent of the time to teach 20 per cent of the students.

Panic

Parkinson's disease

Parkinson's disease is a disease that is marked by a tremor of the limbs, weakness of the muscles, and a peculiar gait. Also known as paralysis agitans, the disease is named after the British physician *James Parkinson* (1755–1824), who first described it in 1817.

Parkinson's law

The observation in office organization known as Parkinson's law states that 'work expands so as to fill the time available for its completion'. This was first formulated in the 1950s by the English historian and author *Cyril Northcote Parkinson* (b. 1909). In *Parkinson's Law* (published 1957), Parkinson also noted that 'subordinates multiply at a fixed rate regardless of the amount of work produced' and his law of triviality: 'the time spent on any item on the agenda will be in inverse proportion to the sum involved'.

Pascal

The French mathematician and philosopher *Blaise Pascal* (1623–62) had an early interest in mathematics that led to his formulation of what has become known as *Pascal's triangle*, used in probability theory. He later made discoveries in fluid mechanics and also invented a hydraulic press and a calculating machine. Coming under Jansenist influence, he entered the convent at Port Royal in 1655. His most well-known writings are *Lettres provinciales* (1656–7), a defence of JANSENISM, and *Pensées sur la religion* (1670), fragments of a defence of Christianity. Pascal is also remembered by having the pascal, the metric unit of pressure, and PASCAL, the high-level computer programming language, named in his honour.

pasteurize

When milk or another drink or a food is pasteurized, bacteria in it are destroyed by a special heating process. The word pasteurize derives from the name of the French chemist and bacteriologist *Louis Pasteur* (1822–95).

The son of a tanner, Pasteur studied chemistry, but was graded as only a mediocre student. He became a teacher and lecturer, and in 1854 was appointed dean of the faculty of science at Lille University. Pasteur first developed the process now known as pasteurization on wine and beer. He found that certain micro-organisms caused wine to ferment very quickly and that the fermentation could be prevented if the wine was subjected to heat and then cooled rapidly.

Pasteur also devised methods of immunization (*pasteurism* or *Pasteur treatment*) against anthrax and rabies.

Paul Jones

The dance known as the Paul Jones, in which couples change their partners is probably named after the American naval commander *John Paul Jones* (original name *John Paul*; 1747–92).

Born in Scotland, Jones went to America where he was commissioned into the American navy and was involved in several naval exploits against the British in the American War of Independence. In 1779, commanding the ship the *Bon Homme Richard*, Jones defeated the British frigate *Serapis* in a long battle. Refusing to surrender, even though his ship was on the verge of sinking, Jones is said to have uttered to the British captain Richard Pearson, 'I have not yet begun to fight.'

After the War of Independence, Jones served in the navies of Russia and France. The dance was probably named after Paul Jones in honour of his exploits.

Paul Pry

A Paul Pry, someone who is inquisitive and interfering, comes from the character of that name in the farce *Paul Pry* (published 1825) by the English dramatist John Poole (*c.*1786–1872). Brewer describes the figure Paul Pry as 'an idle, meddlesome fellow, who has no occupation of his own, and is always interfering with other folk's business'. He constantly enters with the apology, 'I hope I don't intrude'.

pavlova

The Russian ballerina *Anna Pavlova* (1885–1931) is remembered for her popularizing of ballet throughout the world. At the age of 21 she was the prima ballerina at the Russian Imperial Ballet and later she joined Diaghilev's Ballets Russes for a short time. From 1914, Pavlova began to tour throughout the world with her own company, and she is particularly remembered for her roles in *Giselle* and *The Dying Swan*. To celebrate her ballet performances in Australia and New Zealand, chefs in these countries popularized Pavlova – a meringue cake topped with cream and fruit.

Pavlovian

The Russian physiologist *Ivan Petrovich Pavlov* (1849–1936) is remembered for his studies of digestion and condition reflexes. In his experiments with dogs, Pavlov showed that a reflex response could be evoked by a stimulus that was different from the one that usually produces it. He found that dogs produced saliva in response to the sight of food accompanied by a bell. Eventually they would learn to associate the bell with the appearance of food and would produce saliva in response to hearing the bell alone. The adjective Pavlovian has therefore come to refer to something that is predictable or is evoked automatically as a response to a stimulus (*a Pavlovian reaction*).

Pavlov later applied his theories to cover other aspects of human and animal behaviour, such as learning. Although he persistently criticized the communist regime, the authorities continued to fund his work, and his studies have influenced the behaviourist school of psychology.

peach melba see MELBA TOAST

pecksniffian

The character *Seth Pecksniff* in the novel *Martin Chuzzlewit* by Charles Dickens (published 1843–4) has given his name to the adjective pecksniffian. In the story, Pecksniff is a smooth-talking hypocritical figure who gives an appearance of kindness and benevolence but is in reality mean, selfish, and treacherous.

peeping Tom

A peeping Tom, a voyeur or a man who takes pleasure in secretly looking at women undressing, derives from the name of a legendary English tailor. The traditional story relates how Leofric, the eleventh-century Lord of Coventry imposed crippling taxes on his people. Leofric's wife, Lady Godiva, pleaded with him to ease the tax burden on the citizens. Eventually he said he would on condition that Lady Godiva rode naked through the streets. Lady Godiva agreed and, having asked the citizens to keep the shutters on their windows closed, she rode naked through the streets on a white horse. Everyone respected her request except for the tailor, *Tom*, who peeped – only to be struck blind for his brazenness.

Pennsylvania

Pennsylvania, the state in north-eastern USA, is named not, as is sometimes believed, after William Penn, founder of the original colony, but after his father *Sir William Penn* (1621–70), an admiral in the British navy. It seems that the younger William Penn asked King Charles II for an area of land in America in settlement of a debt owed by the King to Penn's father. The land was to become a colony for Protestant Quakers who were being persecuted. Penn suggested the name Sylvania and the King, in honour of Penn's father, added Penn to it. The younger Penn tried to get the name changed but to no avail.

peony see PAEAN

Père David's deer see BUDDLEIA

Pestalozzi

The emphasis of the Swiss educationalist *Johann Heinrich Pestalozzi* (1746–1827) on observation in learning has had a profound influence on primary education. Born in Zurich into a wealthy family, Pestalozzi studied the writings of Rousseau and later attempted to establish schools for poor children. In spite of the apparent failure of the schools, his writings, including his book *Wie Gertrud ihre Kinder lehrt* (1801) have affected later educational developments. *Pestalozzi International Children's Villages* have also been established, for example in Sedlescombe, East Sussex.

Peter Pan

A Peter Pan is a man who never seems to grow up or who is unwilling to give up boyish or immature ways. The name is taken from the character in the play *Peter Pan, or The Boy who Wouldn't Grow Up* by the Scottish dramatist and novelist Sir James Matthew Barrie (1860–1937). The play, an immediate success when first performed at the Duke of York's Theatre in London, was developed from fantasy stories Barrie had created for the young sons of friends. Barrie became famous because of his writings, especially *Peter Pan*, and was made a baronet (1913) and awarded the Order of Merit (1922) and several honorary degrees. From 1930 he was chancellor of Edinburgh University.

See also WENDY HOUSE.

Peter Principle

'In a hierarchy, every employee tends to rise to the level of his incompetence.' This humorous semi-scientific statement is known as the Peter Principle, after the Canadian educator *Dr Laurence J. Peter* (b. 1919) and Raymond Hull (b. 1919) in their book *The Peter Principle – Why Things Always Go Wrong*, published in 1969.

Peter's pence

Peter's pence was originally an annual tax of one penny formerly levied on all English householders for the maintenance of the Pope. Dating from the ninth century, it was abolished by King Henry VIII in 1534; it is now a voluntary contribution made by Roman Catholics to the Pope. The phrase derives from the tradition that the apostle Peter was the first Pope.

petersham

Petersham, a tough, corded ribbon used, for example, in belts and hatbands takes its name from the English army officer *Charles Stanhope, Viscount Petersham, 4th Earl of Harrington* (1780–1851).

Viscount Petersham, it seems, was something of a dandy; he designed and popularized a kind of overcoat made of a heavy woollen cloth; the coat and cloth and then the ribbon coming to be known by his name. It is also said that he invented an original mixture of snuff.

Petrarchan sonnet

The Petrarchan sonnet, also called the Italian sonnet, originated in thirteenth-century Italy and was associated with the Italian poet *Petrarch* (Italian name, *Francesco Petrarca*; 1304–74). The 14-line poem is divided into two parts: the first eight lines rhyme abbaabba and the remaining six lines rhyme cdecde.

Born the son of a notary in Florence, Petrarch spent most of his life in Provence. He travelled throughout Europe and is particularly noted for *Canzoniere*, a series of love poems addressed to Laura, and also his humanist and spiritual writings. In 1341 he was crowned poet laureate in Rome.

See also SHAKESPEAREAN.

philippic

Philippic, meaning bitter and biting denunciation, derives from the name of the speeches in defence of Athenian liberty by the Athenian orator and statesman *Demosthenes* (384–322 BC) against King Philip II of Macedon (382–336 BC). In the three orations, known as the *Philippics* ('speeches relating to Philip'; 351, 344, 341 BC), Demosthenes attacked Philip's ambitions to make Athens part of his kingdom, and attempted to arouse the citizens against their cruel ruler. Philip, however, defeated Athens at the Battle of Chaeronea in 338, thus ending the self-government of the Greek city states and making his conquests of Greece complete. Philip was, however, assassinated two years later.

Later, Cicero's eloquent speeches against Mark Anthony were referred to as philippics, and now philippic refers to passionate speech against anyone.

Pickwickian

The adjective Pickwickian is used to allude to the character *Mr Pickwick* in the novel *Pickwick Papers* by Charles Dickens (first published 1836–7). In particular, Pickwickian is used to mean 'kind and generous in a simple manner' and also, to describe a word or expression that is not used in its ordinary or literal sense, from the scene in the opening chapter in which Mr Pickwick and Mr Blotton appear to insult each other, whereas in reality they respected each other greatly.

pinchbeck

Pinchbeck, was originally an alloy of copper and zinc – five parts copper and one part zinc – used to imitate gold in cheap jewellery. The word derives from the name of the English watchmaker *Christopher Pinchbeck* (*c.*1670–1732). Pinchbeck used the alloy in the manufacture of watches and jewellery. Later, the word came to be used for anything counterfeit or shoddy, probably partly because the pinch in the name has association of cheapness.

Plantin SEE BASKERVILLE

platonic

A platonic relationship is a close relationship between a man and a woman that does not involve sex. Such platonic love – spiritual or intellectual in contrast to physical – was first described by the Greek philosopher *Plato* (*c.*427–347 BC), in his *Symposium*, originally with reference to the pure love of Socrates towards young men.

Born into a wealthy Athenian family, Plato was known as a poet and athlete before becoming a follower of Socrates. Following Socrates' death, Plato travelled widely before returning to Athens to found his Academy in about 385 BC, teaching philosophy, mathematics, and government. Many of his writings survive, in which ethical and philosophical matters are discussed.

Plimsoll line; plimsoll

The Plimsoll line is a set of markings on the side of a ship that show the various levels that the ship may safely be loaded to. The pattern of lines is named in honour of the English leader of shipping reform *Samuel Plimsoll* (1824–98).

Originally the manager of a brewery, then a coal dealer, Plimsoll was elected M P for Derby in 1868. He called the overloaded ships of his day coffin-ships and determined to make maritime transport safer. His book *Our Seamen* was published in 1872 and following his insistent efforts a bill providing for rigorous inspection of ships became law in 1876. The Plimsoll line was adopted in that same year to mark the limit to which a ship may be loaded.

Plimsoll is also honoured in the light rubber-soled canvas shoe that bears his name, since the top edge of the rubber was thought to resemble a Plimsoll line.

poinsettia

The traditional Christmas evergreen plant known as poinsettia takes its name from the American diplomat *Joel Roberts Poinsett* (1779–1851). Born in Charleston, South Carolina, Poinsett was educated in Europe. He left his medical and legal studies, however, preferring to travel. During the course of his wanderings he is said to have met several political leaders including Napoleon, Metternich and the Tsar of Russia. When Poinsett returned to the United States, he was sent by President Madison to be consul to South America, where, however, he supported the Chilean revolutionaries.

Following several years' service as a Congressman, he was appointed as American Minister to Mexico (1825). He is said to have sent back to the United States specimens of the fiery plant now named after him, although it seems that it had already been introduced into the country. Because Poinsett was a well-known public figure at that time, the plant was named in his honour.

Poinsett later became Secretary of War in the cabinet of Van Buren and a Unionist leader in the Civil War.

Pollyanna

A person who is constantly optimistic is sometimes described as a Pollyanna. The name was originally that of the heroine in the novel *Pollyanna* (published in 1913) by the American writer Eleanor Porter (1868–1920).

Pollyanna is an eleven-year-old orphan who is sent to her very strait-laced Aunt Polly – who only takes her in as it is her duty. When young, to cope with the very poor life they lived as a missionary family, her father had taught Pollyanna the 'glad game' – in whatever unhappy circumstances one finds oneself always to look for something to be glad about. The result is that she is always a happy, smiling child.

Pollyanna passes on the 'glad game' to every needy person she meets in the village of Beldingsville with some quite startling results. A Pollyanna is therefore someone who can find something good in even the blackest circumstances.

pompadour

The word pompadour was used originally for a woman's hair style that was fashionable in the early eighteenth century, in which the hair was raised back, usually over a pad, into loose rolls round the face. A similar later style, in which the hair is combed straight up from the forehead, came to be worn by men and women. The name of the hair style derives from *Marquise de Pompadour*, title of *Jeanne Antoinette Poisson* (1721–64), mistress of Louis XV of France. From 1745 until her death, Mme de Pompadour exerted great influence on political matters. She was to a great extent responsible for the French defeats in the Seven Years' War (1756–63). Mme de Pompadour also served as patron to scholars such as Voltaire and Diderot.

The French court was renowned for its wasteful extravagance at that time and after being reproved for such excesses, Mme de Pompadour is said to have replied with the now famous words, 'Après nous le déluge' (literally, 'after us the flood').

praline

A praline, a confection of nuts – usually almonds – and sugar, is named after *César de Choiseul, Count Plessis-Praslin* (1598–1675). Count Plessis-Praslin was a French field marshal, and it seems that it was his chef who first concocted the confection. Later, the Count served as Minister of State under Louis XIV. Originally known as a praslin, in time the spelling became praline.

Pre-Raphaelite

A Pre-Raphaelite is the term used for a member of a particular artistic group known as the Pre-Raphaelite Brotherhood (PRB) – a group of artists, including Dante Gabriel Rossetti, John Everett Millais, and William Holman Hunt, founded in 1848. This group aimed to emulate the earlier Italian schools, in reaction to the contemporary taste for the Italian painter *Raphael* (original name *Raffaello Santi*; 1483–1520). The Pre-Raphaelite Brotherhood sought to oppose what they saw as the superficial conventionalism of much painting at that time by returning to a faithfulness to nature. Their works depict moral or religious scenes, and are marked by fine detail and vivid colours.

Prince Albert

A Prince Albert is a man's long double-breasted frock coat. It is named after *Prince Albert Edward*, later King Edward V I I of England (1841–1910). He is said to have worn the formal coat at afternoon social functions and so established it as a fashionable garment.

Procrustean

Procrustes was a robber in Greek mythology who forced his victims to lie on a bed. If they were too long, he would lop off their limbs; if they were too short, he would stretch their bodies to the necessary length until they fitted the bed. The name *Prokroustēs* literally means 'the stretcher', and the adjective Procrustean has come to describe something designed to enforce or produce conformity to a particular teaching by violent or arbitrary methods. Similarly, *a Procrustean bed* (or *a bed of Procrustes*) has come to refer to a predetermined system or standard to which a person or thing is forced to conform exactly.

Promethean

The adjective Promethean is used to describe something that is exceptionally creative or original. The word derives from *Prometheus*, a demigod in Greek mythology who is known for his bold, skilful acts: he made mankind out of clay, stole fire from Olympus, gave it to man, and taught man many arts and sciences. Zeus punished him by chaining him to a rock in the Caucasus mountains where during the day an eagle fed on his liver, only for it to grow again each night. Eventually Prometheus was freed from this torture by Hercules.

protean

Proteus was the sea-god of Greek mythology who tended the flocks of Poseidon. He was noted for his ability to take on different shapes at will. The adjective protean, deriving from his name, has therefore come to mean 'variable or diverse' or 'capable of assuming different shapes, sizes, or roles', as in a protean personality.

Pulitzer prize

The Pulitzer prizes are prizes awarded annually for outstanding achievements in journalism, literature, and music. The awards take their name from the Hungarian born U S newspaper publisher *Joseph Pulitzer* (1847–1911). Persuaded to emigrate in 1864, Pulitzer served for a year in the Union army before settling in St Louis, where he set up the *Post-Dispatch* newspaper in 1878. He later moved to New York where he founded the *World* (1883). The prizes were established by Pulitzer's will, in which he provided a fund to Columbia University, for the setting up and endowment of a school of journalism. The prizes have been awarded since 1917; since 1943 a prize for musical composition has also been presented.

Pullman

A Pullman, the luxurious railway passenger coach, is named after the American inventor *George Mortimer Pullman* (1831–97). Originally a cabinet-maker, Pullman began improving railway coach accommodation in the 1850s and, with his colleague Ben Field, built the first sleeping car, the Pioneer, in 1864. This cost $20,000 and had chandeliers, walnut woodwork, painted ceilings, a heavy-pile carpet, and folding upper berths for the sleeping accommodation.

It was the assassination of President Lincoln in 1865 that brought the Pioneer – and Pullman – to fame. Every area brought out its finest railway transport and so the Pioneer was brought into service to form part of the presidential funeral train. Bridges were raised and platforms narrowed to accommodate the Pioneer and it proved so popular that other railway companies wanted similar carriages. Pullman then formed a company, the Pullman Palace Car Company, to manufacture sleeping and dining cars, the profits from which made him a multi-millionaire.

Next, Pullman had a model town built in Chicago, but he fell into disrepute when the courts found that the rents he was charging were much higher than those for the houses in the surrounding area.

Towards the end of his life Pullman suffered a further blow – the railway workers' strike and riots of 1893–4 in which at least 12 died. His name is, however, still remembered for the special trains that provide comfortable and luxurious accommodation.

Pyrrhic victory; Cadmean victory

A Pyrrhic victory is a victory won at such a great cost that it amounts to no victory at all. It is named after *Pyrrhus, King of Epirus* (312–272 BC), who won several victories against Rome, particularly that of Asculum (279 BC) in which he lost very many of his men. After this battle he is said to have uttered, 'One more such victory and we are undone!'

A Pyrrhic victory is also sometimes known as a Cadmean victory. In Greek mythology *Prince Cadmus* killed a dragon and planted its teeth, from which, later, a race of armed warriors sprang up. Cadmus set the warriors fighting by throwing a stone among them, and only five escaped death. A Cadmean victory thus refers to a victory that is secured at an almost ruinous cost: the allusion being to the victory of the five survivors in the conflict with the multitude of other warriors.

It is interesting to note that this story also gave rise to the expression *sow the dragon's teeth*. One can take a course of action that is intended to be peaceful, such as disposing of the dragon's teeth by burying them, but in reality the course of action leads to dissension or warfare.

Pythagoras' theorem

Pythagoras' theorem states that 'in a right-angled triangle the square of the length of the hypotenuse is equal to the sum of the squares of the lengths of the other two sides'. The theory is named after the sixth-century BC Greek philosopher and mathematician *Pythagoras*, whose work had a significant effect on the development of mathematics, music, and astronomy. It seems, however, that the ancient Egyptian surveyors, and also the Babylonians at least 100 years before Pythagoras, were already familiar with such triangles, but it was Pythagoras or one of his followers who developed the actual theorem that has been named after him.

python

The large non-venomous snake that winds itself around its prey and then crushes it by constriction is known as a python. The word derives from the name of the monstrous serpent *Python* of Greek mythology. This dragon arose from the mud after the flood that Deucalion survived and guarded Delphi. It was after killing Python that Apollo set up his oracle at Delphi.

Q

quassia

Quassia is used to refer to the genus of tropical trees and shrubs that have a bitter bark and wood, and also the bitter drug obtained from this bark and wood. The drug was formerly used as a tonic and vermifuge and is now used as an insecticide. The name quassia honours an eighteenth-century Surinam Negro slave *Graman Quassi*, who in about 1730 discovered the medicinal value of the tree.

Queen Anne is dead; Queen Anne

Queen Anne is dead is a saying used as a reply to mean 'your news is stale; everyone knows what you've said already'. Born in 1665, *Queen Anne* was Queen of England and Scotland (Great Britain from 1707) and Ireland (1702–14). The last of the Stuart monarchs, she died in 1714; her death led to the coming of the Hanoverians. The expression *Queen Anne is dead* is first recorded in a ballad of 1722, eight years after her death. Obviously everyone knew of the monarch's passing; to tell stale news needed to be met with such a slighting rejoinder.

Queen Anne is the term used to describe a style of furniture popular in the eighteenth century, marked by plain curves, walnut veneer, and cabriole-legged chairs and also a style of early eighteenth-century architecture, marked by plain red brickwork in a restrained classical form.

Queensberry rules

The Queensberry rules, representing the basis of modern boxing, were written under the sponsorship of *John Sholto Douglas, the 8th Marquess of Queensberry* (1844–1900) and were published in 1867. The Queensberry rules established the use of padded gloves – up to that time fighting had been with bare fists – rounds of three minutes, and limitations on the kinds of blows permitted.

The expression Queensberry rules in also sometimes used to stand for fair play or proper behaviour in sport – or elsewhere.

quisling

A quisling is a traitor who collaborates with an invading enemy. The word derives from *Vidkun Abraham Quisling* (1887–1945), the Norwegian politician who collaborated with the Germans in the Second World War.

Having served as a military attaché in Russia and France, Major Quisling worked for the League of Nations, entering politics as a zealous anti-communist in 1929. A Defence Minister in the Norwegian government (1931–3), Quisling resigned to form his right-wing National Unity party in 1933, which met with little success, however.

When Hitler invaded Norway in April 1940, Quisling became 'puppet' Prime Minister, and later Minister President. Under his rule, 1000 Jews were sent to concentration camps. He lived in a reinforced 46-room villa on an island near Oslo; he was so paranoid that all the food he ate had been previously sampled by others.

When the Germans surrendered in Norway on 15 May, Quisling was arrested. He was found guilty of war crimes and was shot by a firing squad on 24 October 1945.

The Queen ... ry Ru...

To be a fair ... ... hoxing match
... -four fo... ... r that size as

No ... ... in the ...

The rounds ... 6. No...

... one minu... ... nutes ... 7. Shou...

... either m... ... ...able int...

must get ... ssisted ... akness ... place a...

... to do s... ... ... o that th...

... corner ... other man ... e backers

... e roun... ... when the... en ma...

... be resume... glove ... best q...

... the th... ... inutes ha... ... hired. Rule 9. ... uld

must be repla...

Rule 10. A man

down, and if struck...

Rule 11. No shoe...

... n hang... allowed.

... his toes

Rule 12. The conte...
governed by the revise...
Prize Ring.

Quixotic; Don Quixote

Someone who is carried away by the impractical pursuit of romantic ideals and who has extravagant notions of chivalry is sometimes referred to as quixotic. The word comes from the name of *Don Quixote*, hero of the novel *Don Quixote de la Mancha* (published in two parts 1605, 1615) by the Spanish novelist Miguel de Cervantes Saavedra (1547–1616). The novel tells how Don Quixote, infatuated with stories of chivalry, feels himself called to roam the world in pursuit of noble adventures.

The expression *tilt at windmills*, 'to attack an imaginary enemy, in the belief that it is real' comes from part 1, chapter 8, of the romance. Don Quixote travels through the countryside attacking windmills, in the belief that they are giants.

Quonset hut see NISSEN HUT

Queensberry rules

R

Rabelaisian

Rabelaisian is sometimes used to describe coarse humour or, less commonly, fantastic extravagance or sharp satire. These features are considered characteristics of the works of the French writer *François Rabelais* (1483–1553).

A Franciscan and then a Benedictine monk, Rabelais left the monastery to become a physician. Renowned for his fine scholarship and satirical wit, he wrote many works, of which the most famous are *Pantagruel* (1532) and *Gargantua* (1534) – the source of the word GARGANTUAN.

Rachmanism

The unscrupulous exploitation of tenants by a landlord known as Rachmanism takes its name from *Peter (Perec) Rachman* (1920–62), a Polish-born British landlord, who indulged in such a practice.

Under the 1957 Rent Act, rents in Britain were kept at an artificially low level compared with the market value of property as long as the property remained in the hands of the tenant. This led to unscrupulous practices by some landlords who harassed tenants in order to evict them. The property could then be sold or re-let at an exorbitantly high rent.

Rachman was one such landlord who bought cheaply rented houses in London in the early 1960s and used blackmail, intimidation, and physical violence to evict the tenants. He then let the properties out at very high rates to prostitutes, etc., or sold them to businesses, making a great profit.

Rafflesia

The genus of parasitic Asian herbs known as Rafflesia is named after the British colonial administrator *Sir Thomas Stamford Raffles* (1781–1826), who discovered it. After a renowned administrative career in Penang and Java, Raffles acquired Singapore for the East India Company in 1819. The famous Raffles Hotel in Singapore is named after him.

The species *Rafflesia arnoldi* has the largest bloom in the world, measuring up to three feet in diameter, and weighing up to 15 pounds. This mottled orange-brown and white flower – also known as stinking corpse lily – grows on the roots of vines in south-east Asia. Only the bloom of the plant can be seen above the ground. Its growing fungus below the ground smells of rotting meat and attracts carrion flies that act as pollinators.

raglan

A raglan, a loose-fitting coat that has sleeves (*raglan sleeves*) that extend to the collar without shoulder seams, is named after the British field marshal *Fitzroy James Henry Somerset, 1st Baron Raglan* (1788–1855). Raglan served in the Napoleonic Wars, and when wounded at the Battle of Waterloo and had his arm amputated, he is alleged to have said, 'I say, bring back my arm – the ring my wife gave me is on the finger!'

Raglan later became secretary to the Duke of Wellington, then Commander-in-Chief of the British forces, and field marshal. Despite his success at the Battle of Inkerman in the Crimean War, his tactics at the Battle of Balaclava were heavily criticized. It was during the Crimean War that Raglan became known for wearing his raglan overcoat.

See also CARDIGAN.

raise Cain; the mark of Cain; the curse of Cain

The expression *to raise Cain*, 'behave in a wild, noisy manner; to cause a loud disturbance; to protest angrily' derives from the biblical *Cain*, the eldest son of Adam and Eve, the brother of Abel and the first murderer in the Bible (Genesis 4:3–12). It seems that in earlier times, Cain was a euphemism for the devil, religious people preferring *raise Cain* to *raise the devil*.

Two expressions derive from the judgement of God on Cain after he killed Abel. *The curse of Cain*, the fate of someone who is forced to lead a fugitive life, wandering restlessly from place to place, derives from the punishment mentioned in Genesis 4:11–12: 'And now art thou cursed from the earth . . . a fugitive and a vagabond shalt thou be in the earth'.

The mark of Cain is a stain of a crime on one's reputation, with reference to the protective mark God gave him to prevent him from being killed himself, mentioned in Genesis 4:15: 'And the Lord set a mark upon Cain, lest any finding him should kill him'.

Rastafarian

Haile Selassie (1892–1975) became Emperor of Ethiopia in 1930. His title *Ras Tafari* (*Ras*, meaning 'Lord' and *Tafari*, a family name) was adopted by Black West Indians, who venerated Haile Selassie as God, and wanted deliverance for the Black race and the founding of a homeland in Ethiopia. Rastafarian beliefs were developed by the Jamaican founder of the Back to Africa movement Marcus Garvey (1887–1940).

Haile Selassie lived in exile in England from 1936 to 1941 during the Italian occupation of Ethiopia. He was finally deposed in a military rising in 1974.

Réaumur scale

The Réaumur scale is a scale of temperature in which the freezing-point of water is 0° and the boiling-point of water 80°. It is named after the French scientist *Réne Antoine Ferchault de Réaumur* (1783–1757) who devised it. A naturalist as well as a physicist, Réaumur studied the chemical processes of animal digestion and also developed a method of tinning iron that was used in French industry.

rehoboam see JEROBOAM

Reuters

Baron Paul Julius von Reuter (original name *Israel Beer Josaphat;* (1816–99) founded the first news agency. Born in Germany, Reuter began a continental pigeon post in 1850, to fly stock-market prices between Brussels and Aachen to complete the final part in the growing European telegraph system. In 1851 Reuter moved to London. England and the continent were linked with the opening of the Dover–Calais submarine cable; so enabling Reuter to send stock prices between Paris and London. He then extended his coverage to include general news items to many European newspapers. In 1865 Reuters Telegraph Company was registered; it became a private company, Reuters Ltd, in 1916, and in 1984 it became a public company, Reuters Holdings PLC.

rhesus monkey; Rh factor

A rhesus monkey, *Macaca mulatta*, is a south Asian monkey that is widely used in medical research. It seems that the description rhesus was chosen arbitrarily in honour of *Rhesus*, the King of Thrace in Greek mythology. The Greek hero Odysseus and King Diomedes killed Rhesus and 12 of his men, carrying off his splendid horses, because an oracle had said that if Rhesus' horses had tasted

Trojan pasture and drunk of the River Scamander, Troy would not fall.

The Rh (or rhesus) factor in blood derives from rhesus monkeys, in which it was first discovered. The Rh factor is a blood protein that is present in the red cells of most people, those who do have it being classified as Rh-positive and those who do not Rh-negative. It can cause strong reactions in the blood during pregnancy or blood transfusions.

Richard Roe see JOHN DOE

Richter scale

The Richter scale, a scale for expressing the magnitude of earthquakes, is named after the American seismologist *Charles Richter* (1900–85). Richter devised the scale in 1935 in association with the German Bruno Gutenberg (1889–1960), thus it is sometimes called the *Gutenberg–Richter scale*. The logarithmic scale ranges from 0 to 10; a value of 2 can just be sensed as a tremor, while earthquakes that measure values greater than 6 cause damage to buildings. The strongest earthquake so far recorded measured 8.6 on the Richter scale.

Rip van Winkle

Someone who has outdated views and is completely out of touch with contemporary ideas is sometimes referred to as a Rip van Winkle. The description comes from the character in the story *Rip Van Winkle* (published in 1819) by the American author Washington Irving (1783–1859). In the story, Rip van Winkle falls asleep for 20 years and wakes to find his home in ruins and the world utterly different.

Washington Irving used to write using the pseudonym Knickerbocker: see KNICKERBOCKERS.

ritzy

The adjective ritzy is used in informal English to mean smart, especially in a showy manner. This usage derives from *Ritz* hotels, a chain of luxury hotels established by the Swiss hotelier *César Ritz* (1850–1918).

The original Ritz hotels in Paris (founded 1898) and London (1906) were known for their elegance and luxury. The 1920s saw the growth of 'Plazas and Astorias and Ritzes all over the hinterland' (H. L. Mencken), and also the development of the word ritzy with association of ostentatious smartness. The word Ritz also featured in the song by Irving Berlin, 'Putting on the Ritz', sung by Fred Astaire.

robin

The British robin, the songbird related to the thrush that has an orange-red breast and brown back, was originally called a robin redbreast. It seems that the name *Robin*, nickname for Robert, was chosen arbitrarily to stand for this bird. The name is now used for a number of different species of red-breasted birds in different countries.

Roland (a Roland for an Oliver)

Roland and *Oliver* were two of the legendary 12 peers or paladins who attended King Charlemagne, King of the Franks (*c*. AD 742–814). Roland, Charlemagne's nephew, once fought Oliver in a duel that lasted several days. The knights were so evenly matched, each man answering the other's blows in kind, that the duel was declared a draw and the two knights became ardent friends. The expression *a Roland for an Oliver* thus came to mean an effective retaliation or tit for tat.

Both knights were slain at Roncesvalles in north-east Spain in 778. The early-twelfth-century French epic poem *Chanson de Roland*, describes the heroic stand of the knights at this battle.

Rolls-Royce

Rolls-Royce, the trademark for a type of luxurious car of outstanding quality, is also applied to something that is considered to be the foremost of its kind. The car is named after its designers, *Charles Stewart Rolls* (1877–1910) and *Sir Frederick Henry Royce* (1836–1933).

Royce originally established an engineering business in Manchester in 1884, where he manufactured electric dynamos and cranes. In 1904 he began to build cars and so impressed Rolls that they formed a partnership, the Rolls–Royce Company, in 1906. Royce was the engineer, while Rolls promoted the cars.

The partnership ended abruptly when Rolls was killed in a flying accident in 1910. Royce was forced, because of poor health, to move to the south of France, where he designed some of their most famous cars and also the aero-engine that was developed into the Merlin engine that was used in Spitfires in the Second World War.

Romeo

A romantic lover is sometimes known as a Romeo, after the hero in Shakespeare's tragedy *Romeo and Juliet*. The two most important families of Verona, the Montagues and the Capulets, are great rivals; Romeo, son of Lord Montague falls in love with Capulet's daughter, Juliet. Shakespeare based his play on Arthur Brooke's poem 'The Tragicall Historye of Romeus and Juliet' (1562).

röntgen

A röntgen (roentgen), the former unit of dose of ionizing radiation, is named after the German physicist, *Wilhelm Konrad Röntgen* (1845–1923). Röntgen was awarded the first NOBEL PRIZE for physics in 1901 for the outstanding achievement of the discovery of X-rays (formerly known as *roentgen rays*). While professor of physics at

Würzburg University, Bavaria, Röntgen accidentally discovered the mysterious rays when he was undertaking research into the luminescence of cathode rays in 1895. Because the phenomenon of X-rays was unknown to him, he borrowed the symbol X from algebra to describe them. The discovery that X-rays pass through matter was quickly appreciated by the medical world and they soon became used in medical diagnosis.

Rorschach test

The Rorschach test is a psychological test in which the interpretation by a subject of a series of inkblots reveals aspects of the subject's personality. The test is named after the Swiss psychiatrist *Hermann Rorschach* (1884–1922), who devised it in 1921.

Roscius; Roscian

Quintus Roscius Gallus (*c.*126–62 BC), was a famous Roman actor. A friend of Cicero, he became regarded as the most distinguished Roman comic actor. The name Roscius is thus sometimes applied to an outstanding actor; and a *Roscian performance* is one that displays great theatrical mastery.

Rubik's cube

Rubik's cube is a puzzle consisting of a cube, each face of which is divided into nine small coloured squares that can rotate around a central square. The aim of the puzzle is to rotate the squares on the cube such that the whole of each face shows one colour only. The total number of positions that can be reached on the Rubik's cube is 43,252,003,274,489,856,000.

Rubik's cube is named after its inventor, the Hungarian designer, sculptor, and architect *Ernö Rubik* (b. 1944). Originally intended to help Rubik's students understand three-dimensional design, it first became generally known to mathematicians at a Mathematical Congress at Helsinki in 1978. In the following few years it quickly became a craze throughout the world.

Rudbeckia

The Rudbeckia genus of flowers has showy flowers with yellow rays and dark-brown to black conical centres. Also called coneflowers, several of the plants of the genus, particularly *Rudbeckia hirta*, are known as black-eyed Susan.

The name Rudbeckia derives from the Swedish botanist *Olof Rudbeck* (1630–1702) and his son, also *Olof Rudbeck* (1660–1740). Olof Rudbeck the senior was noted for his discovery of the lymphatic system and also his book *Atlantica* in which he argued that Sweden had been the site of Plato's Atlantis.

rutherford

The rutherford, a unit of radioactivity, honours the British physicist *Ernest Rutherford, 1st Baron Rutherford* (1871–1937).

Born in New Zealand, Rutherford was educated at Christchurch and later Cambridge. He is known for his pioneer research into the nature of radioactivity – initially in Montreal, then in Manchester and Cambridge, where he was director of the Cavendish Laboratory. Most well known for his discovery of the atomic nucleus in 1911, he was awarded the NOBEL PRIZE for chemistry in 1908, the Order of Merit in 1925 and made a baron in 1931.

S

Sabin vaccine; Salk vaccine

The American microbiologist *Jonas Edward Salk* (b. 1914) developed the first successful vaccine against polio, which came to be named after him, and was used initially in 1954. The Salk vaccine was widely used but by the 1960s it was replaced by the Sabin vaccine, which provided greater immunity from polio and for a longer period. The Sabin vaccine is named after the Polish-born American microbiologist *Albert Bruce Sabin* (b. 1906), who developed it in 1955. Sabin vaccine is administered orally.

sadism

Sadism – the pleasure derived from inflicting pain on others – is named after the French soldier and writer *Count Donatien Alphonse Françoise de Sade*, known as *Marquis de Sade* (1740–1814). De Sade's writings depict sexual perversion. His most famous writings include *Les 120 Journées de Sodome* (1785) and *Justine* (1791), composed during the 1780s and 1790s while he spent many years imprisoned for sexual offences. The final years of de Sade's life were spent in a mental asylum in Charenton.

St Anthony's fire

St Anthony's fire is the name of a disease causing inflammation or gangrene. Known technically as ergotism or erysipelas, the diseases were named after *St Anthony* in the sixteenth century because it was believed that praying to him led to healing.

St Anthony of Egypt (*c*. AD 251–256) was known as a hermit and also as the founder of Christian monasticism. At the age of about 18, he gave up all his possessions and withdrew some years later to the desert, to be tempted by demons disguised as wild animals. He emerged in about 305 to organize his followers into a monastic community.

St Bernard dog

The Italian churchman *St Bernard of Menthon* (923–1008) founded hospices on two alpine passes, which came to be named after him, the *Great St Bernard Pass* between Italy and Switzerland and the *Little St Bernard Pass* between Italy and France. The monks of the hospice at the Great St Bernard Pass used to keep a breed of large working dog that was trained to track down travellers lost in blizzards and so the breed came to be named after the founder of the hospice.

The breed is the heaviest breed of domestic dog in the world, the heaviest recorded example weighing 22 stone 2 pounds (140.6 kg).

St Elmo's fire

The expression St Elmo's fire refers to the luminous discharge sometimes seen in stormy weather at points that project into the atmosphere, such as a church spire or the mast of a ship. Known

St Bernard dog

technically as corposant, the luminous appearance derives from small electrical discharges.

St Elmo's fire is probably so called because it was associated with *St Elmo*, an Italian alteration of the name *St Erasmus* (d. 303 BC), the Italian bishop and patron saint of Mediterranean sailors. According to one legend, in reward for being saved from drowning by a sailor, Erasmus is said to have promised that a light would be displayed to indicate an impending storm.

St Leger

The St Leger horse race is a flat race for three-year-old colts run annually in September on the Town Moor, Doncaster, South Yorkshire. Founded in 1776, it is named after a leading local sportsman of that time, *Lt.-Gen. St Leger* of Park Hill, Doncaster.

St Luke's summer; St Martin's summer

St Luke's summer and St Martin's summer both refer to periods of exceptionally warm weather in the autumn. The summery weather associated with the saints is associated with the times of their feast-days, St Luke's Day being 18 October, and St Martin's Day 11 November.

St Luke, traditionally regarded as the author of the third Gospel and also the Acts of the Apostles, was the Gentile doctor who accompanied Paul on his missionary journeys. *St Martin* (*c*.315–397) was Bishop of Tours. Born into a non-believing family, it is said that he became a Christian after dividing his cloak into two to give half to a beggar.

St Vitus' dance

St Vitus' dance is the non-technical name for chorea, the disease of the central nervous system marked by involuntary jerky movements. The disease is named after *St Vitus*, a child who was martyred with his nurse and tutor in the persecutions of Christians by the Roman Emperor Diocletian in about 303. The description of the disease as St Vitus' dance arose in the seventeenth century, when sufferers prayed to St Vitus for healing, dancing around a statue of him.

Salk vaccine see SABIN VACCINE

Sally Lunn

A Sally Lunn, a slightly sweetened tea-cake, is said to have been named after a late-eighteenth-century English baker. It seems that *Sally Lunn* used to advertise her wares by shouting out her name in the city of Bath. A resourceful local baker named Dalmer developed mass production of the buns and also wrote a song to express their delights; so their fame spread.

salmonella; salmonellosis

Salmonella is the name of the rod-shaped bacteria that cause diseases including food poisoning (salmonellosis) in humans. The genus of bacteria has nothing to do with the fish but is named after the American veterinary surgeon *Daniel Elmer Salmon* (1850–1914), who first identified it. Many cases of salmonellosis are thought to have been caused by inadequate thawing of frozen poultry before being cooked.

Sam Browne belt

A Sam Browne belt is the military officer's leather belt supported by a light strap that passes over the right shoulder and designed originally as a belt for supporting a sword or pistol. The belt is named after the British army officer *Sir Samuel J. Browne* (1824–1901) who designed it.

Born in India, Browne had a distinguished military career. His decisive role in the Indian Mutiny (1857–9) earned him the Victoria Cross and in 1888 he was promoted to general.

A version of the belt is worn by cyclists, etc., to increase their visibility.

samarskite

Samarskite, the velvet-black mineral discovered in Russia in 1857, is named after a Russian mine official *Colonel M. von Samarski*. When, in 1879, the French chemist Lecoq de Boisbaudrian discovered a new lanthanide element spectroscopically, he named the element *samarium* after samarskite, since it contained this mineral. Thus a little-known mine official is remembered by having a chemical element named in his honour.

Samoyed

Samoyeds are a breed of working dogs, strongly built with husky-like features, and a dense white or cream coat. The dogs take their name from the *Samoyed* people, a group of Siberian people who live in the coastal regions of north central USSR.

See also HUSKY.

Samson

A man of great strength is sometimes known as a Samson, with reference to the biblical judge of Israel. *Samson's* outstanding feats of strength included the tearing of a lion apart with his bare hands, catching 300 foxes and then tying them tail to tail in pairs, and striking down 1000 men with a jawbone of a donkey.

When the treacherous DELILAH eventually discovered that the secret of his strength lay in his hair, she had it all shaved off and so his strength left him. The Philistines seized him, gouging out his eyes.

Samson's final act was to entertain the Philistines at the temple of Dagon. Samson's hair had grown since it was shaved off, and so calling upon God, he braced himself against the two central pillars that supported the temple; above him were about 3000 people. Pushing with all his strength, the temple was destroyed, killing himself and more Philistines in his death than the total he had killed during his life.

sandwich

Sandwich is one of the most famous eponyms in the English language. The name of the snack consisting of two slices of buttered bread with a filling between them derives from the English diplomat *John Montagu, 4th Earl of Sandwich* (1718–92).

The Earl was addicted to gambling, some of his gambling sessions lasting as long as two days non-stop. He was so compulsive a gambler that, rather than leave the gaming table to take food, and so interrupting the game, he would order his valet to bring him food. Invariably, he would be brought food that consisted of slices of cold beef between two slices of bread. Within a few years the snack became generally known as a sandwich, although it had of course been eaten before this time.

The Earl of Sandwich was also notorious for his part in the prosecution of his former friend John Wilkes, and the inadequacy of the English navy during the American War of Independence is attributed to the corruption that was current while he was First Lord of the Admiralty.

Sanforized

Sanforized is the trademark used for a process of pre-shrinking a fabric before it is made into articles, such as clothes. In the process, the fibres are compressed mechanically. The word derives from the name *Sanford Lockwood Cluett* (1874–1968), the American director of engineering and research of a firm of shirt and collar manufacturers, Cluett, Peabody, and Co., of Troy, New York.

Saturday

Saturday, the seventh day of the week, derives its name from the Roman god of agriculture *Saturn*. The Old English name *Sæternes dæg* was a translation of the Latin *Saturnī diēs*, day of Saturn.

saxophone

The saxophone, the keyed woodwind instrument with a brass body and a single-reed mouthpiece, is named after its inventor, the Belgian musical-instrument maker *Adolphe Sax* (1814–94). It seems that it was while working in the musical-instrument workshop of his father Charles Joseph Sax (1791–1865) in the early 1840s that Adolphe invented several instruments, the most famous of which was to become known as the saxophone.

The instrument was first shown to the public in 1844, and enjoyed a great deal of success. Composers such as Berlioz and Bizet wrote music for the instrument and today the sax is most commonly used for jazz and dance music.

Scrooge

A miserly person is sometimes called a Scrooge, after the character *Ebenezer Scrooge* in the story *A Christmas Carol* (published in 1843) by Charles Dickens. On Christmas Eve Scrooge is visited by the ghost of his former business partner Marley. He sees visions of the past, present, and future, including one depicting his own death unless he quickly changes his ways, which he then proceeds to do.

Scylla (between Scylla and Charybdis)

The expression *between Scylla and Charybdis* is used to refer to a situation in which one is faced with two equally dangerous alternatives: avoiding one danger immediately exposes one to the other. The expression originally referred to the narrow sea passage between Italy and Sicily. In Greek mythology, the female sea monster *Scylla* was believed to live in a cave off the Italian coast. On the other side of the Strait of Messina lived *Charybdis*, the monster in the whirlpool. Thus, sailors who tried to avoid one danger were exposed to the other.

sequoia

The most massive tree in the world, the Giant Sequoia, is named after the American Indian *Sequoya* (*c.*1770–1843). The name Sequoia, referring in fact to either of two giant Californian coniferous trees, the big tree (Giant Sequoia) or the redwood, was so called by the Hungarian botanist Stephen Ladislaus Endlicher in 1847.

Sequoya – who believed himself to be the son of a white trader and so adopted the name George Guess – was sure that the power of the white man lay in his possession of a written language. He therefore set about writing down his own language. Over a period of 12 years, Sequoya established a writing system of 86 characters that represented all the sounds in the Cherokee language. Thousands of Cherokees quickly mastered the writing system and soon a weekly Cherokee newspaper was published and a constitution written in the Cherokee language.

Shakespearean

The adjective Shakespearean (or Shakespearian) is used to describe *William Shakespeare* (1564–1616) or his writings, particularly when considered to show great vision and power. The name of the famous English dramatist and poet is also remembered in the *Shakespearean sonnet*, a 14-line poem in the form abab cdcd efef gg. Also known as the *English sonnet*, it is a variant of the PETRAR-CHAN SONNET.

Shavian

The adjective Shavian describes the life, works, or ideas of the Irish dramatist and socialist George Bernard Shaw (1856–1950). GBS, as he was known, disliked the adjective Shawian, so coined Shavius as the Latin form of Shaw, then derived the adjective Shavian from it. Shavian wit is sometimes used to describe the particular style of humour of Shaw's plays.

Sheraton

The English furniture-maker Thomas Sheraton (1751–1806) is remembered for a style of furniture named in his honour. The style is known for its elegance, straight lines, and inlaid decoration.

Sheraton is particularly famous for his writings, especially *The Cabinet-Maker and Upholsterer's Drawing Book* (published in four volumes, 1791–4) and *The Cabinet Dictionary* (1802). He taught drawing, but there is no record that he ever owned a workshop where he undertook furniture design.

shrapnel

The explosive device known as a shrapnel, the projectile that contains bullets or fragments of metal and a charge that is exploded before impact, takes its name from the English artillery officer *Henry Shrapnel* (1761–1842) who invented it.

Shrapnel spent many years developing this deadly weapon, which was originally known as the spherical case shot. It was eventually adopted in about 1803, was first used in action against the Dutch in Surinam (Dutch Guiana), and was important in the defeat of Napoleon at Waterloo in 1815.

Shrapnel gained promotion for his efforts – he was finally a general – but he received scant financial reward for all his work.

shyster

A shyster is a person who is unscrupulous in the pursuit of his or her profession; the word is used chiefly in American English to describe a lawyer or a politician. The word possibly derives from the name *Scheuster*, a mid-nineteenth-century lawyer who on several occasions was admonished in a New York court for pettifoggery. Other authorities suggest the ultimate origin as German *Scheisse*, 'excrement'.

Shylock

A pitiless and extortionate money-lender is sometimes referred to as a Shylock. The name was originally that of the ruthless usurer in Shakespeare's *Merchant of Venice*. The expression have, get, etc., one's *pound of flesh* also derives from the play. *Shylock* agreed to lend the merchant Antonio money against the security of a pound of Antonio's flesh, but as the debt could not be repaid when due, Shylock demanded his pound of flesh.

sideburns

Sideburns refers to the hair that grows down the sides of a man's face reaching from the hair-line to below the ears. The word comes from *Ambrose Everett Burnside* (1824–81).

After a short time as a tailor's apprentice and a brief period of military service, Burnside set up in business to manufacture a breech-loading rifle that he had invented. The business failed, however.

Later, he became a general, fighting for the Union in the American Civil War, and was renowned for the defeats under his command at Fredericksburg (1862) and Petersburg (1864). Despite these failures, Burnside remained popular and was elected Governor of Rhode Island (1866–69) and as US Senator from 1875.

The General is notably remembered for his shaving habits: he sported so-called burnsides, full side whiskers joining the moustache. With the passage of time, the side whiskers became shorter and the two parts of the word mysteriously changed places to give sideburns.

siemens

Siemens, the metric unit of electrical conductance, is named after the German electrical engineer *Ernst Werner von Siemens* (1816–92). A pioneer in telegraphy, Siemens is known for his work in laying a government telegraph line from Berlin to Frankfurt. With his three brothers, Friedrich Siemens (1826–1904), Sir William Siemens (Karl Wilhelm Siemens; 1828–83) – who invented the open-hearth process of making steel – and Karl Siemens (1829–1906) he created the immense Siemens industrial empire.

It is curious that the siemens unit was formerly known as a *mho* – a word formed by reversing the letters of another eponymous, word OHM.

silhouette

A silhouette, the outline of a dark shape set on a light background, takes its name from the French politician *Étienne de Silhouette* (1709—67), but the precise reason for this is uncertain.

As Controller of Finances (1759), Silhouette had to restore the French economy after the Seven Years War. He therefore instituted a series of stringent tax revisions, which made him unpopular. His measures were seen as niggardly and the phrase *à la silhouette* meaning 'on the cheap' became current. The sense of parsimony was then applied to the partial shadow portraits that were fashionable at that time.

Other sources suggest that the brevity of Silhouette's period of office as Controller-General – he was forced to resign after only nine months – is the origin of the incompleteness of the portraits.

Still others claim that Silhouette's hobby was in fact making such outlines and he is said to have displayed many examples of this art form in his château.

silly-billy

The word silly-billy is sometimes used in informal English – particularly by or to children – to describe someone who is foolish or silly. The expression, deriving from *Billy*, the nickname for William, may well have first been applied to *King William IV* of England, formerly Duke of Clarence (1765–1837). He was known as silly billy, from, it seems, his carefree attitude towards his Royal responsibilities. The nickname was also given to the nobleman *William Frederick*, Duke of Gloucester (1776–1834).

simony

Simony, the practice of buying or selling of church or spiritual benefits or offices, derives from *Simon Magus*, a first-century AD sorcerer. After becoming a Christian, Simon tried to buy the gift of spiritual power from the Apostles, but was strongly rebuked by Peter (Acts 8:9–24).

slave

The word slave came via Old French from Medieval Latin *sclavus*, meaning quite simply, 'a Slav'. In the Middle Ages a large number of Slavonic people in central Europe were conquered and held in bondage, so the name *Sclavus* gained the additional sense of 'slave'.

smart alec

A smart alec (or aleck) is a conceited know-all: *I don't want any smart alec coming in here to tell me how to run this business, thank you very much.*

The expression can be traced back to about the 1860s, but it is not recorded who the first smart Alec was: he seems to have been intelligent enough to conceal all the evidence of his identity. An expression with the same meaning is clever Dick.

smithsonite; Smithsonian Institution

Smithsonite, the whitish mineral that is an important ore of zinc, takes its name from the English chemist *James Smithson* (original name *James Lewes Macie*; 1765–1829).

Smithson left a bequest that an institution named after him should be set up in Washington, DC: 'for the increase and diffusion of knowledge among men'. The American Congress spent many years discussing whether to accept the bequest and finally agreed to do so. The Smithsonian Institution was founded in 1846, and today conducts scientific research and maintains several art galleries and museums.

Socratic method; Socratic irony

The Greek philosopher *Socrates* (*c.*470–399 BC) wrote no philosophical works himself, his beliefs only being known through the works of his pupils, Plato and Xenophon. His supposed method of reasoning (*Socratic method*) involved questions and answers designed to evoke truths that he considered every rational person knew, even if only implicitly.

The expression *Socratic irony* derives from his pretended ignorance in arguments, so leading the person answering his questions to be easily defeated by his skilful interrogation.

In 399 Socrates was condemned to death by the Athenian government for impiety and corruption of youth. He was forced to commit suicide by drinking hemlock.

Sod's law see MURPHY'S LAW

Solomon (*the wisdom of Solomon; Solomon's seal*)

Solomon, the tenth-century BC King of Israel and son of David and Bathsheba was noted for his great wisdom and wealth. His wisdom has become proverbial, being evident in expressions such as *need the wisdom of Solomon* and *as wise as Solomon*. The wisdom was seen when two women came to him each claiming that a particular baby was her own. Solomon's suggestion that the baby be divided in two revealed the true mother: the one who would rather hand the baby over to her rival than see her own baby killed (1 Kings 3: 16–28).

Solomon's seal is the name given to any of the genus *Polygonatum* of the lily family that have greenish-white flowers, long smooth leaves, and a fleshy white underground stem. The underground stem is marked with prominent leaf scars, which are said to resemble seals – hence the name. Solomon's seal is also the name of a mystic symbol, the *Star of David*, that is traditionally associated with Solomon.

sop to Cerberus

In Greek mythology, Cerberus was the three-headed dog that guarded the entrance to Hades. Cerberus allowed the dead to enter; some were greeted in a friendly manner, others were met with ferocious snarls. Friends used to put a cake in the hands of those who died, to be given to Cerberus; thus securing safe passage. So it is that figuratively *a sop to cerberus* is a bribe or gift given to appease a potential source of trouble or danger.

sophist; sophistry; sophism

The *Sophists* were ancient Greek itinerant teachers of the fifth and fourth centuries BC who taught various subjects, particularly public speaking and philosophy. Although their name comes from a Greek word meaning wise man or expert, because of the methods of some of the teachers, the word sophist came to stand for someone who used unscrupulously clever arguments in persuasion. Thus our modern word sophistry means deceptively subtle reasoning and sophism is an instance of this.

soubise

Soubise, a white or brown sauce containing a purée of onions, takes its name from the French nobleman *Charles de Rohan, Prince de Soubise* (1715–87). It seems that the sauce was probably named in the Prince's honour by his chef Marin. The Prince de Soubise was a renowned military leader and general and became Marshal of France in 1758 through the influence of Madame Pompadour.

Sousa

sousaphone

A sousaphone, the large tuba that encircles the player with a forward-facing bell, is named after its inventor, the American bandmaster and composer *John Philip Sousa* (1854–1932).

Known as 'The March King', Sousa was appointed leader of the US Marine Corps band in 1880, and 12 years later formed his own Sousa Band, which toured the world, gaining him great fame. Sousa composed over a hundred popular marches, including 'The Stars and Stripes Forever', 'The Washington Post', and 'Liberty Bell'.

spaniel

Spaniel, the name of any of several breeds of smallish short-legged dog that have long drooping ears, comes ultimately from the Old French word, *espaigneul* or *espaignol*, meaning 'Spanish'. The dog is thought to have originally come from Spain.

Spartacist

In 73 BC a Thracian gladiator named *Spartacus* successfully led a slave revolt against Rome. Two years later he and his followers were defeated by the Roman politician Marcus Licinius Crassus.

During the First World War the German socialists Karl Liebknecht and Rosa Luxemburg formed a radical socialist group known as the *Spartacus League* (which developed into the German Communist Party), Karl Liebknecht adopting the name Spartacus. Members of the group were called Spartacists. Both leaders were murdered following the unsuccessful communist revolt of 1919.

spencer

A spencer – a short, waist-length, close-fitting jacket, which was fashionable in the late eighteenth and early nineteenth centuries – takes its name from the English politician *George John Spencer, 2nd Earl of Spencer* (1758–1834). According to one account, the Earl won a bet that he could set a new fashion simply by appearing in the streets wearing a new kind of garment.

While Lord of the Admiralty under the Prime Ministership of William Pitt the Younger, Earl Spencer chose Nelson to command the Fleet in the Mediterranean – which led to the British victory in the Battle of the Nile (August 1798).

Spenserian stanza; Spenserian sonnet

The English poet *Edmund Spenser* (*c*.1552–99) is noted for his moral allegory *The Faerie Queen* (1590; 1596). It consists of nine-line stanzas that have come to be known as Spenserian stanzas: eight lines in iambic pentameter followed by an iambic line of six feet, rhyming ababbcbcc. Spenser also developed a form of sonnet with the rhyming scheme abab bcbc cdcd ee, which came to be known as the Spenserian sonnet.

spinet

The spinet, a type of small harpsichord with one manual, may take its name from the sixteenth-century Italian musical instrument maker *Giovanni Spinetti*. It is said that Spinetti invented this instrument at the beginning of the sixteenth century. Alternatively, the word spinet may possibly derive from Italian *spina*, a thorn, with reference to the thorn-like quills used in plucking the strings of the instrument.

Spode

The British potter *Josiah Spode* (1754–1827) was famous for a type of porcelain that came to bear his name.

His father, also Josiah Spode (1733–97), had started his own works at Stoke-on-Trent in 1770. The son succeeded his father in 1797, developing porcelain (1800) by introducing bones into the paste as well as feldspar, and stone china tableware in about 1805.

spoonerism

The *Rev. William Archibald Spooner* (1844–1930) was, it seems, renowned for slips of the tongue in which the initial sounds of words were accidentally transposed, often with a comical effect. Some examples of such spoonerisms, as they came to be called, attributed to the clergyman included: *a half-warmed fish* instead of *a half-formed wish*; *Kinkering Congs* instead of *Conquering Kings*; *a well-boiled icicle* instead of *a well-oiled bicycle*; reference to God as a *shoving leopard* instead of a *loving shepherd*; and to Queen Victoria as *our queer old dean* instead of *our dear old Queen*.

Stakhanovite

A Stakhanovite is an industrial worker in the USSR who is awarded with special incentives in recognition for producing an output that is greater than the norm. The word Stakhanovite, a member of the movement known as *Stakhanovism*, derives from the Russian coal-miner *Alexei Grigorievich Stakhanov* (1906–77). In 1935 Stakhanov reorganized his coal-mining team, so greatly increasing the production.

Stalinism

Stalinism describes the form of communism developed by the Soviet leader *Joseph Stalin* (original name *Josef Vissarionovich Dzhugashvili*; 1879–1953). A variant of Marxism–Leninism, Stalinism is marked by a policy of establishing socialism in one country, strict bureaucracy, extensive use of terror, and devotion to Russian nationalism.

Succeeding Lenin as head of the Communist Party, Stalin (his name means 'steel') created a totalitarian state in the USSR. He introduced rapid collectivization of industry and agriculture. Notorious for his ruthless dictatorship, Stalin crushed all opposition, particularly in the purges of the 1930s. By the outbreak of the Second World War Stalin was in complete control of the country. By the time of his death the Soviet Union had been transformed into a world power.

After his death, Khruschev denounced Stalin and a process of de-Stalinization followed. Stalin's body was transferred from Lenin's mausoleum and the names of all places honouring him were changed.

See also LENINISM, MARXISM, TROTSKYISM.

Star of David see SOLOMON

Sten gun

The Sten gun, the light 9-millimetre sub-machine-gun used in the Second World War, is named using the initials of the surnames of its inventors: *Major R. V. Shepherd*, a 20th-century English army officer and *H. J. Turpin*, a civil servant, plus the 'en' of *England* (or *Enfield*, London).

stentorian

If someone speaks in stentorian tones, he or she is speaking extremely loudly. The adjective derives from the name *Stentor*, the herald in Greek mythology who, according to Homer's *Iliad*, had a voice as loud as the voices of 50 men. Stentor died when he lost a shouting contest with Hermes, herald of the gods.

stetson

The stetson, the wide-brimmed, high-crowned, felt hat, was named after the American hat-maker *John Batterson Stetson* (1830–1906), who designed it.

When Stetson travelled in the western USA at the time of the Civil War, it occurred to him that hats suitable for the needs of the cowboys were not being manufactured. When he returned to Philadelphia in 1865, therefore, he started to mass-produce a wide-brimmed hat that became popular with cowboys and was known as a stetson or a John B.

stoic

If someone behaves in a stoic or stoical way, then he or she endures hardship or pain without letting their feelings show. The word derives from the *Stoics*, the ancient Greek philosophical school taught by Zeno of Citium. Amongst the teachings of Stoicism was the repression of emotion and the belief that wisdom lay in mastery of oneself.

The school was known as the Stoic school, since it met at the Painted Portico (in Greek, *Stoa Poikilē*) in Athens.

stonewall

If you stonewall, then you act in an obstructive or defensive manner. The expression gained currency as a result of the nickname of the US Confederate general in the American Civil War, *Thomas Jonathan Jackson*, known as *Stonewall Jackson* (1824–63). In the first battle of Bull Run (1861), he and his forces were considered as 'standing like a stone wall' against the Federal troops.

From Jackson's name derived *stonewalling*, the obstruction of something with stubborn resistance. The word is found particularly in cricket, to describe cautious defensive batting, and also in discussion where a speaker talks for a long time, especially in order to stop other people from expressing their opinion.

Swedenborgian

The Swedish scientist and theologian *Emanuel Swedenborg* (original surname *Svedberg*; 1668–1772) is known for his system of teachings showing the importance of the spiritual structure of the universe.

Originally a mining engineer and mineralogist, Swedenborg became more spiritually orientated in about 1743, claiming to have mystical visions. His works include *Arcana Coelestia* (1756) and *Divine Love and Wisdom* (1763). The religious group known as the New Jerusalem Church also known as the New Church or Swedenborgians, was established after his death in 1787.

sweet Fanny Adams

Sweet Fanny Adams now means 'nothing at all': '*What's been happening while I've been away?*' – '*Sweet Fanny Adams.*' It is sometimes shortened to sweet f.a.

The expression comes originally from the name of a girl who was murdered in Alton, Hampshire in 1812. Her body was found in the River Wey, cut into pieces.

Fanny's name became popularized by sailors talking about a distasteful meal of tinned mutton – it is said that a sailor found a button in a tin of mutton and with gruesome humour called the tin's contents Fanny Adams. From this slang usage, the meaning of the word developed to refer to something of little value and then the current meaning.

Swiftian

Swiftian is sometimes used to mean satirical in a keen and bitter way: *The appointment of a mathematician to lead the enquiry into the teaching of English language shows an undeniable Swiftian logic.* The adjective clearly derives from the name of the Anglo-Irish clergyman, poet, and satirist *Jonathan Swift* (1667–1745) whose numerous writings included the satires *A Tale of A Tub* (1704), on 'corruption in religion and learning', and the famous *Gulliver's Travels* (1726), a satire on the human condition, particularly the politics of that period.

sword of Damocles

In classical legend, the courtier *Damocles* declared enviously that the tyrant of Syracuse, Dionysius the Elder (405–367 BC) was the happiest of men. Flattered by this remark and wanting to teach Damocles a lesson, Dionysius invited Damocles to a banquet, where he could see the ruler's happiness. Damocles accepted the invitation, and sat down to a sumptuous feast, but above him was a sword, suspended by a single hair. Damocles was so troubled that he could not enjoy the banquet.

The moral was that fears and threats of danger constantly prevent those that have power from fully enjoying that power. The expression *sword of Damocles* has thus come to refer to an imminent danger.

syphilis

The venereal disease syphilis derives from the name of a character in a poem published in 1530 with the title *Syphilis sive Morbus Gallicus* ('Syphilis or the French Disease') by the Italian physician and poet Girolamo Fracastro (1483–1553).

In the poem Syphilis, the hero of the book and a shepherd, angers the Sun god to such an extent that he is struck down by this disease. Fracastro probably coined the word Syphilis from Greek *suphilos* 'lover of pigs' or 'swineherd'.

T

tam-o'-shanter

Tam-o'shanter, the brimless cap of Scottish origin that usually has a pom-pom on the top, is named after the hero of the poem *Tam o' Shanter* (published 1791), by the Scottish poet Robert Burns (1759-96). Often shortened to tam or tammy, it is possibly the only item of male headgear that takes its name from a poem.

Tammany Hall

Tammany Hall is the headquarters of the Tammany Society, the central organization of the Democratic Party in New York City. Originally founded in 1789, it was notorious for its political corruption in the nineteenth and early twentieth centuries.

The society is named after *Tammanend* (also known as *Tammenund* or *Tammany*), a Delaware Indian chief, who, it seems, may have negotiated with William Penn over the transfer of land that eventually became PENNSYLVANIA.

tantalize

Tantalize, to tease someone by offering something desirable to view and then withholding it, derives from Greek mythology. *Tantalus*, the mythical King of Phrygia, was punished for offences

276

against the gods. In Hades he was condemned to stand in water that receded whenever he tried to drink it and under branches of fruit that moved away whenever he tried to grasp them.

Tarmac see MACADAM

tartar

A person who is thought to be very formidable, fearsome, or exacting is sometimes known as a tartar. The world tartar comes from the *Tatars*, a Mongoloid people who conquered Asia and eastern Europe to establish an immense and mighty empire from the thirteenth to the sixteenth centuries.

It seems that the change of spelling from Tatar to Tartar came about in the Middle Ages under the influence of *Tartarus*, Latin for 'hell', since their deeds were so savage that it seemed as if they had come from hell.

Tasmania

Tasmania, the island in the south Pacific, south of mainland Australia, is named after the Dutch navigator *Abel Janszoon Tasman* (1603–59). Appointed by the Dutch Colonial Administrator Anthony van Dieman (1593–1645), Tasman explored the south Pacific Ocean for trading purposes (1642–44). Tasman sighted the island that is now named in his honour, originally calling it *Van Dieman's Land* after his patron. The island was known as this until 1856, when its name was changed to Tasmania.

tawdry

The queen of Northumbria, *St Audrey* (*Ethelrida*) (died 679) was patron saint of Ely. In olden times a fair was held annually on 17

October in her honour. The fair was noted for its good-quality jewellery and fine silk scarves, which in time came to be known as *St Audrey's laces*. Later, however, the fine scarves were replaced by cheap, gaudy imitations and so the word tawdry developed, a shortening and alteration of (Sain)t Audrey('s laces), a term that is now applied to anything that is cheap and showy.

Some versions of the story add that St Audrey died of a tumour in her throat, which she considered a punishment for wearing showy jewel necklaces as a child.

teddy bear

The teddy bear, the soft stuffed toy bear, takes its name from the US President *Theodore Roosevelt* (1858–1919), who was nicknamed *Teddy*. Well known as a hunter of bears, it is said that on one occasion Roosevelt spared the life of a brown bear cub while on a hunting expedition. The story was later depicted in a cartoon in the *Washington Post* by the cartoonist Clifford K. Berryman, and stuffed toy bears became known as teddy bears.

The President's association with teddies remained. He presented several bears to the Bronx Zoo, and when, in 1911, he received an honorary degree at Cambridge University, a large teddy bear was lowered from the ceiling onto his head while he stood on the platform.

Teddy boy

Teddy boys, young men in Britain of the 1950s, wore tightly fitting trousers and long jackets that were fashionable during the reign of *King Edward VII* (1841–1910; reign 1901–10), Teddy being the nickname for Edward.

Associated with early rock-and-roll music, the Teddy boys were known for their unruly or violent behaviour. Young men who

Teddy boy

278

nowadays wear clothes in this style are also sometimes known as Teddy boys, and the association with bad or rebellious behaviour remains.

tesla

Tesla, the metric unit of magnetic flux density, is named after the Croatian-born American electrician and inventor *Nikola Tesla* (1857–1943). Tesla is known for his work on the distribution of alternating electrical current and many inventions including a transformer, dynamo, and a generator.

Thatcherism

Thatcherism is the term used to describe the policies of the Conservative government of the U K under the Prime Ministership of *Margaret Thatcher*, from 1979 onwards.

Born in Grantham in 1925, Margaret Hilda Thatcher studied chemistry at Oxford University. After studying and practising law, she was elected M P for Finchley in 1959. She served as Secretary of State for Education and Science (1970–74) and became leader of the Conservative Party in 1975 and Prime Minister in 1979.

As Prime Minister, she has led a firm government that has adopted a monetarist economic policy, seeking generally to reduce public expenditure, and policies of privatizing nationalized services and industries.

Thespian

The late-sixth-century BC Greek poet *Thespis* is traditionally thought to have been the founder of Greek tragic drama. Up to that time performances had been given only by a chorus; he is said to have introduced an actor who represented a historical or legendary figure. Thespis is also said to have toured the country with his plays. From his name comes Thespian, used as a name for an actor, and as an adjective to refer to drama.

Thursday

The name of the fifth day of the week comes from Old English *Thursdæg*, the day of *Thor*, the Norse god of thunder. Thor is said to have made thunder with a chariot that was pulled by he-goats across the sky. Armed with a massive hammer, he was considered the strongest and bravest of the Norse gods.

titan; titanic

The *Titans* were 12 primeval gigantic gods and goddesses in Greek mythology, the children of Uranus (sky or heaven) and Gaea (earth). There were six Titans (Oceanus, Coeus, Crius, Hyperion, Japetus, and Cronus) and six Titanesses (Thea, Rhea, Themis, Mnemosyne, Phoebe, and Tethys).

The Greeks believed that the Titans once ruled over the earth in a golden age. The youngest of the 12, Cronus, became their leader when he overthrew his father Uranus. Later, Cronus was himself overthrown by his son, Zeus.

The noun titan and the adjective *titanic* have come to describe a person or thing that is extremely large or strong. The *Titanic* was, of course, the luxury passenger ship that struck an iceberg near Newfoundland on its maiden voyage on the night of 14–15 April 1912, with the loss of 1513 lives.

titchy

Someone or something that is described as titchy is very small. The word derives from *Little Tich*, the stage name of the English actor *Harry Relph* (1867–1928). The word *Tich* may derive from the *Tichborne case*, a legal case of the 1870s, in which a certain podgy Arthur Orton was found to have impersonated a *Roger Charles Tichborne* (1829–54), the heir to a vast fortune, who was presumed lost at sea. Eventually Orton was discredited and imprisoned (1874–84).

Titian

The adjective Titian is sometimes used to describe bright golden-auburn hair. The word derives from the Italian painter *Titian* (original name *Tiziano Vecellio; c.*1487–1576). A renowned artist of the Venetian school, Titian is noted for his mythological and religious works, frescoes, and portraits. In many of his works, Titian depicted a model with hair of a reddish-brown hue that came to be named after him.

tom; Tom, Dick, and Harry; Tom Thumb

The male of various animals, especially the cat, is known as a tom, a shortened form and nickname of *Thomas*. The name *Tom* also occurs in such words as *tomboy* and *tomfoolery*.

The expression *Tom, Dick, and Harry* refers to different kinds of ordinary people, often when they are unsuitable or unqualified: *We won't allow any Tom, Dick, and Harry to come and set up a stall in the market.*

A Tom Thumb, a person of restricted growth, derives from the tiny hero of nursery tales. *General Tom Thumb* was the stage name of the American person of restricted growth, Charles

Sherwood Stratton (1838–83), who was exhibited by P. T. Barnum in his circuses. He was 3ft 4in (102 cm) tall.

Tom Collins

A Tom Collins – the tall iced drink consisting of gin, lime (or lemon) juice, sugar, and soda water – is said to have been named after a bartender, but his exact identity is unclear. A possible candidate is the nineteenth-century bartender at Limmer's public house in London.

tommy; Tommy Atkins; Tommy gun

Tommy, a representative British soldier, especially a private, is the shortened form of the name *Thomas Atkin*. Use of the name Thomas Atkins dates back to the early nineteenth century: it first appeared on sample army enlistment forms in 1815.

The name of the lightweight sub-machine-gun known as a Tommy gun comes from a different source. It was invented by the American army officer general *John Taliaferro Thompson*, hence *Tommy*; (1860–1940), the American navy commander John N. Blish, and others towards the end of the First World War. First manufactured in 1921, the Tommy gun was popularized by the Chicago gangsters of the Prohibition era (1920–33).

tontine

Tontine, a financial scheme that provides life annuities to a group of subscribers, is named after the Italian banker *Lorenzo Tonti* (1635–90), who devised the scheme and introduced it to France in

1653. Under the scheme, a number of people subscribe to the tontine. When one of the subscribers dies, his share is divided among the remaining members, until the last surviving member takes the whole income. The scheme was used by governments to raise money, particularly in the seventeenth and eighteenth centuries.

Tony

Tony, the medallion awarded annually for 'distinguished achievement' in the American theatre, is named after the American actress *Antoinette Perry* (1888–1946), known familiarly as *Tony*. Making her debut in 1905, Perry became a successful actress and producer and was appointed to the chair of the American Theatre Council.

tradescantia

The genus of flowering plants known as *Tradescantia*, with striped leaves and usually grown as house plants, includes the popular varieties known as wandering Jew and spiderwort. The genus is named after the English traveller and gardener *John Tradescant* (*c.*1570–1638), who was gardener to Charles I. John Tradescant travelled widely with his son, also John Tradescant (1608–62), and introduced into Britain many vegetables, fruits, trees, and flowers, including figs, runner beans, oranges, lupins, and the lilac. He established his own nursery in Lambeth, London.

trilby

Trilby, the soft felt hat with an indented crown, derives from the dramatized version of *Trilby*, the novel (published in 1894) by the

English artist and writer George du Maurier (1834–96). In the original stage version of the novel (1895), the heroine, *Trilby O'Ferrall*, wore such a hat.

Trotskyism

Trotskyism is the theory of communism of the Russian revolutionary *Leon Trotsky* (original name *Lev Davidovich Bronstein*; 1879–1940). Trotsky called for permanent worldwide revolution, in contrast to Stalin's insistence on the establishing of socialism in one country in isolation.

A leader with Lenin of the October Revolution (1917), Trotsky was Commissar of Foreign Affairs and War (1917–24) and built up the Red Army. On Lenin's death, he was ousted by Stalin, and was expelled from the Communist Party in 1927. Banished from the Soviet Union, he eventually settled in Mexico, where he was assassinated, probably by Soviet agents.

See also LENINISM, MARXISM, STALINISM.

tsar

Tsar (or czar), used as a title of the rulers of Russia from 1547 to 1917 or to describe someone who exercises authority, derives ultimately from the Latin *Caesar*, 'emperor'.

The title *kaiser*, adopted by the Emperor of the Holy Roman Empire and also the Emperors of Germany and Austria, similarly derives from Caesar.

Opinions are divided, however, on which Roman statesman is the source of this expression. Some sources propose *(Gaius) Julius Caesar* (100–44 BC); others, more probably, suggest his adopted son, Augustus, known as *Gaius Julius Caesar Octavianus* (63 BC–AD 14), the first Emperor of Rome (see also AUGUST).

trudgen

The trudgen (or trudgen stroke), is a type of swimming stroke that uses a double overarm action and a scissors kick. It is named after the English swimmer *John Arthur Trudgen* (1852–1902), who introduced it in 1893.

Tuesday

The name of the third day of the week comes from Old English *Tīwesdæg*, the day of *Tiw* (or *Tyr*), the Anglo-Saxon god of war and the sky. Latin writers, beginning with Tacitus, identified Tiw with Mars, the Roman god of war – hence the Latin name for Tuesday, *dīes Martis*, day of Mars.

Tweedledum and Tweedledee

Tweedledum and Tweedledee – two individuals or groups that can scarcely be distinguished – were first applied to the musicians George Frederick Handel (1685–1759) and Giovanni Bononcini (1670–1747), when a rivalry arose between them. The probable first occurrence is in an epigram by John Byrom (1692–1763):

> Some say, that Signor Bononcini
> Compar'd to Handel's a mere ninny;
> Others aver, to him, that Handel
> Is scarcely fit to hold a candle.
> Strange! That such high dispute should be
> 'Twixt Tweedledum and Tweedledee.

The names were popularized by the fat twin characters in *Through the Looking Glass* (published in 1872) by the English writer Lewis Carroll (1832–98).

U

Uncle Sam

Uncle Sam is a personification of the United States of America, its people, government, or national spirit. The expression is probably a humorous expansion of the letters U S (abbreviation of United States) stamped on the side of some containers for military provisions. It is also noted that in 1812 a meat-packer named *Samuel Wilson* (1766–1854) at Troy, New York, was jocularly called Uncle Sam by his employees, in reference to the U S stamped on the side of the cases.

The expression Uncle Sam spread quickly during the war of 1812, to oppose John Bull, the symbol of the British Army. It was nearly 60 years later, however, that the first picture of Uncle Sam as he is recognized today appeared in *Harper's Weekly*. Uncle Sam was depicted as clothed in top hat and striped suit and enjoying his victory over John Bull.

Uncle Tom

Uncle Tom is a derogatory term for a Black person who wants to co-operate with and win the favour of Whites. The name was originally that of the Black slave in the abolitionist novel *Uncle Tom's Cabin* (published in 1852) by the American author Harriet Beecher Stowe (1811–96). The novel aroused strong anti-slavery feelings; and Abraham Lincoln is alleged to have said that the novel helped to start the Civil War.

V

valentine

Valentine – a card sent anonymously to one's sweetheart on 14 February – derives from either of two third-century A D Christian martyrs. One *St Valentine* was a Roman priest who was martyred for assisting persecuted believers. He is said to have been martyred on the Flaminian Way, the road from Rome to Ariminum (Rimini) in about 270. The other *St Valentine* was a bishop of Terni, martyred in Rome at about the same time.

The connection between the feast of St Valentine (14 February) and courtship is not associated with either saint, however. The traditions linked with St Valentine go back to the Roman feast of Lupercalia (15 February) and the popular belief that 14 February is the date that birds select their mates.

Van Allen belt

The Van Allen belts, two regions of electrically charged particles surrounding the earth in the outer atmosphere, are named after the American physicist *James Alfred Van Allen* (b. 1914). It was during International Geophysical Year of 1958 that, as the Carver Professor of Physics at Iowa University, Van Allen inferred the

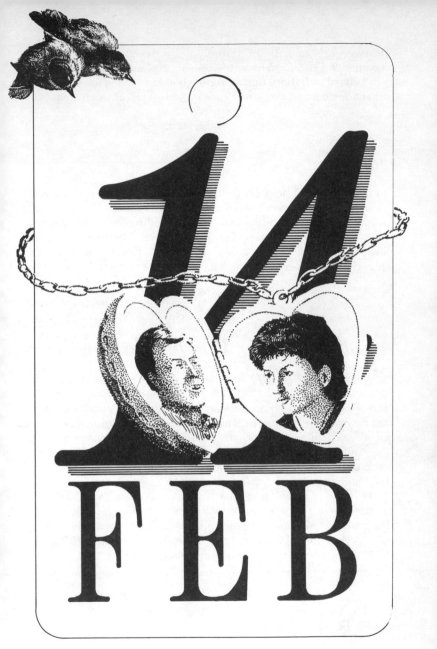

existence of two belts of radiation. By examining the readings recorded by the *Explorer* satellites, he explained the existence of two belts of radiation, one at 1000–5000 km (620–3100 miles), the other at 15,000–25,000 km (9300–15,500 miles), above the equator.

vandal

Someone who deliberately destroys or damages property is known as a vandal. The word derives from the *Vandals*, the Germanic people who moved southwards from Scandinavia in the first four centuries AD, overrunning Gaul, Spain and North Africa in the fifth century and sacking Rome in 455. The devastation that they caused was so severe that their name has ever since stood for those who bring about wanton destruction.

Vandyke beard; Vandyke brown; Vandyke collar

The Flemish painter *Sir Anthony Van Dyck* (or Vandyke; 1599–1641) was court painter to King Charles I. His paintings are noted for their depiction of portraits bearing a trim pointed beard (Vandyke beard) and a wide collar with deeply indented points forming a border (Vandyke collar). Vandyke brown is a dark brown colour that the artist liked to use.

Born one of 12 children to a rich silk merchant, Van Dyke was by the age of 19 an assistant to Rubens. In 1620 he first came to England and worked for King James I. After travels round Europe, he returned to England in 1532 to be court painter to Charles I (1632–41), who conferred on him a knighthood.

venereal; Venus

The word venereal is most often used in the expression *venereal disease*, a disease spread by sexual intercourse, for example gonorrhoea or syphilis. The word venereal derives from Latin *venus* 'sexual love', from *Venus*, the Italian goddess. Originally the goddess of gardens and fertility, Venus became identified with the Greek Aphrodite as goddess of love: see also APHRODISIAC.

Venus occurs in many compounds, particularly in the names of flowers and plants, such as *Venus's flytrap* (*Dionaea muscipula*), and even the small creature *Venus's flower basket*, a deep-sea sponge, genus *Euplectella*.

Venn diagram

A diagram in which circles and other shapes are drawn to overlap at certain points in order to represent mathematical and logical relationships is known as a Venn diagram. The name honours the English mathematician and logician *John Venn* (1834–1923), who devised the system.

Venus see VENEREAL

vernier; vernier rocket

A vernier is a small additional scale that is attached to a measuring instrument to allow measurements to be taken that are finer than those on the main scale. The scale is named after the French mathematician *Pierre Vernier* (1580–1637), who described it in a treatise that he wrote in 1631. The scale was in fact a development of the *nonius*, invented by, and named after, the Portuguese mathematician *Pedro Nuñez* (1492–1577).

A vernier rocket (or vernier engine) is an alternative term for a rocket thruster, the small engine or gas nozzle that makes fine adjustments to the speed, altitude, or direction of a space vehicle or missile.

Very light; Very pistol

The Very light is a coloured or white flare used as a signal. It is fired from a special pistol, a Very pistol. The light and pistol are named after the American naval officer *Edward W. Very* (1847–1910), who invented them in 1877.

vesta; vestal

The kind of short match known as a vesta is named after the Roman goddess *Vesta*. Vesta was the goddess of the hearth, who was venerated by every Roman household. The *Vestal virgins* were the virgin priestesses who kept the sacred fire at the altar in the Temple of Vesta constantly aflame.

Victorian

The adjective Victorian is sometimes used to refer to the moral standards or behaviour popularly associated with the reign of *Queen Victoria* c. 1819–1901; reign, 1837–1901). Some examples of the use of the word are: *She rebelled against her strait-laced Victorian upbringing*; *traditional Victorian values*; *the solid Victorian virtues of self-help and hard work*. The qualities regarded as typically Victorian are thus seen to emphasize 'good' morals, often to the point of prudery, and strict discipline. The divergence between moral standards and practices during Queen Victoria's reign is reflected in the word's further associations of narrow-mindedness and hypocrisy.

Queen Victoria instituted the *Victoria Cross* (VC) in 1856, the highest military decoration awarded to members of the armed forces of Britain and the Commonwealth for bravery in battle. The Queen also gave her name to numerous places including the *Victoria Falls, Victoria state, Lake Victoria*.

Queen Victoria is further honoured in the word *victoria* itself which is used variously to refer to a light, four-wheeled carriage with a folding hood, a kind of water-lily, and a large sweet variety of plum (*victoria plum*).

volcano; vulcanize

A volcano, an opening in the earth's crust out of which molten matter issues in an eruption, derives from *Vulcan* the Roman god of fire and metalworking. As Ernest Weekley comments, '*There was . . . for the ancient world, only one volcano . . . Etna . . . in the bowels of which Vulcan and the Cyclopes forged the thunderbolts of Jupiter*' (*Words and Names*).

Vulcanize, to treat natural rubber chemically, in order to increase its elasticity, hardness, etc., also derives from the god Vulcan.

volt

Volt, the metric unit of (electric) potential, is named after the Italian physicist *Count Alessandro Volta* (1745–1827). Volta is particularly noted for his invention (1800) of what was the first real battery (the *voltaic cell* or *pile*), and the electrophorus (1775) a device that accumulates electric charge. Widely praised for his experiments, he received numerous awards and medals from many countries; Napoleon conferred a countship on him in 1801.

vulcanize see VOLCANO

W

Wagnerian

The adjective Wagnerian, used to mean grandiose or intense in a dramatic manner, derives from the music of the German composer *Wilhelm Richard Wagner* (1813–83). Particularly noted for his origination of the music drama, Wagner's operatic cycle *Der Ring des Nibelungen* was first produced in 1876.

Walter Mitty

The expression Walter Mitty is used to refer to an ordinary person who indulges in extravagant day-dreaming and fantasies in an attempt to escape from reality. The description derives from the hero of the short story *The Secret Life of Walter Mitty* by the American humorist and cartoonist James (Grover) Thurber (1894–1961).

Wankel engine

The Wankel engine, a type of internal-combustion engine that has a triangular-shaped rotating piston with slightly curved convex sides, is named after its inventor, the German engineer, *Felix Wankel* (b. 1902).

Wankel gained his engineering skills in private study and

through correspondence courses. His interest in a rotary engine dates back to 1924 and he developed the engine before and during the Second World War. Cars powered by the Wankel engine were produced by the early 1960s but the engine's inherent design problems have never been fully overcome.

Washington

The name of the American statesman and first president of the United States, *George Washington* (1732–99; President 1789–97), is the most frequently used place name in the USA. The capital of the USA, Washington state, Lake Washington, Mount Washington . . . all honour him. In Britain, Washington (new town) in Tyne and Wear was the home of George Washington's forebears before they moved to Sulgrave, Northamptonshire.

Born into a rich Virginian family, Washington was a surveyor before serving in the French Indian War (1754–63). He became a strong opponent of British government policy in the Continental Congresses and when the American War of Independence broke out, he was appointed Commander-in-Chief of the American forces. Having gained the final victory over Cornwallis at Yorktown in 1781, Washington became President of the Constitutional Convention in 1787.

The popular story that the young George Washington virtuously admitted to his father that he had felled the cherry-tree is probably an invention. He is alleged to have said, 'Father, I cannot tell a lie. *I* did it.' The story seems to have originated in the biography of Washington by the American clergyman Mason Locke Weems, first published in the fifth edition of the book (1806).

Wassermann test

The Wassermann test (or reaction), a test for detecting syphilis, is named after the German bacteriologist *August von Wassermann* (1866–1925), who invented it. An assistant to Robert Koch at his Institute for Infectious Diseases in Berlin, Wassermann later became director of the department of experimental therapy and serum research. In 1906, he developed a test for syphilis, which, using the 'complement-fixation' technique, indicates the presence or absence in the blood of a specific antibody. Wassermann is also noted for his development of a diagnostic test for tuberculosis.

Watt

Watt, the metric unit of power, is named after the Scottish engineer and inventor *James Watt* (1736–1819). Watt is particularly famous for his development of the steam engine.

Born at Greenock, Scotland, Watt worked at Glasgow University. While repairing a model of the Newcomen steam engine (1765), Watt realized that it would be more efficient if it were fitted with a separate condenser. Thus Watt's steam engine, developed in 1769, soon replaced the Newcomen model. From 1774–5 he worked in partnership with the businessman and engineer Matthew Boulton (1728–1809) to manufacture steam engines.

Watt's other inventions included a centrifugal governor and manuscript copying machine; the term horsepower was coined by him and Boulton.

Watteau back; Watteau hat

A Watteau back (or dress) has broad back pleats that fall from the neckline to the hem without a girdle. A Watteau hat is one that has shallow crown and a wide brim that is turned up at the back to hold decorative flowers. Both features are named after the French painter *Antoine Watteau* (1684–1721), in imitation of characteristics of his art.

Originally training as a painter of scenery for the theatre, Watteau later had the opportunity of studying Rubens' work, which proved to be highly influential in the development of his style. He became famous in England and France for his scenes of gallantry (*fêtes galantes*).

Wedgwood

Wedgwood is a trademark used to describe a kind of ceramic ware made originally by the English potter Josiah Wedgwood (1730–95). Wedgwood pottery is known for its classical ornamentation in white relief particularly on a blue (*Wedgwood blue*) background.

Born at Burslem, Staffordshire, Wedgwood was handicapped as a child when his right leg had to be amputated, but he nevertheless experimented with clays and firing and worked in the family's small pottery shop. He eventually founded a firm in Staffordshire which produced a wide range of ceramic ware that was to become famous throughout the world. He collaborated with the sculptor John Flaxman (1755–1826) and built a factory – and village for his workers – at Etruria in Staffordshire.

Wednesday

The fourth day of the week comes from Old English *Wōdnes dæg*, Woden's day. Known also as Odin, *Woden* was the god of wisdom, culture, and war. He was also the god of the heroes who died in battle and were brought to Valhalla by his personal attendants, the Valkyries. His yearning for wisdom was so great that he surrendered his right eye so that he could drink from Mimir's fountain of knowledge.

wellington boot

The wellington boot was originally a leather boot which covered the front of the knee and was cut away at the back. Nowadays the wellington is a waterproof rubber boot without fastenings that reaches to the knee. The boot is, of course, named after the British soldier and statesman *Arthur Wellesley, 1st Duke of Wellington* (known as the Iron Duke; 1769–1852). Wellington is known for his victory against the French in the Peninsular War (1814) and, with Blücher, for the final defeat of Napoleon at Waterloo (1815). He

served as Prime Minister (1828–30) but his opposition to parliamentary reform led to his resignation. He was Commander-in-
Chief of the British army (1827–28; 1842–52).

Apart from the boots named in his honour – he is said to have
worn the boots during his military and political careers – the
capital of New Zealand is named after the Duke, as is the *wel-
lingtonia*, the giant Californian coniferous tree, known also as the
'big tree'.

Wendy house

A Wendy house is a small model house that children can play in.
It is named after the house built for Wendy, the girl in the play
Peter Pan, or The Boy who Wouldn't Grow Up by the Scottish dramatist
and novelist Sir James Matthew Barrie (1860–1937).

See also PETER PAN.

Wesleyan

John Wesley (1703–91) was the English preacher who founded
Methodism, the word being used to describe his followers, especially the branch of Methodism known as *Wesleyan Methodists*.

Born the 15th son of a rector in Epworth (now Humberside),
John was ordained in 1735. After a conversion experience in 1738,
he determined to devote the rest of his life to evangelistic work.
From 1742 he travelled throughout Britain, and is said to have
preached over 40,000 sermons and travelled 250,000 miles before
he died.

His brother Charles (1707-88) is known for his composition of
several thousand hymns, including 'Jesus, lover of my soul'; 'Love
divine, all loves excelling'; and 'And can it be that I should gain'.

Wightman Cup

The Wightman Cup, the annual tennis competition between British and US women's teams, is named after the donor of the trophy, *Hazel Hotchkiss Wightman* (1886–1974). A very successful tennis player herself – she was American national singles champion 1909–11 – Wightman bought the silver cup in about 1920, when preliminary efforts were under way to stage a competition similar to the Davis Cup. These plans proved fruitless but in 1923 a competition was arranged between British and US women's teams, which has been played every year since.

See also DAVIS CUP.

will-o'-the-wisp

The expression will-o'-the-wisp is used to describe a light that sometimes appears over marshy ground at night. Known also by a variety of other terms – *friar's lantern, jack-o'-lantern* and *ignis fatuus* – the light is believed to be caused by the spontaneous combustion of gases formed by organic decomposing matter. Figuratively, the expression will-o'-the-wisp is used to refer to an elusive person or someone who cannot be depended on. The original seventeenth century expression was 'Will with the wisp', *Will* – the short form for William – being chosen as alliterative with *wisp*, 'a twist of hay, etc. burning as a bright light'.

Winchester rifle

Winchester rifle is the trademark of a type of repeating rifle with a tubular magazine below the barrel. The name derives from its American manufacturer *Oliver Fisher Winchester* (1810–80). The Winchester was first made in 1866, at his factory in New Haven, Connecticut. The Winchester became well known as a cowboy rifle, in the Wild West period of American history.

Winchester's original line of business was the manufacture of men's shirts; his special competence lay in the adaptation of the inventions of others. In fact, the Winchester rifle was a development of the *Henry rifle*, a repeating rifle invented by *Benjamin Tyler Henry* (1821–98).

wisteria

Wisteria, the genus of twining climbing plants with purple flowers in hanging clusters, are named after the American anatomist *Caspar Wistar* (1761–1818).

The son of a well-known glass-maker, Wistar was a Philadelphian Quaker who was professor of anatomy at the University of Pennsylvania. He wrote America's first textbook on anatomy. It was, it seems, an error by Thomas Nuttal, the curator of the botanical garden in Harvard in 1818, that resulted in the misspelling of Wistar's surname in the designating of the plant as wisteria.

X

Xanthippe

Socrates' wife, *Xanthippe*, was notorious for being bad-tempered and nagging; so an ill-tempered or irritable woman or wife is sometimes referred to in the same way. Shakespeare refers to her in *The Taming of the Shrew* (Act 1, Scene 2):

> Be she as foul as was Florentius' love,
> As old as Sibyl, and as curst and shrewd
> As Socrates' Xanthippe, or a worse,
> She moves me not.

Xanthippe's nagging is discussed in different ways by various authors. Some see it as the cause of Socrates' delight in outdoor discussions, while others argue that Socrates was such an unconventional husband that living with him must have taken up all his wife's patience.

Y

Yale lock

Yale, the trademark for a type of cylinder lock, is named after the American locksmith *Linus Yale* (1821–68), who invented it. Yale invented numerous other kinds of locks in the 1840s–1860s, but it is for the lock which has a revolving barrel that he is particularly remembered. Yale set up a company, the Yale Lock Manufacturing Company to produce locks at Stamford, Connecticut in 1868.

Yankee

Yankee, someone from the USA in British English in a derogatory sense, and someone from the northern USA – particularly New England – in American English, probably comes from a Dutch name. Yankee may well originally have been *Jan Kass*, a derogatory nickname for a Hollander, meaning 'John Cheese'.

After the Dutch settled in New York, they applied the term to the neighbouring English settlers in north Connecticut. By the time of the American War of Independence, the term was used by the British to describe any colonist. (The song 'Yankee Doodle' originally mocked the poorly clad colonial forces, but the colonial troops changed the song's lyrics and used it as a marching song).

In the American Civil War, the South used Yankee as a derisive term for a Union soldier, and by the outbreak of the First World War, all American soldiers were known as Yankees (or Yanks) by the rest of the world. From that time on, Yankee and Yank have been used to describe an American.

yarborough

A yarborough is a hand in bridge or whist in which none of the cards is higher than nine. The word comes from *Charles Anderson Worsley, 2nd Earl of Yarborough* (d. 1897). An enthusiastic card-game player, Lord Yarborough is said to have betted 1000 to 1 against the dealing of such a hand. In fact, the true mathematical figure has been calculated as 1827 to 1 against.

Z

zany

Something that is comical, especially in a fantastic or absurd way, may be described as zany. The word comes from Italian *zanni*, originally a traditional masked clown in the Italian *commedia dell'arte*. The buffoon was known as *Zanni* – an alteration of the name *Giovanni* (John), one of the traditional names for a clown. Zanni's role was to mimic the clown's tricks and generally to play the fool.

Zeppelin

A Zeppelin is an airship, and in particular a large rigid cylindrical airship built in Germany in the early twentieth century. It takes its name from the German general and aeronautical pioneer *Count Ferdinand von Zeppelin* (1838–1917). Zeppelin served in the American Civil War and the Franco-Prussian War. On retiring from the army in 1891, he developed his earlier interest in airships, and by 1900 had built the first rigid airship. Between 1910 and 1914 Zeppelins were widely used in Germany to carry passengers. During the First World War, the Germans used these airships to bomb Britain, the first raid being over Great Yarmouth in 1915. From that time onwards, the story of airships was generally one of disaster – notably the British R101 disaster (1930) and the German

Zeppelin

Hindenburg (1937) – but in more recent times, airships are again being used, using non-flammable gas.

zinnia

Zinnia, the annual or perennial plant native to tropical America of the family Compositae, is named after the German botanist and anatomist *Johann Gottfried Zinn* (1727–59). A professor of medicine, Zinn published in 1753 what is reported to have been the first book to describe the anatomy of the eye.

Zoroastrianism

The pre-Islamic Persian religion of Zoroastrianism was founded in the sixth century BC by the prophet *Zoroaster* (in Avestan, *Zarathustra*). Zoroaster (*c.*660–583 BC) received at the age of about 30 a vision of Ahura Mazda who inspired him to teach a new religion proclaiming that he was the god of light.

Zoroastrianism recognizes two principles, good and evil, which are personified by Ahura Mazda (god of light, wisdom) and Ahriman (or Angra Mainyu; prince of darkness; the destroyer). Life is considered as a struggle between these two spirits, which will be won in the eventual triumph of good over evil.

The scriptures of Zoroastrianism are the Avesta. Written in Old Iranian, its five books contain prayers, hymns and songs (Gathas), and teaching on ritual, worship, and law. Zoroastrianism survives in India amongst the Parsees and in Iran.

Zwinglian

Zwinglian is used to describe the teachings of the Swiss theologian *Ulrich Zwingli* (1484–1531), especially his understanding of the holy communion. In contrast to Luther, Zwingli had a purely symbolic interpretation of the eucharist.

Ordained as priest in 1506, Zwingli became a preacher in Zurich in 1519, strongly criticizing Roman Catholic teachings. His New Testament lectures marked the beginning of the Swiss Reformation. His conflict with Luther was seen at the Colloquy of Marburg (1529), which failed to bring about a union between the two men and a united Protestantism became impossible. The Reformation divided Switzerland and in the civil war that followed, Zwingli, serving as a chaplain, was killed.